UNDERSTANDING RESEARCH IN EARLY CHILDHOOD EDUCATION

Understanding Research in Early Childhood Education: Quantitative and Qualitative Methods prepares readers to be informed consumers of early childhood research. Rather than following the traditional format of covering quantitative and qualitative methods separately, this innovative textbook offers side-by-side coverage and comparison about the assumptions, questions, purposes, and methods for each, offering unique perspectives for understanding young children and early care and education programs.

Understanding Research in Early Childhood Education is broadly based across the major research paradigms, and numerous examples are offered throughout the text. Through the use of this book, students will be able to more knowledgeably read, evaluate, and use empirical literature. These skills are becoming more important as early childhood educators are increasingly expected to use evidence-based research in practice and to participate in collecting and analyzing data to inform their teaching.

Nancy File is Kellner Early Childhood Professor in the Department of Curriculum and Instruction at the University of Wisconsin–Milwaukee, USA.

Jennifer J. Mueller is Associate Professor and Chair of Early Childhood Education in the Department of Curriculum and Instruction at the University of Wisconsin–Milwaukee, USA.

Debora Basler Wisneski is John T. Langen Early Childhood Professor in the Department of Teacher Education at the University of Nebraska–Omaha, USA.

Andrew J. Stremmel is Professor and Department Head of the Department of Teaching, Learning, and Leadership at South Dakota State University, USA.

UNDERSTANDING RESEARCH IN EARLY CHILDHOOD EDUCATION

Quantitative and Qualitative Methods

Nancy File
Jennifer J. Mueller
Debora Basler Wisneski
Andrew J. Stremmel

Routledge
Taylor & Francis Group

NEW YORK AND LONDON

First published 2017
by Routledge
711 Third Avenue, New York, NY 10017

and by Routledge
2 Park Square, Milton Park, Abingdon, Oxon OX14 4RN

Routledge is an imprint of the Taylor & Francis Group, an informa business

Library of Congress Cataloging-in-Publication Data
Names: File, Nancy.
Title: Understanding research in early childhood education : quantitative and qualitative methods / Nancy File [and three others].
Description: New York : Routledge, 2016. | Includes bibliographical references and index.
Identifiers: LCCN 2016002364 | ISBN 9780415714389 (hardcover) | ISBN 9780415714396 (pbk.) | ISBN 9781315882734 (ebook)
Subjects: LCSH: Early childhood education—Research—Methodology.
Classification: LCC LB1139.225 .F55 2016 | DDC 372.21—dc23
LC record available at http://lccn.loc.gov/2016002364

ISBN: 978-0-415-71438-9 (hbk)
ISBN: 978-0-415-71439-6 (pbk)
ISBN: 978-1-315-88273-4 (ebk)

Typeset in Galliard
by Apex CoVantage, LLC

Printed and bound in the United States of America by Edwards Brothers Malloy on sustainably sourced paper

CONTENTS

CONTENTS

ACKNOWLEDGMENTS

This very beginning to the text is being written at the end, actually. It is now that we can gather our thoughts about the work and what we have done together, with many people standing beside and/or behind us.

Research has been a significant part of our careers. We each pursued doctoral degrees after years of being in the classroom with children. Our classroom experiences pushed each of us to find new ways to pursue understanding and to continue to ask and find answers for our questions. And so for years we have identified as scholars in one of our job roles.

Each of us, however, also identifies strongly as a teacher. We no longer teach young children, but the role of teaching is important to our identities. This is where this text was conceived. Some of the students we have worked with in our professional lives are preparing for careers as researchers. Many of the master's-level students in our courses are teachers and will remain teachers for the time being, though. For them the undertaking is focused on gaining depth of knowledge in their work. The literature in the field adds to that depth of knowledge, but learning how to understand and use it requires effort and practice.

We have written this text because of our interest in helping early-career professionals learn about research. The text comes from our own teaching, the concepts we have discussed with students, the big ideas and take-away messages we have introduced to them. And so, while we have written this text from our roles as researchers, we have also written strongly from our roles as teachers.

Unsurprisingly, then, we must acknowledge the many students we have taught in the course of our careers. Their questions, their frustrations and confusion, and their growing clarity of understanding have shaped our own understanding of how students can learn about research. It has been a privilege to walk alongside our students and watch them learn.

In addition, we must thank some particular individuals, current students who have played a part in producing this text. Meghan Johnson, a doctoral student in the University of Wisconsin–Milwaukee's School Psychology program, took on the job of writing the glossary. We very much appreciated being able to let go of one of our tasks! Amanda Hanrahan, another doctoral student in the same program, did invaluable editing on our writing. If explanations are clear, she is to credit for letting us know when they were not, before going to press! In addition, Amanda located articles and took on the task of editing and alphabetizing a reference section that began as a conglomeration of information from four authors. Patti Drewes and Jennifer Eldridge Weatherly, graduate students in the University of Nebraska–Omaha's Educational Leadership program, helped review research, took notes, and provided their perspectives in understanding paradigms in research. Their small contributions made a big impact on the third chapter.

We also want to acknowledge our Routledge editor, Alex Masulis. He has shown us support and immense patience throughout this project.

The four of us have worked together and from a distance for a number of years. We have known each other as we've grown as scholars, and it has been a mutually supportive and beneficial web of professional and personal relationships. None of us could have done this without the others, and we all appreciate that together we end up places none of us could go alone.

Individually, we each have further acknowledgments.

Nancy: I must thank my family, Jim, Mallory, and Peri. Their love and support were what I needed to see this through. I want to acknowledge the person who served as my mentor during my introduction to research, the late Susan Kontos; her voice is indelibly present in my mind. I've learned from so many others as well. A rich set of friends within the profession has supported my ongoing growth for years, and I look forward to many more conversations with them about the important stuff and laughter about the rest.

Jennifer: Of course I need to thank my family—those who live in my house and the extendeds. Lots of patience and doing life without me has been necessary, and I appreciate all the love, texts, memes, and beverages. Here I will also thank one of my most challenging kiddos from my teaching days—Herman Williams. He was one of those children who pushed one to their limits and made me learn more about myself as a teacher than I thought possible. He also was the child who inspired me to go to graduate school so that I could make a 'bigger' impact. As always, big thanks to all of my students, who continually brighten my day and make me hopeful for the future of early childhood education.

Debora: I would like to thank my family: Aron, Henry, and William. I remember with much gratitude the professors and former students/colleagues of the University of Texas–Austin, particularly of the internal review board of the *International Journal of Qualitative Studies in Education* and the Early Childhood Education Program, during my graduate school years. The experiences with these wonderful people taught me how research can be employed with great mindfulness, compassion, and intellect. A thank you to my students in Texas, Wisconsin, and Nebraska who thoughtfully continue the conversation.

Andy: I would like to thank the many students, teachers, and faculty who have inspired me over the years and taught me the value of working with student teachers as researchers and collaborators in generating new understanding of what it means to be a teacher. I wish to thank, in particular, Gail Perry, who was a pioneer and staunch advocate for teachers, seeing them as theorists, researchers, reflective thinkers, and decision makers. She championed the notion that early childhood teachers must understand and study their own practice in order to enhance the status of our profession.

1

INTRODUCTION

"The research . . ." There are many ways that this sentence is completed. Perhaps some of the following are familiar. "The research. . .

- suggests . . ."
- proves . . ."
- is inconclusive . . ."
- raises questions . . ."
- adds to our understanding . . ."
- implies that . . ."
- leads to these conclusions. . ."
- contradicts earlier research . . ."
- supports earlier research . . ."
- fails to show . . ."
- has limits . . ."

These examples are drawn from both the way that researchers discuss their work and the way that research is presented in popular media outlets. We live in a society in which individuals are exposed to research through many means. One can read original research reports written for professional audiences, read versions of research reports written more specifically for a lay audience, and hear or read about research as interpreted by others, such as journalists, professional development providers, and even marketers.

Within this environment, it is common to hear a variety of claims about research. Anyone paying attention is bound to have questions. Does research prove something? Why does research result in contradictory findings? What does it mean if research fails to show something? Why do researchers sound so cautious or tentative—can't they just take a stand? Is research about finding answers or generating more questions? How does research lead to implications?

One might be led to declare: "JUST TELL US!" (and, *please*, in language we can understand). The truth of the matter is that it is not that simple. Research does result in contradictory findings across different studies. When research findings are described, sometimes it can feel a bit 'underwhelming.' Research is almost always limited by the manner in which it was conducted. Limitations might relate to who participated, what types of data were collected, and the degree to which the findings might be similar if the study was conducted with other people or in another place. In general, research is driven by questions, and it is likely that questions will lead to more questions.

Finally and importantly, research is difficult to approach for those who are not researchers. The processes involved are intricate, and much of the professional terminology sounds like so much gobbledygook to the uninitiated. We have found when discussing research with students that they are likely to admit that when reading a quantitative study, marked by displays of numerical results presented in tables, that they "just go to the discussion section" at the end of the study, for an interpretation presented in words. And although they might feel more comfortable reading a qualitative study, described solely through verbal means, it often happens that the vocabulary and conceptual knowledge required to comprehend the work can get the better of them.

With this text, it is our intent to provide guidance for understanding research. As professionals, teachers in the early childhood education field are expected to have some knowledge of the literature. Inquiry is a highly valued activity in teaching; good teachers continually ask questions about their work and the children they serve. The literature produced by researchers is a useful tool for teachers to consult in their inquiry process. Understanding the literature also provides teachers with a chance to participate in dialogue with others about where and how research links to practice.

Thus, we believe that being a skilled consumer of research literature is an important competency for teachers. Not all research is created equally. It is important to be able to evaluate the methods used within a study and decide how much trust to place in the findings. Each study has a unique profile of strengths and limitations, and often one must look below the surface to identify these. Additionally, readers of research must make the translation to their own situations. How might the results apply? What implications are warranted? Capable consumers of research understand research more deeply. They can follow the processes involved, evaluate the decisions made in the study, and decide what the work means to their own understanding and practice.

Research in Society

What Is Research?

Research defines a particular form of inquiry intended to extend our understanding. For some, this understanding is meant to be a more complete or thorough understanding of the topic of inquiry, an understanding that can be generalized to other situations. For others, understanding is defined as a way of making meaning about that topic in ways that acknowledge the unique nature of situations and the variety of ways that one can choose to make meaning, all of which lessen generalizability.

Research revolves around questions, and typically in the search for more understanding, more questions arise. For some, the research process begins with clearly delineated questions, often formed from an understanding of the research conducted to date. For others, the questions are less specific at the outset, allowing the study and the questions to evolve as they proceed.

Research procedures are meant to result in data, as research is an evidence-based process. In other words, evidence, in the form of data, is generated and then analyzed to develop findings and implications. For some researchers the evidence is reflected via numbers, with numeric descriptions of the phenomena and statistics used to analyze the data. For others, the evidence is expressed in words, and the analysis allows for the identification of descriptions and themes.

Research follows forms of logic. In presenting the results of a study, the researcher is working to explain the decisions and theory that led the study forward, allowing others to agree or not with those processes. Additionally, the logic stems back to very basic philosophical positions about the world. At the very beginning are questions about reality and how we know what we know. For some, what we can perceive is our reality. It can be measured and assessed and 'known' in objective ways. For others, reality is what we construct as we work to make meaning about the world.

2

There are processes to be followed in research, rules of the road that are taught to successive generations of researchers. Although the processes exist within separate schools of thought or paradigms and thus differ, they act similarly in any school of thought to enclose the project within a shared definition of what that form of research means. Not unexpectedly, though, there are always some who push against those boundaries and work to define new understandings of what procedures mean and could mean.

To summarize what research is, we offer the following. Research is a form of inquiry that relies on evidence, or data. It is complex because, in part, there are many accepted ways to do research. And yet 'accepted' is a key word, because research is governed as a particular form of inquiry with defined processes, differentiated from other ways of knowing about the world such as wisdom, reflection, or craft knowledge. Research is conducted through a variety of processes. Its scope can be very finely focused, for example, a case study of a single child. Or it might be wide ranging, such as the impact of a policy change on kindergarteners.

Furthermore, research is traditionally conducted within a setting of accountability and scrutiny. The traditional standard for publication of a research article is the peer-review process. Typically, prior to publication other researchers read the article, without the authors being identified. Their evaluation of the article (returned to the authors also without the reviewers being identified) may raise questions and suggest concerns about how the research was conducted, oftentimes leading to a new draft of the article. Through this review process, the editors of journals decide which research articles will be published and which will be rejected.

In addition, foundations, think tanks, or private entities can self-publish the findings of their own research. This has always been the case, but in an Internet-dominated world, these reports are more easily accessible than ever. It is absolutely true that many of these reports reflect skilled research. At the same time, the reports have not undergone the peer-review process, leaving more responsibility on the shoulders of the reader to evaluate and decide upon the quality of the study.

The Impact of Research

Science and the processes of research are revered in our society. Information gained through research is typically assumed to have credence among the public. After conducting a poll of both the public and scientists, the authors of the report wrote (Pew Research Center, 2015),

> Science holds an esteemed place in the public imagination and in the minds of professionals. Americans are proud of the accomplishments of their scientists in key fields and, despite considerable dispute about the role of government in other realms, there is broad public support for government investment in scientific research.

Yet, as mentioned earlier, scientific research can be perplexing, particularly when viewed from the 'outside.' For example, different studies focused on the same topic can vary one from the other in the process details, which can impact the findings. The chains of logic utilized by researchers vary among studies, including what assumptions are accepted. New methods are developed that produce different results. To illustrate, consider a story reported in the *New York Times* in 2014 that detailed how the latest research on mammography for detection of breast cancer raised new questions about its effectiveness. The newest research used a large group of women and was described as "meticulous" in this article. The newest study reported that the death rate from breast cancer was almost the same between the group of women who had mammograms and those who did not. Still, there were many unanswered questions. The study resulted in a set of findings, but these findings did not answer questions about 'why' mammograms did not offer the health benefits that are widely assumed of their use. Was it because of newer, more effective treatments for cancer? Or because women are now more aware of breast cancer and thus more proactive in their health care? What more do we know about detecting and treating cancer over time? What questions do we not know to ask yet? Because of the mixed results and the unanswered questions, the reporter stated that it was unlikely that recommendations for regular mammogram screening would be changing soon (Kalota, 2014). In this case, a single study, even one described as well done, was not enough to change practice.

This story illustrates a central point about research. When examining complex subjects, the answers are often partial and accompanied by cautions. In regard to medical research, the human body is indeed an intricate system. Some research findings provide us with averages, but rarely do these researchers describe the individual processes of one person's genetic inheritance, life habits, environment, and reaction to medications used in treatment. There are often many potential reasons results might vary from one study to another. To account for these differences, some researchers specifically state that their findings are not generalizable to others.

Similarly, intricacies abound in educational research. Each classroom is made up of many children, all from unique families and each with a distinctive relationship with the teacher. Each child enters the classroom with an individual set of background experiences, while also subgroups of individuals may share cultural norms and expectations. Thus, there is a complex mix of similarities and differences among children. Similarly, each teacher is an individual. During any particular learning activity, some children may be deeply engaged while others are tired, out of sorts, or disinterested. Accordingly, results may vary from study to study, and most often what we know through educational research is incomplete.

In sum, our society has a history of holding scientific research in high esteem. And who can argue with the impact of research on many aspects of our lives? Nonetheless, research often does not provide us with the clear and absolute answers we might desire and that those uninitiated to the complexities of research feel they can expect. Continued questioning, new methods, and different perspectives all contribute to the tentative nature of 'what we know' via research. So researchers cannot "just tell us," as we mentioned earlier. What they can do is tell us about their work. The rest is up to those who read the study—to understand the work, put it alongside other work, consider its implications, and thus make meaning of it within their own understandings of teaching young children.

Research in Early Childhood Education

Anyone who has read an introductory textbook in the field might remember that it is commonplace to look back across the centuries to attribute contributions to early childhood from figures such as Locke, Rousseau, and Pestalozzi. Philosophical stances and ideologies regarding childhood and learning do indeed have a long history. In contrast, the history of research as a way of knowing about children and education is much briefer, only slightly longer than a century.

Even with a relatively brief history of research, there has been much change over time. What we will help the reader better understand in this text is how the ideas and phenomena that are valued in research are greatly influenced by larger social and cultural contexts. What we believe to be important, what we value, and what we need to understand as a society or as a culture at any point in time is shaped by historical moment, dominant political ideologies, technology of the time, and the prominent paradigms of thought. It follows that early childhood education, as an institution of our society, has moved through different phases in terms of what we have believed to be its purpose and main goals and so follows the purposes of and needs for educational research.

In order to be a competent consumer of research in early childhood education, it is important to realize and understand how larger social contexts have come to bear in the research endeavor over time within the field. We will help the reader understand how the two main approaches to research—quantitative and qualitative—have at different points defined the field, determining what it is we value and study and what it means to be a child in a classroom and an early childhood educator. But we also will discuss how social conditions and the needs of young children in educational settings have pushed a need for different kinds of study and different voices being heard in the research endeavor. In the early childhood field, we have moved back and forth with various goals of research, from finding overall universal truths that allow us to explain and predict what it is children need to know and do in their learning settings to examining more fine-grained and deeper understandings of localized situations and phenomena.

As we will explore in the coming chapters, those who operate in these differing paradigms, quantitative and qualitative, start from different places. They have different answers to questions about what reality is and how we come to know what we know. They pose different questions and work to answer them with different methods. Most importantly, they provide us with different perspectives about what it means to be a young child within a family and ever-enlarging contexts, including an early childhood program.

Outline of the Book

Our intent in this text is to prepare readers to be informed consumers of early childhood research. To that end, we will include information across the major models for conducting research. We include both quantitative and qualitative methods so that readers may access all of the available literature. We will coach readers in how to understand the research literature and make evaluations about the trustworthiness and applicability of studies. It is possible to become a competent evaluator of research with a single text. The task of learning how to do research is more complex and requires multiple texts and courses across both paradigms, however.

To make this work most relevant, we will be drawing our examples from the early childhood literature. Our purpose is to equip readers with the background knowledge needed for understanding research; because we draw our examples from the field, we hope readers will also learn about the exciting work being done in our field.

We will begin by examining the structures of research. In Chapter 2, we describe the basic foundations of research, the epistemology that drives researchers' perspectives on questions such as: How is reality defined? What assumptions are held about what we know and how we know it? In Chapter 3 we discuss in more detail the context within which research is conducted and used, as well as the cultures of research. Focal topics include the ethics of conducting research and how research and policymakers interface.

Beginning with Chapter 4, we introduce the major paradigms of qualitative and quantitative research. We will compare the major tenets of the research process within each paradigm, including the researcher's role, standards of rigor, and assumptions about the implications of studies. In the two chapters that follow, we describe how qualitative research is conceptualized and processes for generating data, as well as how to understand presentations and interpretations of data. We follow a similar set of goals for Chapters 7 and 8, which examine the conceptualization of quantitative studies and processes for data collection, as well as understanding the presentation of findings in a quantitative study. In this group of chapters, we will also present information on how to read and evaluate research studies.

The second major section of the book consists of a set of five chapters that bring to life the logic and modes of inquiry used in early childhood research. In this section, our structure is around the 'unit of analysis,' or the focus of the study. Thus, there are chapters that center on questions about children, questions about the adults in children's lives, questions about classrooms and curriculum, and questions about institutions and policy. In each of these chapters, we compare the perspectives and work of qualitative and quantitative researchers. For instance, we note the types of questions they ask and the types of data generated in each area. Each of these chapters is a conversation back and forth across the paradigms. The final chapter in this section is a look at teacher research.

Our concluding chapter is a look at research through the lenses of promise, pitfall, and limitation. Research is a very human enterprise, and throughout the text, we encourage a multifaceted examination that will support readers to decide for themselves what a study means rather than uncritically accepting all statements that begin, "The research says. . ."

We come at this enterprise having been educated ourselves in different research paradigms. Both Nancy and Andy earned their degrees through programs in child development with a singular focus on quantitative research. Jennifer and Debora earned their degrees in education programs and both conducted qualitative research during their schooling while being educated about both paradigms. We have all continued to grow and question ourselves as researchers, both singularly and together. A part of this book's structure was 'birthed' as Jennifer and Nancy cotaught a course in understanding research. We found our ability and willingness to simultaneously talk across paradigms with students was invigorating and, we think, helpful to their understanding. In relation to any one topic, we explored questions about what would interest researchers within the two paradigms and how they would make meaning of the phenomenon. We knew after this experience that we could not create a book in which the two paradigms constituted two separate sections, never to meet.

We have included two other features to maximize the usefulness of this book to readers. First, we have included short essays from colleagues in which they answer the prompt, "How I have used research to find out about. . ." These essays appear in the second section of the book to illustrate the unique perspectives offered by varying types of research. Also, we have included a glossary at the end of the book. Research is marked by terminology, no matter the paradigm. We hope that readers consult the glossary freely until they feel they have mastery over these many words and concepts.

As a final word, we encourage readers to think about research as a story. We do not intend to draw analogies between research and the elements of story. Rather, we suggest readers consider questions such as these: What is the story here? Who is it about? What happened? The beauty of stories is that they are accessible. Stories draw us in, even if they are not always simple and straightforward. It may help readers to regard research as a story to make a study more comprehensible, giving them an approach that aids in understanding. This disposition, along with the knowledge gained in the coming chapters, can reduce many of the barriers toward understanding research and research-to-practice links.

Part I

STRUCTURES OF RESEARCH

2

HOW DO WE KNOW?

Research has become an integral part of early childhood education and care as seen through the adopted policies and practices of local, state, and national institutions. We may hear a teacher defend her classroom practice by stating, "Developmental *research says* children at this age learn through hands-on play." Or a school district may adopt a certain packaged curriculum over other options because "this curriculum is research based." For example, on its website, the Creative Curriculum, a widely used package, demonstrates via a chart the links its creators made between practices in the curriculum model and research. The Creative Curriculum document "Research Foundation: Language and Literacy" states, "By directly translating into practice the most current research on how children develop and learn language and literacy skills, teachers using The Creative Curriculum for Preschool *can be certain* that they are focusing on what matters most for a child's success, in language and literacy as well as in other curricular areas" (italics added by author; Teaching Strategies, 2010, p. 6). Another example can be found on the website of the National School Boards Association, with this statement: "Research *has proven* that high-quality prekindergarten programs can raise student achievement and close achievement gaps" (italics added by author; National School Boards Association, n.d.).

We can see how research is relied upon for decision making, sometimes based on definitive statements about what we know, such as the research 'proves' something to be true. This may give administrators, policy makers, teachers, and the larger community a sense of security that they are making the correct decisions. For many beginning to read and use research in education, we find ourselves assuming that any published research *proves* a point or case. However, as one becomes more informed and begins to explore issues through multiple studies, we find that a research study may *suggest* a finding and shows evidence of knowledge from one standpoint, which provides *some* insight into the issue, but seldom definitive and universally applicable answers.

What accounts for these discrepancies, uncertainties, or differences in research? One of the main reasons we find complexity in research is that not all researchers come to an issue or problem with the same types of questions. A researcher's assumptions of the nature of knowledge—how we know what we know—affects what type of question is asked, how the researcher searches for the answer to the question, and how the researcher makes sense of the findings. A researcher's values and ethics will also influence what and how she will conduct a study. For example, if a researcher values academic achievement through success on standardized tests, she may define academic achievement through test scores. Or if a researcher values the perspectives of children and mothers, she may design a study that includes ways to capture and share those perspectives.

So what is reality? How is reality defined? How do we know what we know? What types of questions are considered possible and valuable? What types of evidence are important? These are big philosophical questions that might seem quite farfetched and superfluous to some. However, these questions are at the crux of doing research whether a researcher explicitly takes the time to interrogate his or her own world view or not. We share the position with Mertens (2014) that

> a researcher's philosophical orientation has implications for every decision made in the research process, including the method of choice. . . . Therefore, to plan and conduct your own research, read and critique the research of others, and join in the philosophical, theoretical, and methodological debates in the research community, you need to understand the prevailing paradigms, with their underlying philosophical assumptions.
>
> (pp. 7–8)

We also contend that educators or practitioners who are using research to understand their work or making decisions based on research must also understand these philosophical stances. In this chapter we will explore these assumptions, beliefs, and theories underlying research processes so that readers can reach an understanding of why questions are asked differently, what assumptions are carried by researchers, and how that affects the choices of methods in studies.

The Elements of Research Paradigms

The word most commonly used to describe a researcher's worldview is *paradigm*. This concept is taken from Thomas Kuhn's thesis on the philosophy of science called "The Structure of Scientific Revolutions" (1962/2012). A paradigm is a philosophical stance in which our thinking and action are embedded. Philosophers and scholars have pondered the nature of knowledge for centuries, and thus we have different and ever-changing answers to these questions. As these philosophical debates and inquiry have evolved, educational scholars have attempted to categorize the major paradigms, or worldviews, to provide a framework in making sense of the research. To help differentiate and distinguish these worldviews, Lincoln, Lynham, and Guba (2011) defined research paradigms based on four belief systems. Those four beliefs, the foundation of all research paradigms, are the following:

Axiology—the nature of ethics and what is of value: What is valued and what is the most ethical way we can come to know something?
Ontology—the nature of reality: What is reality?
Epistemology—the nature of knowledge: How do we know what we know? How do we know reality?
Methodology—the system of inquiry or approach used to gain new knowledge: How can we find out the knowledge or new understanding that we want to know?

In the following sections, we will explain further what these four beliefs are and how they influence research.

Axiology

Axiology is the nature of ethics. What is of value or what knowledge is valued, and what is the most ethical way we can come to know something? What a researcher values will determine what is important to know and search out. One researcher may question the effectiveness of a particular type of curriculum in regard to academic performance, while another researcher may want to understand how children interpret and feel about participating in a certain type of education program. Each question shows what the researcher values most.

Furthermore, ethics has become important in the processes of research and coming to gain new knowledge. Due to past cruelties done to people in the name of research throughout history, ethical guidelines have been established. The most influential guiding report of research ethics is *The Belmont Report*, created by the National Commission for the Protection of Human Subjects of Biomedical and Behavioral Research in 1978. This report set the stage for an approach to ethics used today by institutional review boards that grant permission to researchers to implement their studies. The three main ethical principles are that (1) research should be for the benefit of society, science, and the individuals participating in the study, and risk and harm should be diminished or avoided; (2) people should be treated with respect; and (3) procedures should not exploit participants and should be just (Mertens, 2014). All researchers are obligated to consider the beliefs, values, and ethical principles that guide their research.

Ontology and Epistemology

As the title of this chapter asks, how do we know what we know? The concepts of ontology, or the nature of reality, and epistemology, the nature of knowledge, answer the question for us. In other words, how we view reality and how we believe the world works shape our worldview/paradigm of research.

There have traditionally been different approaches or answers to the ontological and epistemological questions. The answers fall into three different categories: objectivism, constructionism, and subjectivism. Objectivism is the idea that truth and meaning are independent of our consciousness and lie within the object observed. In other words, the concept or meaning of an object lies within the object, whether or not humans are aware of it. When humans discover an object, we are made aware of what was always there. Truth, therefore, is objective. Objectivity is critical and obtainable. Reality can be reduced to the smallest parts that can be observable.

Constructionism is the idea that meaning does not lie in the object one is observing but that the observer him or herself gives meaning to the object. Therefore, there is no one true meaning, but multiple truths that are influenced by the context of the object and subject. As stated by Crotty (1998),

> It is the view that *all knowledge, and therefore all meaningful reality as such, is contingent upon human practices, being constructed in and out of interaction between human beings and their world, and developed and transmitted within an essentially social context.*
>
> (p. 42, italics in original)

Thus, there is interplay between the known and knower (or the object and subject). Rather than striving for objectivity, the researcher must consider context and interpretation.

Subjectivism takes a further step from constructionism and holds the belief that all knowledge is solely subjective and there is no real objective truth. Meaning comes from the subject (the knower) imposing it on the known (object). And the subject (or knower) is vulnerable to the context and discourses he or she inhabits. Any attempt to try to come to a "truth" is fraught with contradictions. Thus, all truths are relative and cannot be generalized to similar situations or even knowable. Therefore, the subjectivist attempts to reveal contradictions and challenge what we think we know.

One way to see the differences in ontology and epistemology is how one might approach the very idea of childhood. For example, from an objectivist worldview, childhood is a specific time within the life span, generally from birth to the late teen years. It is also defined as a distinct time of life different from adulthood. This can be known because the child (or the 'object') itself holds the quality of being a child.

From a constructionist worldview, the concept of child is socially constructed by the society and culture in which a child resides. As James, Jenks, and Prout (1998) stated,

> To describe childhood, or indeed any phenomenon, as socially constructed is to suspend a belief in or a willing reception of its taken-for-granted meanings. . . . Such knowledge of the child and its lifeworld depends on the predispositions of a consciousness constituted in relation to our social, political, historical, and moral context.
>
> (p. 27)

While a constructionist may view children as people at the beginning of their lifetime chronologically, the constructionist recognizes that different cultures or groups may view the child or childhood in very different ways. For example, for some, early childhood is a time of innocence and vulnerability in which a person is in need of protection and incapable of taking care of him- or herself. For others, young children are viewed as highly capable members of society who can contribute to the larger community in many ways and are included in community life from work to leisure.

From a subjectivist worldview, childhood and adulthood are a constructed binary (or opposites) that can be deconstructed and called into question. A subjectivist is not comfortable defining childhood as a coherent or continuous concept. From the subjectivist point of view, we (as the knower) are defining the other (the child) based on our own histories and identities, so rather than attempting to definitively or even contingently say what "childhood" is, we can only show ways in which we complicate our ideas of childhood.

Readers may begin to imagine how a researcher's view of reality must heavily influence how that researcher will design a study and what information or data the researcher will consider 'real' and 'knowable.' An objectivist will begin by defining the object of research with specific categories that are observable and controllable that leads to a finding which can thus be generalizable to similar situations. The constructionist will begin defining the object of research broadly and explore multiple perspectives, contexts, and experiences in defining the object, thus demonstrating there is no ultimate or absolute reality of the object of inquiry. Yet we can come to a better understanding if we consider multiple social constructions. The subjectivist will explore an object of research with caution and be reluctant to state any definitive finding but will lead the reader to question the understanding of the object of research. This leads us to the final aspect of a paradigm as defined by Lincoln et al. (2011): how the researcher goes about finding the knowledge he or she wishes to understand—the methodology.

Methodology and Methods

Once a researcher has a question in mind about an issue, he or she must decide how to design an investigation in response to the question. This research design is called the methodology, or the system of inquiry or approach used to gain new knowledge. The tools that are used to collect the data and analyze the data are called the methods. While there are several different epistemologies that guide research studies, there are two major forms of methodology used to design a study, quantitative and qualitative methodologies. The quantitative designs are generally associated with those with an objectivist worldview, and the qualitative designs are generally associated with the constructivist and subjectivist worldviews.

Quantitative research is defined by Creswell (2014) as "an approach for testing objective theories by examining the relationship among variables. These variables, in turn, can be measured, typically by instruments, so that numbered data can be analyzed using statistical procedures" (p. 4). The methods used in this approach are based on reducing human experiences to observable behaviors and objective attitudes that are measured in a quantifiable manner and with tools that can be validated and reliable (we will discuss validity and reliability in Chapter 4). Studies are performed while using instruments that transform data into numerical form. Then a statistical analysis of such data is employed to test the hypothesis or theory upon which the researcher based the study.

Qualitative research seeks to observe and interpret human experiences by generating rich description of what has been experienced. The qualities of this data are reviewed for evidence to patterns or themes in order for the researcher to make meaning of the phenomenon. Qualitative research has evolved over time, but a general definition used by Denzin and Lincoln (2008) best describes this methodology:

> Qualitative research is a situated activity that locates the observer in the world. It consists of a set of interpretive, material practices that make the world visible. These practices transform the world. They turn the world into a series of representations, including field notes, interviews, conversations, photographs, recordings, and memos to the self. At this level, qualitative research involves an interpretive, naturalistic approach to the world. This means that qualitative researchers study things in their natural settings, attempting to make sense of, or interpret, phenomena in terms of the meanings people bring to them.
>
> (p. 4)

Qualitative methodologies vary and are diverse due to the myriad research disciplines and philosophies from which qualitative research emerged. Disciplines such as ethnography, sociology, history, anthropology, social psychology, linguistics, cultural studies, and feminist studies, just to name a few, are the roots from which qualitative methodologies have arisen. Because qualitative researchers are looking from and for multiple perspectives, there are a variety of methods of collecting data that attempt to capture those perspectives, such as interviews, focus groups, narratives, audio and visual representations, and written texts.

In the following sections, we will briefly describe different types of paradigms that frame research in early childhood studies and the methods employed while also giving an example of a research study that exemplifies each paradigm.

Paradigms and Examples of Research in Early Childhood Education

The elements just described have been drawn upon to construct several different paradigms within which research can be situated. Various researchers and social scientists have attempted to distinguish the differences between research paradigms and to name the paradigms themselves. It is important to recognize that these names and categories are nuanced and not static. Furthermore, the social scientists who explore the concepts within research do not always agree on how to categorize the various paradigms. However, in order to understand the context in which research is done and the particular language used in different studies, it is helpful to have a general understanding of the oft-used paradigms. In this section, we will give a brief description of a paradigm, its common names, and an example of a study within that paradigm. The descriptions and labels used in this chapter are created by synthesizing the work of Creswell (2014), Crotty (1998), Guba and Lincoln (2005), Lather (1991, 2006), and Mertens (2014).

We include the following paradigms: postpositivist, constructivist, transformative, postmodern, and pragmatic. Each paradigm is based on many years of philosophical discussions and reflections. Thus, each paradigm has a rich historical context. Multiple disciplines and theories have shaped each paradigm as well. We do not attempt to completely or thoroughly explore these theories or histories in this text but rather give a general description to help readers understand the foundational differences. For further exploration, we recommend the aforementioned listed references from which the descriptions have been synthesized. For a condensed view and summary of the paradigms and their components, please refer to Table 2.1 at the end of the chapter titled "Research Paradigms in Early Childhood." To demonstrate how the different beliefs about the nature of knowledge influence what questions researchers ask and how they attempt to find out the answers with different methods, we have chosen to briefly examine research studies on a topic familiar to early childhood professionals: play.

Postpositivist

Since the beginning of early childhood research, the positivist paradigm guided the way research was done. Positivist beliefs held that social research (research on individual people or groups of people in society) could follow the same scientific research methods of the natural world in which researchers could employ experiments, observe, and measure behaviors and find an objective constant truth and universal 'laws' that can become generalized to all. However, in the latter half of the 20th century, some researchers began to question if the science of the natural world could be applied to the complexities of human behavior and experience. Thus, a postpositivist paradigm evolved that recognizes that while we cannot claim absolute truth, we can design studies using the traditional scientific method. Essentially, postpositivists have made a step back from the certainty of claims in the positivist paradigm. Their work begins by developing a hypothesis, collecting data that can be quantified with careful observations using measurements or instruments that have been validated. It continues with analyzing the data for verification through statistical procedures deemed appropriate for the type of hypothesis and measurement used. Postpositivists choose to study problems that "reflect the need to identify and assess the causes that influence outcomes" (Creswell, 2014, p. 7). The following example of a postpositivist study on play by Conner, Kelly-Vance, Ryalls, and Friehe (2014), shows how the researchers attempted to look at how play skills influence language skills of very young children. Two groups of children (one with play intervention and one without) were used for comparison of results to test a hypothesis that play intervention would increase language skills.

Conner, J., Kelly-Vance, L., Ryalls, B., & Friehe, M. (2014). A play and language intervention for 2-year-old children: Implications for improving play skills and language. *Journal of Research in Childhood Education*, 28(2), 221–237.

Research Problem: Lack of research in play interventions in which the participants are under 3 years old.

Research Question: Does reading and modeling increase play skills and language development in 2-year-old children?

Methodology: Quantitative

Methods: Assessing play and language skills in 2-year-old children. Before and after the intervention the children were given the Play in Early Childhood Evaluation System (PIECES), Preschool Language Scale (PLS), and a vocabulary assessment made up of 40 words. Children broken into two groups for the 4-week intervention that was administered twice per week in the morning. One group was the intervention group and the other was the comparison group. Intervention processes included a story read to participants, a toy set, modeling by the instructor of how to play with the toys, 5 minutes of free playtime facilitated by the instructor, and 5 minutes of play without facilitation.

Findings: Play increased in three out of five children in the intervention group and decreased in four out of five in the comparison group. Vocabulary gains were made by the children in the intervention group in both the PLS and vocabulary assessment. PLS scores for the children in the comparison group went down, while vocabulary assessment scores increased in comprehension and expression.

Discussion: The intervention helped the majority of the children improve in complexity of play skills, which related to higher cognition levels and language skills. The length of the intervention may have been too short for the young age of the children to retain the skills. Limitations include small sample size and little emphasis on adult interaction to affect play and language skills.

Constructivist

Researchers framing their studies within a constructivist paradigm reject the notion that there can be an objective truth. Rather, constructivists see knowledge as being socially constructed and, as well, not outside the values and context of the researcher. Therefore, the constructivist research process is an effort to understand the complexities of the human experience from the multiple perspectives of the people who are part of the studied experience. The research process is interactive between the researcher and the 'researched.' There is not an attempt to find a single answer or solution to the problem. Rather, the goal is to illuminate the context in which the researcher and the researched live and the interpretations or meanings that the participants construct from their experiences, developing a deeper understanding of a human experience. As seen in Sherwood and Reifel's (2010) study, the researchers attempted to understand preservice teachers' beliefs about the play of young children. Based on interviews and observations, the researchers demonstrated the differences in definitions of play based on past experiences and context.

Sherwood, S.A.S., & Reifel, S. (2010). The multiple meanings of play: Exploring preservice teachers' beliefs about a central element of early childhood education. *Journal of Early Childhood Teacher Education, 31*, 322–343.

Research Problem: Preservice teachers have a wide range of beliefs about the definition and role of play in the classroom that affect how they teach.

Research Questions: What do preservice teachers believe constitutes play?

Methodology: Qualitative

Methods: Seven preservice teachers participated in the study, which included one-on-one interviews, direct observations, and analysis of university course–related documents. Emphasis was on one-on-one interviews.

Findings: Preservice teachers defined play differently based on their individualized experiences and philosophies. While there was some overlap in words used to describe play, the definitions and examples varied among the seven participants.

Discussion: The preservice teachers' individual experiences led to their unique definitions of play, what leads to play, and what activities count as play. The definitions seen in this study show that there was no universal definition of play among preservice teachers because their experiences led them to their own understanding of play in their classroom and at home.

Transformative

Some researchers have critiqued the constructivist paradigm for not fully considering the perspectives of marginalized groups or the politics and power dynamics that shape the context of the lives of those researched. These researchers (many who have come from marginalized groups themselves, such as women, minorities, Indigenous groups) recognize that knowledge is socially constructed, but that knowledge is created in a context of oppression. Studies conducted within this paradigm are often positioned within a theoretical perspective that provides a foundation for understanding marginalization and power dynamics. The following historic theories have been used in transformative research and shaped how research is conducted in this paradigm: feminist theory, Marxist theory, cultural standpoint theories, critical theory, and queer theory. Thus, the methodology utilized directly focuses on challenging oppressive powers, and the researcher openly recognizes his or her position within the power dynamics of the context that is studied. The goal of transformative (or emancipatory) research is to liberate a particular group of people from the power structures that oppress them through a deeper understanding of human experience that also supports change. In a study of Thai children's play spaces by Truong and Mahon (2012), the young children of a community center were considered to be adversely affected by the social and political changes in their village. The study was designed to include the children's perspectives of their play environment and how they would change it to meet the children's needs and desires, not considered by the adults who created the center.

Truong, S., & Mahon, M. (2012). Through the lens of participatory photography: Engaging Thai children in research about their community play centre. *International Journal of Play*, *1*(1), 75–90.

Research Problem: The changing landscape of childhood in Thailand due to globalization and urbanization.

Research Question: How do Thai children experience play and sense of place at a children's center located in an urban low-income congested community?

Methodology: Qualitative action research

Methods: This study focused on the process of using children's photographs as a means for communication and study. Each time students met, they were given an assignment on a topic, sent out to take pictures, asked to select three images to discuss at the next meeting, and asked to make notes about why they took and chose each picture. Topics included different things to do/play at the center, favorite places to play at the center, how the child would change the play center, and others. Focus was put on children's pictures and conversation.

Findings: The children in this study focused on several categories of play: active play, quiet space for imaginative play, natural features such as trees and sandbox, and play equipment. Many also mentioned the lack of open space for free play. Play with friends and socialization was looked at differently from natural spaces and play equipment. Safety was also a part of the discussion about the center's space and outside play spaces as well.

Discussion: There was a difference between designed play spaces for children and where they felt safe and wanted to play. The distinction was made in their responses and desire for open space that was safe to imagine and explore in. Listening to the children's voices was important in this study.

Postmodernism

The postmodern paradigm has emerged for researchers who call into question our ability to make any knowledge claims with surety. The term 'postmodernism' is sometimes used interchangeably with poststructuralism. While the philosophical histories of each of these concepts are unique and complex, they are often considered similar based on their comparable views of the world. While poststructuralists focus mostly on individual agency and postmodernists focus on the larger society, both paradigms view individuals and societies as incapable of developing coherent or continuous meanings of the world (Hughes, 2010). Meaning, power, and identity are always changing, and the postmodernist explores those complexities. The goal of postmodern research is to deconstruct or call into question what we think we know for sure. For many postmodern researchers, this is to reach a goal similar to transformative researchers, addressing power differentials and oppression of groups. In the case of study on children's and adults' views of play, Nicholson, Kurnik, Jevgjovikj, and Ufoegbune (2015) attempted to call into question what adults think they know about children's play.

Nicholson, J., Kurnik, J., Jevgjovikj, M., & Ufoegbune, V. (2015). Deconstructing adults' and children's discourse on children's play: Listening to children's voices to destabilise deficit narratives. *Early Child Development and Care*, *85*(10), 1569–1586.

Research Problem: Discourse between adults' and children's view of the role of and decline of play in today's society.

Research Questions: 1. What discourse do adults use to speak about children's play today? Their own childhood play? 2. What discourse do children use to speak about their play? 3. How aligned and/or divergent are these discourses representing children's play? 4. What are the consequences of these alignments and divergences, especially in relation to children's rights?

Methodology: Qualitative

Methods: Combine data from two studies: Children's Play Narratives Project (CPN) and Global Play Memories Project (GPMP). CPN gathered information from 98 child interviews about their perspectives on their own play and their ideas about adults' play. GPMP gathered information from 135 adults from 21 countries about their play memories.

Findings: CPN children regarded their own play using names of specific toys and games, such as dolls, Legos, Monopoly. They described their favorite types of play using words such as 'fun,' 'run,' 'hang out,' 'playdate,' etc. Few children mentioned digital forms of play, and when they did, it was in a group context and not by themselves. GPMP described a large discrepancy between adults' and children's definitions of play. Adults used many negative terms (such as 'don't,' 'won't,' 'can't,' 'not') to describe children's play, while many of the same statements were given without the negatives by children. Adults brought up the use of digital forms of play more often than did children. Adults also described their own play in negative terms, while most gave excuses of money and situational reasoning.

Discussion: The differences in discourse between adults' views of children and children's ideas of play were vast. Because of the differences in discourse, children should be included in the conversation on play to provide their voice and inform our understanding of critical problems that impact their lives. The children's perspective challenged adults' understanding of play. Children's perspectives can broaden our dialogues socially and politically to become more equitable.

Pragmatism

Pragmatism is a worldview that does not commit to one single system of philosophy or reality. According to Creswell (2014), pragmatists freely choose methods that help answer the questions. Thus, reality or 'truth' is simply what works at the time. While context and historical and social perspectives are considered, sometimes pragmatists will take on social justice. The goal of pragmatic research is to solve a human problem at hand. The unique indication of a pragmatic paradigm is the use of qualitative and quantitative methodology to find the answers to solve the problem identified. In Trawick-Smith and Dziurgot's (2010) study, the researchers recognized that the quality of preschool experiences for children was linked to the quality of teachers' interactions with children during play. The researchers wanted to know if teachers who were professionally educated were better at interacting with children during play in an effort to solve the problem of providing quality preschool experiences for children. The study included using quantitative analysis of the observed teacher interactions with children and the qualitative analysis of interviews with the teachers.

Trawick-Smith, J., & Dziurgot, T. (2010). Untangling teacher–child play interactions: Do teacher education and experience influence "good-fit" responses to children's play? *Journal of Early Childhood Teacher Education, 31*(2), 106–128.

Research Problem: What characterizes high-quality preschools?

Research Questions: Do levels of teacher education and experience influence how teachers respond to children's play needs in the preschool classroom?

Methodology: Mixed methods

Methods: Eight early childhood professionals from full-day preschool classrooms. Four or five 30 minute sessions were videotaped to observe and categorize the adult interactions with children's play. Also, the teachers were interviewed as a second data source.

Findings: Teachers with more experience and high education showed commitment to assessing and enhancing children's outcomes during play. They were successful in using good-fit interactions that facilitated independent play. Low-education and high-experience teachers were more variable in their interactions, sometimes being overly directive. Teachers with low education and low experience stated the main reason for play intervention was for fun and to just play. The low-experience and low-education group also had unpredictable reactions to children's play needs.

Discussion: The researchers used Vygotsky's work as the theoretical orientation. The skills and thoughtfulness required to provide good-fit interactions are worth developing in teachers.

Summary

When one speaks of 'research' in early childhood education, there must be caution in not overgeneralizing or assuming too much for what 'the research says.' As shown by the play research studies in early childhood displayed here, studies vary widely. They are unique in the questions, the values guiding the studies, the worldviews, and the methodologies. However, what all peer-reviewed and published research and evaluation studies most have in common is a documentation of the process or steps taken in doing the research, often in the following order:

- Identifying and situating the problem, leading to a specific question or series of questions.
- A literature review: a summary and synthesis of the research around the topic of inquiry chosen. This may also be the place in which the researcher briefly describes the theoretical framework in which the current study is based.
- Methodology: the design of the study is identified (quantitative, qualitative, or mixed); the participants and sources of data are identified and defined.
- Methods: the data collection methods and/or instruments used to collect the data are described.
- Analysis and findings: how the data were analyzed is described, and what was found through that process is discussed.
- Discussion and implications: how the researcher makes sense of the findings and how those understandings can be used for further research or practice in the field of study.

Table 2.1 Research Paradigms in Early Childhood

	Postpositivism	Constructivism	Transformative/ Emancipatory	Postmodern	Pragmatic
Other Associated Labels	Experimental Quantitative Correlational Randomized-control trials	Naturalistic Interpretivist Phenomenological Hermeneutic Qualitative Ethnographic Grounded theory	Critical Freierian Neo-Marxist Feminist Action Research Queer theory Indigenous Disability Theory	Poststructural Deconstructionist Postcolonial	Post Paradigmatic Mixed methods
Purpose	To predict	To understand	To liberate	To deconstruct	To solve problems
Axiology— what is valued	An attempt to be free of values; objectivity; distance from the researched and the researcher	Context and a balance of multiple perspectives	Promotion of social justice Positionality of researcher and researched	Breaking down the grand narratives and questioning reality and systems of "reality"	
Ontology— what is the nature of reality	There is one reality that is knowable.	Reality is socially constructed. There are multiple realities.	There are multiple realities that are created based on power positioning. Some realities are privileged over others, and this leads to oppression.	Reality is subjective, incoherent, and discontinuous.	Some may reject any claim to truth. Truth is what is useful. There is one reality, but everyone has their own interpretation of reality. What is most important is "what works."
Epistemology— how we know what we know	Objectivity is critical and obtainable. Reality is reduced to smallest parts that can be observable.	There is a relationship between the researcher and the participants that is made explicit. Meaning is constructed together, with attention given to context and complexity.	There is a relationship between the researcher and participants. Action and change are part of the process of knowing.	Meaning is given to the object by the subject. Exploring contradictions	Relationships are defined by what the researcher views as important to solving the problem at hand.

Methodology— an approach or system of inquiry	Quantitative Interventionist Decontextualized	Qualitative Contextualized Case study Ethnography	Qualitative (perhaps quantitative) including historical and political factors. Issues of power and trust are highlighted to address oppression. Examples: participatory action research critical discourse analysis critical ethnography	Foucauldian archeology Critical discourse analysis	Qualitative and quantitative applied to the appropriate questions
Types of Methods— the tools and procedures used to collect and analyze data	Survey Instrument-based questions Performance data, census data Statistical analysis	Interview Observation Participant-observation Focus group Audio/visual artifacts Documents Narrative	Many of the same tools as constructivist with attention to reflexivity and praxis	Reviewing and deconstructing dialogue, historical text, and media	Mix of quantitative and qualitative
Examples of Research in EC	Meisels, S. J., Xue, Y., & Shamblott, M. (2008). Assessing language, literacy, and mathematics skills with work sampling for Head Start. *Early Education and Development, 19*(6), 963–981. Forry, N., Iruka, I. U., Tout, K., Torquati, J., Susman-Stillman, A., Bryant, D., & Daneri, M. P. (2013). Predictors of quality and child outcomes in family child care settings. *Early Childhood Research Quarterly, 28*(4), 893–904.	Graue, M. E., Whyte, K. L., & Karabon, A. E. (2015). The power of improvisational teaching. *Teaching and Teacher Education, 48,* 13–21. Sherwood, S. A., & Reifel, S. (2013). Valuable and unessential: The paradox of preservice teachers' beliefs about the role of play in learning. *Journal of Research in Childhood Education, 27*(3), 267–282.	Adair, J. K. (2014). Examining whiteness as an obstacle to positively approaching immigrant families in US early childhood educational settings. *Race Ethnicity and Education, 17*(5), 643–666. Quintero, E. (2010). Something to say: Children learning through story. *Early Education and Development, 21*(3), 372–391.	Blaise, M. (2005). A feminist poststructuralist study of children "doing" gender in an urban kindergarten classroom. *Early Childhood Research Quarterly, 20*(1), 85–108. Kinard, T. A. (2015). Anonymous green painting: An artifact of resistance as danger and hope in an early childhood educational setting. *International Journal of Qualitative Studies in Education, 28*(2), 195–215.	Dillon, D. R., O'Brien, D. G., & Heilman, E. E. (2000). Literacy research in the next millennium: From paradigms to pragmatism and practicality. *Reading Research Quarterly, 35,* 10–26.

Source: Adapted from Creswell (2014), Crotty (1998), Lincoln et al. (2011), Lather (1991, 2006), and Mertens (2014)

3

THE CULTURE AND CONTEXT OF RESEARCH IN EARLY CHILDHOOD EDUCATION

In this chapter we consider the contexts of research. By 'context' we mean the larger social, cultural, political, and historical influences that have shaped how we view research and what kind of research is considered appropriate. We consider how the ideas and values of the larger society and culture shape what and how research is conducted, how researchers have approached their work, and the groups that have been utilized as participants. The goals and aims of education in the United States have changed over time. Accordingly, what the field of education has needed from and expected from research has shifted as well. Early childhood education has followed an interesting path within these contexts, and in this chapter we discuss and explain how this has played out.

Discussing the contexts of research leads us necessarily to questions of ethics related to how, when, where, why, and with whom research is conducted. This will be a second focus of this chapter. There has been a significant shift over time in how researchers conduct their projects and in the stances the researchers take regarding their relationship to the work. We will note how the quest for ethical practices affects inquiry with adults and with children within the differing paradigms of educational research.

Finally, we will illustrate the 'humanness' of the research enterprise, considering the realities of passionate disagreement among researchers and the stakes of the situations within which policy makers and researchers interface. Here we argue that we cannot ignore the "broad moral and political frameworks that undergird research" (Howe & Moses, 1999, p. 32) both in how researchers approach their work and in how that research is ultimately used (or not) to shape policy and practice in educational settings and situations.

Contexts

Social sciences research is a social activity in which we are interested in learning more about the relationships people have with each other, to events in society and social situations, and to the institutions that govern their lives. What we believe to be important, what we value, and what we need to understand as a society or as a culture at any point in time is shaped by a historical moment, dominant political ideologies, technology of the time, and the prominent paradigms of thought. Thus, education as an institution of our society has moved through different phases in terms of what we have regarded as its purpose and goals and so follows the purposes of and needs for educational research. Research in early childhood education has flowed along this stream as well. In what follows, we describe some important and influential moments across the last century that help us to understand from where research has come and where it might help us to go.

In the early years of the 20th century, social institutions were shifting in importance and influence, and the population was rapidly changing. The country struggled to define the aims and goals of education (Kliebard, 2004). The major belief at the time was that that we needed to study education scientifically, which meant that research needed to be entirely empirical and analytical. Those studying social behaviors and phenomena attempted to describe "law-like theories of social behavior" (Bloch, 1991, p. 100), and researchers sought to find a universal truth that was objective and not context specific. Researchers believed they could isolate variables for study without regard to context, leading to the ability to predict future behaviors. There was also a belief that research (theory) was distinctly separate from practice and that theory should serve to inform practice (Popkewitz, 1984). There was conviction in the ability to determine "exactly what should be taught in schools and how educational knowledge should be structured" (Scott, 2008, p. 6).

Early childhood research at this time was heavily influenced by the doctrine of developmentalism. The focus of research was on children's development rather than being directed toward learning and/or curriculum (Saracho & Spodek, 2013). This doctrine held that we could determine exact and universal understandings about how children developed; the goal was to optimize children's development via scientific inquiry (Beatty, 2005). Scientific inquiry would be "the model for truth, [would provide] definitions of valuable knowledge, a way to get factual information about 'normal' child development, and [provide] guidance for pedagogy" (Bloch, 1992, p. 9).

The developmentalist movement was led by G. Stanley Hall and operated from the belief that through careful observation and documentation we could literally catalog what happened in the minds of children. Observable and quantifiable behavior was key, and the research was accomplished via surveys, careful observation, and recording of children's behaviors at various stages of their development. Hall's work was highly influential in advocating for the importance of including children as a worthwhile area of study, and it opened the door to serious attention being paid to children by the fledgling psychological sciences (Brooks-Gunn & Johnson, 2006). Bloch (1991) noted that Hall's notions, "more or less intact were used to begin the child development movement which related psychology to science, psychology to child development, and psychology to the study of pedagogy and curriculum" (p. 100). Another highly influential researcher of the mid-20th century was Arnold Gesell, who charted descriptions of children's development, believed to be genetically programmed and to unfold within an appropriately supportive environment.

Goffin (1996) pointed out that the 'scientism' of research in early childhood at this time in history supported the professionalization of the field. She noted that there was an "undervaluation of children as public responsibility," and great faith was put into the ability of "scientifically derived solutions" in the form of "predictable and achievable child development outcomes" (p. 125) to lead advocacy for higher-quality early childhood settings with better-prepared and better-compensated personnel.

It was also during the early 20th century that nursery schools, first institutionalized in Great Britain, were imported to the United States. Women, both philanthropists and professionals, were key figures in establishing supports for research associated with the growth of nursery schools. For example, Cora Bussey Hillis, a citizen-advocate, led efforts to establish a research station in Iowa focused on children's development. Lucy Sprague Mitchell and Caroline Pratt are often cited in introductory early childhood texts as key early practitioners/leaders within the field. Along with Harriet Johnson, they also made an early impact on research by founding the Bureau of Educational Experiments (Beatty, 2005). In the 1920s, large influxes of funding were distributed to support research associated with nursery schools and the growing number of research institutes across the country via the Laura Spelman Rockefeller Memorial.

These efforts helped clearly establish early childhood research as a field worthy of attention, influenced greatly by developmental psychology. The early decades of research relevant to early childhood were marked by a mission to understand and nurture children's development. There was little attention to context or to diversity among the children and families who participated in this research. Therefore, it was common for generalizations about children's development to be made after studying only white middle-class children.

Interestingly, despite Hall's early dominance, his methods were eventually criticized by some factions as not being scientific enough. Hall's methods had led him (and many of his students) to begin to draw conclusions about biological determinism, the belief that genetic inheritance determines development and learning. If researchers were able to exactly determine the developmental path of a child, curriculum could be developed with a probable destination (Kliebard, 2004) in mind. And these kinds of determinations were roundly critiqued by social scientists in education who had begun to consider how social contexts and social structures could impact a child's access to opportunities.

On the heels of the critiques of biological determinism as a means to shape what occurred in schools, a social meliorist faction in educational research emerged in the middle decades of the 20th century. This shift stemmed initially from the Great Depression, which had engendered an "undercurrent of discontent about the American economic and social system" (Kliebard, 2004, p. 154). This period spawned an increased awareness over time regarding the inequitable distribution of opportunity across social groups, and social unrest resulted. Research in early childhood began to change, with streams of inquiry focused on learning and programmatic interventions that could help improve the lot of children and families who were deemed disadvantaged. Around the same time, psychologists began to study learning processes, influenced by ideas in the modern world that the early years could have an impact on children's developmental course. For example, Piaget's theory and Bloom's assertions that the preschool years were particularly important to learning spurred interest in research (Saracho & Spodek, 2013). Additionally, some early childhood researchers began to define their work more strongly within the educational field, exploring questions about curriculum.

As a result of these research efforts, programmatic interventions for children living in poverty sprang up, framed around the vision during these times that the children were 'culturally deprived.' During the 1960s, research was conducted on intervention programs, including but not limited to Head Start. In addition to attempts to determine program effectiveness, this body of research included examination of various curriculum models (Consortium for Longitudinal Studies, 1983). These researchers utilized more complex designs, such as randomly assigning children to classrooms or classrooms to curriculum models (this is used to create groups that are roughly equivalent). In addition, several types of standardized, direct assessments of children's learning and development were included, such as achievement and IQ tests.

For our purposes as early childhood educators, the importance of this research is that it marks a turning point in expectations for early childhood education. By the 1960s more complex research methods from experimental psychology were being used to examine the impact of educational experiences on children. Additionally, researchers conducted studies that targeted children in particular circumstances, such as living in poverty. This research firmly established the place of quantitative methods in looking for effects deemed to be significant. Hypotheses were proposed and tested via statistical analyses, and the results were assumed to be generalizable to other, similar programs or situations. The goal was to find evidence that early childhood programs provided benefits for young children.

As time went on, quantitative methods were used to answer questions regarding the impact of many programs and policies. For example, following the rise in usage of child care, researchers explored a series of questions, commencing with determining whether being in child care was harmful or beneficial. From there, researchers moved toward questions that complicated the initial suppositions about child care's effects by including attention to differences in quality of care and the family context (Phillips & McCartney, 2005). Currently, with universal prekindergarten programs increasing in number, research examining program effectiveness has emerged (for example, see Wong, Cook, Barnett, & Jung, 2008). Another area of high research activity in the current era has been early literacy learning, spurred in part by federally funded reading initiatives (for example, see National Early Literacy Panel, 2008). Other, smaller-scale studies have examined many aspects of early childhood education, including topics such as, for instance, dual language development, teacher–child interactions, peer play, components of teacher shared book-reading, and children's self-regulation.

Throughout the history of early childhood research, researchers have pursued studies that draw upon quantitative methods, and this has been the dominant form of published research in many research journals. These studies most closely align with what is familiar to the general public regarding 'science'—questions or hypotheses are posed and data are collected in numerical form (i.e., scores on assessments, ratings on observation instruments, counts of behaviors, ratings on surveys or questionnaires) and then analyzed via statistics. This history parallels the history of general educational research's early decades. The importance of quantitative measurement was evident in the early 20th century in the training of educational researchers and among the researchers who founded the American Educational Research Association (Lagemann, 1997).

Bloch (1987, 1992, 2000) helps us understand, however, that the paths of early childhood education and general education research did also diverge during this time. Social reformers/ activists and those desiring to realize the potential of education to address inequalities were more successful in shifting the gaze of, approach to, and goals of education research and curriculum in general education research. Separate schools of education emerged at the university level, and alternative research paradigms proliferated. Meanwhile, in many (if not most) cases, early childhood programs and departments remained within or heavily aligned with developmental psychology, focusing on individual development and family influences in order to remain a 'hard' science. This was perpetuated, in part, by the need to push professionalization of the field (Goffin, 1996), which was highly feminized and so lower in regard.

This means that there are some important moments where early childhood research has diverged from (if not lagged behind) a larger 'interpretive turn' taken in the social sciences and the general education research agenda. According to Rabinow and Sullivan (1987), in the mid-20th century and onward, research took this interpretive turn. Social relationships, writ large and small, became the units of analysis. The goal was to understand human relationships and experiences rather than the outcomes related to proof or prediction. Rather than the almost singular focus on individuals and their behavior, there was a shift to better understand how people engaged with each other and with the social settings within which they moved. The group dynamics of majority and minority groups and how institutions and ideologies both shaped and were shaped by the agentic actions of people came to the forefront as well. The postmodern thought movement began to take hold, and interpretive qualitative methodologies gained prominence with the larger goals of social meliorism and/or goals of social reconstructionism. This required a focus on the local, the situated, and the different conceptions of knowledge, power, and voice.

Marked as a period of 'reconceptualization,' particularly in relationship to curriculum studies (Pinar, 2004), this began a time where the basic assumptions of mainstream educational research were called into question and alternative approaches to research were proposed. Critical analyses of schooling and the power relations within highlighted the force of dominant culture and ideology to circumscribe educational opportunities across identity groups. Sociology of education emerged, and researchers began to carefully document the actual experiences of children in schools, the impact that children and teachers had on curriculum, and inequality of access to quality schooling (e.g., Gracey, 1972; Lubeck, 1985; Rist, 1970). Anthropological studies of children and schooling emerged that provided rich descriptions of the lives of children and families to highlight how a variety of cultural norms interfaced with the dominant cultural norms of schooling (Heath, 1983; Lubeck, 1985).

The numbers of early childhood scholars working within this new paradigm were fewer than in general education, and gaining voice within the field took time. These researchers took the position that it was crucial for us to understand childhood, early childhood education, and classroom practice as inseparable from the larger politicized and value-laden contexts in which the field existed. Research highlighted the important notion that neither early childhood practice nor the study of it was value neutral. Cannella and Bloch (2006) pointed out that this work "crossed disciplinary and geographic boundaries [and] fostered hybrid ways" (p. 6) of understanding early childhood theory and practice. Researchers operating within qualitative research methods brought two things to the early childhood field. First, they offered another way to conduct inquiry (asking different questions, generating different information). Second, they brought to bear the influence of postmodern thought, with the expanding ideas of what counted as knowledge and truth. And it is important to note that while the history of qualitative research in relationship to the field of early childhood education is briefer than that of quantitative research, it is no less important.

We will explore more fully how qualitative studies differ from those influenced by developmental psychology in more detail in upcoming chapters. To briefly set the stage, the approaches used share some characteristics: understanding phenomena in light of complexity, concerns with issues of power, and understanding children and adults through their voices and firmly situated within their unique contexts (Walsh, Tobin, & Graue, 1993). Qualitative studies have given us rich descriptions of children, classrooms, and practice, such as these early exemplars: narratives about the experiences of children who were either African American and enrolled in Head Start or growing up white and middle class (Lubeck, 1985), analyses of how differing communities defined readiness for kindergarten (Graue, 1992), and examinations of children's peer relationships and culture (Corsaro, 1985).

In reality, researchers who do qualitative research have often pushed against the dominance of the quantitative approaches from developmental psychology. Having their work recognized, both professionally and in the political arena, has been met with both challenges and successes. Only a decade after his first book on the use of qualitative methods in early childhood, Hatch (2007) described how changes in federal policy with the No Child Left Behind legislation passed in the early 21st century privileged quantitative approaches. He warned that this perspective impacted the credibility of qualitative researchers. Thus, questions such as 'Is this research valuable? Should it have weight in the world? Should it be supported?' are far from being answered with common agreement among all sorts of researchers and policy makers.

In sum, we have provided a brief overview of how the changing historical, political, social, and cultural contexts of education have and continue to shape our approaches to how we consider, approach, and study the education of young children. Shifts in what early childhood education researchers and teachers want to understand and how we go about research have pushed the field to move beyond the methodological boundaries of developmental psychology. The ties to quantitative research are no less important in the field today, yet the field also has been opened up to a wider variety of research methods to help us grapple with the complexity and the heightened importance placed on the field today. There is little quibble about the social and economic benefits of quality early childhood education (for example, Barnett, 2008). As programming expands and states take more interest in supporting comprehensive early childhood education, we fully support the idea that a wide swath of kinds of research and research methods will only help us to better understand what young children and their families want and need from the field.

Ethics

According to Smith (1990),

> ethics refers to that complex of ideals showing how individuals should relate to one another in particular situations, to principles of conduct guiding these relationships, and to the kind of reasoning one engages in when thinking about such ideals and principles.
>
> (p. 141)

Certainly in relationship to the enterprise of educational research, one can see how ethics can and should arise as an important consideration of the researcher's work. It is the case that when we consider the different paradigms of research, ethics are approached somewhat differently, and the contexts of research have shaped how researchers think about the issues of ethics related to their work.

The history of early childhood research presented here should provide enough basis to engender questions of what it means to be a researcher, particularly in relationship to the people or groups that one might study. We have discussed how research positions range from a belief in objective observation of phenomena for some to a full embrace of the impossibility of neutral objectivity for others; this should beg authentic questions of how researchers might behave as human beings in this endeavor. Questions of ethics are not always highlighted in presentations of research unless there is a particularly vexing ethical dilemma involved in the study. It is certainly not common for a journal-length research report to include a discussion of the ethics involved in the study that challenges the reader to understand. However, we believe that a sense of ethics does and should undergird the work of researchers.

So if we are not required to delve deeply into ethics, why might we choose to do so here? Perhaps the interpretive turn in social sciences research described earlier has provided the contexts in which the ethics of research have become more prominent and even more necessary to consider. In the postmodern paradigm, relationship and trust among researchers and participants have become central, and issues of ethics take on a more intimate flavor. In the field of early childhood, we take the stance that since we are always engaging with questions about young children or about phenomena related to the care and education of young children, we have a particularly keen responsibility to consider the ethical responsibilities and implications of our work—regardless of the research paradigm being used to conduct the research. Research in early childhood education always has the potential to impact educational opportunities and, thus, the lives of children and their families. In research, children are considered to be a 'vulnerable' population warranting particular care so that the best interests of the children involved (whether as the primary target of the research or as those for whom the research has implications) are at the forefront at every step along the way of any research project.

All major research-related organizations in education put forward a general code of ethics for researchers to follow. In the case of research related to early childhood, often these organizations will put forth ethical standards for conducting research that include additional considerations when children are directly involved. For instance, the National Association for the Education of Young Children (NAEYC) puts forth the following standards for all types of research including that: (1) children must never be harmed in any way when involved in research; (2) children and families must be involved in a process of informed consent in which they have the right to full information about the study's processes, including explanation of possible risks and benefits; (3) children can and should be allowed to ask questions about the research being conducted and those questions should be answered in a way that the child/ren can understand; (4) children and families can refuse to participate in research and/or can withdraw from a study at any time; and (5) confidentiality of the participants must be maintained at all times throughout the research process, including when the research is shared or disseminated (National Association for the Education of Young Children, n.d.).

The Society for Research in Child Development (SRCD) adds that (1) not only should research involving children be not harmful, the least stressful methods of data collection should also be used; (2) children themselves should be allowed to assent to the research activities in conjunction with parent consent; (3) any incentives that are used in data collection need to be appropriate to the age of the children involved and "must not unduly exceed the range of incentives that the child normally experiences" (Principle 5, para. 5); (4) deception as method should be used only as deemed essential to the research endeavor, and the process used should have "no known harmful effects" (Principle 6, para. 6) to the child or the family; (5) if anything happens during the research process that puts a child in jeopardy in any way, this must be reported to the family; and (6) researchers have an obligation to take care in the presentation of findings related to children (Society for Research in Child Development, 2007).

In the shifting paradigms of research, it is important to consider how the different paradigms may frame their ethical responsibilities. For those working from a positivist, scientific frame, researchers claim that there is scientific neutrality. The writ-large goals of research in this paradigm are the "traditional utilitarian goals of advancing knowledge . . . and benefitting society" (Howe & Moses, 1999, p. 24). Objectivity itself is a goal of quantitative work, so the goal of any project is to design as much objectivity as possible. Ethical responsibilities are fulfilled via following the standards set by professional organization, such as those noted, and via the process of prestudy research design. Conscientious researchers also consider what to do when they uncover sensitive information. For example, if an instrument measuring depression is used in the research, should there be a response from the researcher if a participant's responses show the potential of higher levels of depression? What are the researcher's responsibilities if s/he sees evidence of potential child abuse or neglect in the course of collecting data? Or observes teachers interacting with children in unprofessional ways? How do promises of confidentiality matter in these situations? Obviously, by becoming privy to information about individuals, researchers, even those who prize objectivity, may find a host of situations that require very thoughtful consideration. Often researchers attempt to consider the possibilities for responding to sensitive information as part of the study design. For example, in a multisite study in which one of us (File) participated, the study protocols called for offering a local mental health hotline number to participants who answered questions on a depression scale in the affirmative.

Overall, "for both quantitative and qualitative research studies, the integrity of the research is determined by the authenticity of data, proper data representation, and political issues surrounding research findings" (Howe & Moses, 1999, p. 29). Following the interpretive turn that social science research has taken over the past century, however, it is the case that questions of ethics have taken on more importance and urgency and more complexity and benefited from deeper consideration (Cannella & Lincoln, 2011). We have moved into paradigms of thought and research that insist that "research is not neutral because all research has embedded in it particular assumptions, and ways of viewing the world; particular positioning to knowledge, knowing and meaning making, and then the types of research relationships that are possible" (Coady, 2010, p. 82). This means that while issues of ethics can and should be an integral part of designing research projects, deep thoughtfulness about ethics and potential ethical dilemmas must be considered throughout the research process, including later impact on participants—all of which were/are less a part of the scientific and positivist research paradigm.

The interpretive turn required a growth and interest in qualitative research methods (Cannella & Lincoln, 2011; Christians, 2011; Rabinow & Sullivan, 1987). Qualitative research at its very core is about understanding and interpreting the perspectives of participants and/or of understanding the whys of human behavior and phenomena. The importance of relationships and connections with study participants in order to most accurately reflect their experiences necessitates that ethical considerations are broader and can be more complex. Since qualitative research is an umbrella paradigm with several movements of thought that fall under it, the considerations of ethics do vary somewhat across the qualitative approaches.

In research in early childhood education, the considerations have a great deal to do with the unit or level of analysis that is occurring within the study—does the research focus on social structures (schools, care settings, policy structures), on cultural groups (children in groups, families, teachers), or on individuals (children, teachers, family members)? Within this, any number of ethical questions can arise that need to be handled. These include issues such as how the presence of the researcher may impact the research setting, how the participants feel about the research questions, how the research process impacts them, if the data that is being collected is enough/appropriate to capture their perspectives, how power dynamics are playing out in the research setting or with the researcher, and what the later impacts of the research findings may be on the group/individuals participating in the project. Added to this is that, in many cases in early childhood research, children are the main focus of the research, and thus an additional element of care in relationship to ethics is imperative. And in all cases in early childhood research, the research will have some impact on children and families in some way, and thus, ethics are important.

In later chapters, we will discuss in more detail some of the methodological devices that both quantitative and qualitative researchers use to address ethical considerations in their work. As mentioned, the building of as much objectivity as is possible into the research design and prestudy implementation is a major way that quantitative researchers incorporate ethics into their work. Carrying out the project according to the plans and protocols that acknowledge and protect against identified potential harm and ensure that informed choice to participate is offered are primary considerations for quantitative researchers. For qualitative researchers, ethical considerations are certainly an ongoing part of study design. Because most qualitative researchers pointedly grapple with objectivity (or do not believe it exists), as questions arise while a study is carried out, ethics must be reconsidered from point to point. And it is the case that ethical questions may cause a researcher to change the study design to reflect or address ethical dilemmas. Qualitative research focuses on relationships, perspectives, and interpretations, and how these phenomena occur and play out can raise unexpected questions, concerns, issues, and situations that need to be addressed.

The Humanness of the Research Enterprise

We end this chapter with consideration of the 'humanness' of the research enterprise, considering the realities of passionate disagreement among researchers and the stakes of the situations within which policy makers and researchers interface. One might believe that with the processes of science underlying the research enterprise, there would be relative agreement about research findings. In other words, if the methods utilized in research reflect accepted conventions about how to do research, how much is there to contest about the findings? In short, there can be intense disagreement and debate among researchers. There are many decision points during the research endeavor that can incite discussion. Researchers disagree about the decisions made. They disagree about the perspectives taken in asking a research question. They disagree about what was *not* included in a research question. Researchers come with their own ideas about what to ask and how to investigate a phenomenon. They also have their own biases about how best to conduct research and what methods make the most sense. In short, at times researchers may take opposing positions or make decisions that will be criticized by their colleagues. As in any human enterprise, there is inherent conflict and passionate discussion. Because so many matters in early childhood can relate to public policy and the decisions made within a democratic society, the context often becomes even more fraught. For instance, when do research findings justify a large outlay of money toward an intervention or program? Or a change in public policy?

A vivid example of this sort of turbulence exists within early childhood research related to infants in child care. In the mid-1980s, Belsky (1986) published a brief article contending that mounting research evidence showed infants who were enrolled in child care on a more-than-part-time basis may be at greater risk for insecure attachment with the mother. The stakes were high, as care for infants was increasing at a rate higher than other age groups; mothers were in the workforce more often and sooner following the birth of a baby. In the words of a *New York Times* reporter, "His statement created a professional uproar, and the subject was hashed out on talk shows and in midnight discussions of countless working parents" (Eckholm, 1992).

Intense discussion and more research followed for years. A couple years after the initial piece, a special issue of the journal *Early Childhood Research Quarterly* was devoted to the topic. Belsky (1988) published another article in this issue clarifying that with more recent research, he viewed the risk as such: Infants who participated in more than 20 hours of nonmaternal care in the first year of life were more likely to show behaviors in a research setting that reflected avoidance of their mother. Belsky (1988) went so far as to write, "I know from experience that this is not a popular point of view within the developmental sciences today. I also know that it is charged with being politically and ideologically driven" (p. 266).

The rest of this issue contained articles from other researchers who discussed their concerns about Belsky's conclusions. For example, the research procedure used at the time to assess attachment in infants and young children was called the 'Strange Situation.' It involved a sequence of events during which the child was with the mother, separated from the mother while with a 'stranger' (the research assistant), and reunited with the mother. It had been devised decades earlier, before children in child care regularly separated from their parents. Two researchers (Clarke-Stewart, 1988; Thompson, 1988) questioned whether this procedure had remained meaningful in the same way in recent research given social change. Clarke-Stewart raised questions about whether the concepts regarding attachment in use at the time were too limited for examining this phenomenon. She also questioned what was known about the effect of employment on mothers, speculating that difficulties or tensions with employment could impact the infant rather than only the experience of child care. Another pair of researchers (Richters & Zahn-Waxler, 1988) raised technical questions about Belsky's reading of the research.

As researchers debated, many in the public were alarmed. Effectively, the barn door was open, as it would have been difficult to reverse widespread employment trends. Were children being harmed? Should there be policy in this area? If so, of what sort—paid leaves for parents or more regulation for quality care settings?

Because this issue was so potent, a large federally funded study (the Study of Early Child Care and Youth Development—SECCYD) was launched by the National Institute of Child Health and Human Development (NICHD). More than 1,300 babies and their families were enrolled in the study, which was conducted through 10 sites located across the country. Data collection continued through the middle school years, and as the data were analyzed, the results were published. The research questions were complex, taking into account what was happening in child care centers and what was happening within families. In an account of the study written for the lay public, results of child care enrollment through children's entry into school were summarized as follows:

> Center-based child care is associated with both positive and negative effects. This type of care is linked to better cognitive development through age 4½ and to more positive social behaviors through age 3. But, center-based and large-group settings are also associated with more problem behavior just before and just after school entry.
>
> (U.S. Department of Health and Human Services, National Institutes of Health, 2006, p. 21)

As publication of the study's findings has continued throughout the years, so has discussion about their meaning and implications. Questions about how much the quality of the child care settings mattered and about what was being emphasized in discussions—the large percentage of children functioning well or the smaller percentage reported as having issues—were replayed in professional and lay outlets. Other questions about the design of the study and how it could and should inform public policy were debated. Because of the public nature of some of these debates, this particular long-term research project has provided a front-row view into a very human story.

Summary

Perhaps a good word to summarize this chapter is 'complexity.' While we hope up front to ensure that readers understand how incredibly complex the research enterprise is, we do so not to create anxiety. Complexity does not render the topic something that is beyond understanding. We hope that it leads readers to a perspective that includes the following big ideas. First, how research has been conducted and what has interested researchers have varied over time, and it is true today that there are very different approaches. Not surprisingly, the value placed on varying approaches differs depending on who is doing the valuing. Second, as is true of any human enterprise, research is a space within which people bring their own biases and preferences. From the beginning, as a study proceeds, the space within which a researcher works is somewhat unique, shared by some and foreign to others. Researchers are no less human than anyone else who might have passionate ideas in response to the question, 'If we know this thing, what does it mean for where we might go from here?'

4

METHODOLOGIES

We have situated research as a human activity and one that people enter with differing agendas. We have also introduced the layers that underlie the research project itself: the researcher's own positions on epistemology and ontology, those larger questions that frame ways of understanding the world. In this chapter, we will introduce the major tenets that govern how researchers work within the qualitative and quantitative paradigms, as well as discuss mixed methods.

Comparing Qualitative and Quantitative Research

In the simplest terms, qualitative researchers base their data and analyses in text and narrative, while quantitative researchers use numerical representations of data and statistical analyses. As shown in the previous chapter, researchers across these paradigms have different beliefs at the core of their work. In this section we will outline the premises of research by drawing comparisons between qualitative and quantitative approaches. More information about how researchers generate, analyze, and present data are discussed in the chapters that follow.

Placing the Study

Research never exists within a vacuum, but instead within a larger body of knowledge or literature. Each study is conducted within a space in which there are studies that preceded a particular project and studies that will follow. How that body of knowledge figures in the researcher's decisions and presentation of the study are considered in what follows.

Quantitative Research

Quantitative researchers tend to be very focused upon the 'long story' of research and the body of literature. Their work typically begins with a consideration of the questions: What do we know now about this phenomenon? What has come before? Where are the gaps? In this way researchers attempt to make the next step in building a body of knowledge. In their presentation of a study, quantitative researchers situate their studies within this long story by beginning with a review of the literature, describing what previous research has found and what questions remain unanswered. Then, in the concluding discussion section, the researchers typically indicate how this study contributed to the body of knowledge and next steps for future research. The picture that emerges is that each piece of research is like a part of a brick wall, contributing to the whole but needing each of the other pieces in order to make sense.

To illustrate, Piasta et al. (2012) conducted professional development with teachers in Head Start and public prekindergartens serving low-income groups. The research group then examined how teachers responsively engaged children in conversation, as well as selected features of the children's language production. They situated the study broadly within a current focus on children's school readiness and achievement gaps. Early on, in stating the purpose of their research, the researchers said their study was "drawing on a large body of research" (Piasta et al., p. 387). In the literature review, the researchers examined what was known from previous research about preschools as language-learning environments, establishing that observational instruments had documented relatively low levels of language development support. Noting the potential of language development supports for children, they stated, "Findings such as these have led researchers to consider the potential benefits of PD [professional development] for enriching the preschool classroom language-learning environment" (Piasta et al., p. 388). They noted few studies had been conducted to examine professional development in this area. In this way, the researchers made the case that their study was the next logical step in the development of the knowledge base. They utilized a particular PD program in which previous research had shown "promising prior reports" (Piasta et al., p. 389) when implemented in Canada. Consequently, their purpose in this study was to examine whether a briefer version of the PD, implemented with teachers serving low-income children in the United States, was effective.

In the discussion section of their paper, Piasta et al. (2012) compared their findings to other studies. For example, they noted, "the findings of the present study converge with prior reports . . ." (p. 397) and "our findings are unique in that . . ." (p. 397) and "the value of the present work, in extending [previous] findings, is . . ." (p. 398). Note how these sorts of statements help the readers understand the place of this study within the larger body of research.

In summary, quantitative researchers tend to regard their work as building upon the information and gaps from other work, illustrated by the metaphor of the brick wall. Showing the structure of that wall to the reader is important.

Qualitative Research

Qualitative researchers also spend time situating their studies within the larger body of literature and research related to their question of study. But we will immediately change the metaphor of the brick wall from the previous section. Qualitative researchers seek less to add bricks to the wall and more to remove the bricks and use them to build new walls (or bridges or fences or roadways). Rather than establishing what it is that we already 'know' about a topic or phenomenon, qualitative researchers situate their work within the larger body of research to help us ascertain what is understood thus far. This understanding points to where deeper, more sophisticated, or more critically derived understandings might be beneficial, a nuanced but important distinction. The existing body of knowledge is not taken for granted as the canon. It is, rather, questioned and contested to explicitly point out what has been left out, voices that have not been considered, and power relations that shape a phenomenon that have not been previously accounted for.

This questioning occurs as a result of most qualitative researchers' epistemological beliefs about the nature of knowledge—that it is local, situated, and framed socioculturally, politically, and historically. Explicating the theoretical framing of a study is a key feature of qualitative work, and this is where the grounding in existing literature is often focused. There are a variety of paradigms of thought and theory that qualitative researchers draw from, and no one school of thought is considered better than or at a higher status than another. In fact, the same corpus of data could be examined from a variety of lenses, each garnering differing values, interpretations, and different kinds of findings. 'Results' are not really a feature of qualitative work. Researchers engage in an accounting of findings and a discussion of their relevance that is consistent with the organizing theoretical framework. This makes the explicit situating of a study within a particular theoretical framework a critical component of this work.

For example, Souto-Manning (2014) examined and described engagement with a 'taboo' topic on the part of a teacher and the children in her preschool classroom. Her goal in this article was to question and critically examine the notion of the 'ideal' early childhood classroom that is presented in more traditional early childhood research. She gave an overview of research related to this notion of 'ideal,' but not with the objective of building upon that as a settled and assumed concept. She took an established concept and pointed out the ways in which it has been culturally derived and is fraught with power relations to dominant cultural ideas, thus leaving what could be productive avenues to supporting children in classrooms.

In order to do this, Souto-Manning (2014) introduced the lens of 'conflict theory' as a mechanism to critically examine what the research currently has established as the 'ideal' classroom. She reviewed previous research to establish how this concept/phenomenon has been discussed. She specifically sought to disrupt the idea using this 'new' theoretical lens, carefully pointing out the ways that conceptualizations thus far have not been complete, indeed excluding the values and norms of a diversity of cultural perspectives. Souto-Manning specifically stated, "I suggest that the normative construct of the 'ideal' early childhood classroom needs to be challenged, deconstructed, and reconceptualized" (p. 610). She situated the study within the framework of conflict theory in order to point out the shortcomings of previous work and to set the stage for her critical examination of her data.

Souto-Manning's (2014) presentation of findings and her discussion were utilized to establish and provide evidence for her interpretations. She used the extant literature base to continue to compare and contrast her lens and interpretations with what has come before rather than to build upon it per se. As we said at the beginning of this section, qualitative researchers seek less to add bricks to the wall and more to remove the bricks and use them to build something new.

Reasoning and Logic

Reasoning and logic are the processes by which researchers move from one point to another, drawing connections and making inferences. While quantitative and qualitative researchers might draw upon both inductive and deductive reasoning models, there are patterns within each paradigm.

Quantitative Research

Quantitative researchers most often use deductive reasoning in their work. To begin, they rely on theories about how things work. Theories provide an explanation and can range from more general (e.g., Piaget's theory of development) to more specific (e.g., a theory of how coaching affects teachers' use of professional development efforts). Researchers then devise questions and methods to test a specific example of the theoretical explanation. Traditionally researchers presented their test of the explanation in the form of hypotheses, relationships that they expected to find (e.g., x leads to y). It is more common now to find research questions or statements of purpose; these questions or statements do not utilize the same formal wording as the hypothesis statement.

Returning to our example from the study by Piasta et al. (2012), we find the general theoretical explanation early in the literature review: "Both theory . . . and recent research . . . suggest that children's language development is contingent upon the quality and quantity of language and communicative acts to which they are exposed" (p. 388). From there, getting more specific, they examined a particular form of teachers' language, conversational responsiveness, which facilitates several turns for each speaker within a conversation. They also centered on the problem of using professional development (PD) to increase the occurrence of these types of conversations, using two groups of teachers, one that received PD in this area and one who did not. Their aims were summarized at the end of the literature review (incidentally where one hopes to find them):

> The first aim was to investigate the extent to which preschool teachers' participation in PD influenced their immediate and sustained use of . . . strategies over the academic year. The second aim was to investigate whether the conversational productivity and complexity of children in PD classrooms was increased as compared to children in comparison classrooms.
>
> (p. 390)

Qualitative Research

Qualitative researchers engage in close study of phenomena in our lived worlds. Inductive reasoning, in which a variety of premises are considered and are valid, guides the work of qualitative researchers. Researchers draw from a theoretical framework to study the particulars of an occurrence in a social setting that then leads to new and more sophisticated understandings and different interpretations about what is going on. The goal is to expand existing theories—sometimes to disrupt, sometimes to add nuance, sometimes to apply a new theory to interpret the phenomena, and sometimes to create entirely new theoretical explanations. Qualitative researchers do not study a situation or phenomenon to prove an existing theory but rather use a theoretical framework to guide their interpretations. Indeed, there is a strand of qualitative research called 'grounded theory' in which the goal is to study a phenomenon fully and from it to derive new and unique theories about the workings of the world related to that phenomenon.

Logic in a qualitative study is steeped in the notion of consistency within the conceptual and theoretical groundings of a study and the conduct of the study. This logic helps draw a thread through a study with which the theoretical framing guides the types of questions asked, the types of data collected or the kinds of situations examined, the manner of the interpretations, and nature of the conclusions that might be drawn or discussions that may ensue. Conclusions that are drawn are done so as a result of providing evidence of the researcher's interpretation of the phenomena under study, which relates to the theoretical framing of the study. It is a weaving together of a story that helps us better understand or differently interpret the phenomena under study.

Returning to the Souto-Manning (2014) example, she stated up front that she engaged in an ethnographic research project. While ethnography is a methodology, it entails a particular set of data collection methods that provide insight into the ways that this researcher considered phenomena and how she theorized the workings of the world. She spent long periods of time in a setting, collecting careful notes and observing what happened in that setting. She interviewed carefully the 'actors' of the setting and collected artifacts that represent the working of the culture in that setting. Her goal is to be able to share some interpretations and draw some conclusions based on this kind of "rich description" (Geertz, 1973).

In the example, Souto-Manning (2014) took a slice of what she observed; qualitative researchers often refer to this as findings 'emerging' from the data. She interpreted the occurrences in a unique manner (i.e., using a fresh theory to examine the data) in order to disrupt more traditional notions of the 'ideal' early childhood classroom. She used conflict theory to reinterpret classroom occurrences, inviting readers to "reconceptualize conflicts as powerful and useful learning spaces potentially leading to responsive and authentic educational experiences" (p. 613).

In this study, Souto-Manning (2014) sought to (re)interpret cultural phenomena in critical ways. To do so, she demonstrated the belief that one must carefully and closely study these phenomena in order to understand them (as best as possible) from the perspective of the 'actors' in the setting. Then she applied a theory (conflict theory) to a unique setting in order to re-interpret a classic notion (the ideal early childhood classroom) in a new and productive way. The logic of her choices drew a thread through her study and her interpretations, deriving from her original theoretical framing.

The Researcher's Role—Objectivity/Subjectivity

For the general public, science is typically considered to be an objective activity. It is up to the scientist to conduct a study that provides unbiased information, data that can be considered dispassionately for what it reveals. In the modern world, in which positivism represented *the* approach to research, it was assumed that value-free neutrality would steer researchers toward objectivity. They could leave aside their beliefs, hopes, and passions and follow the conventions of research. Yet within both the natural and social sciences, there is common agreement that complete objectivity is not possible. Research is conducted by people, who enter the situation with experiences and perspectives. How those experiences and perspectives are handled differs between qualitative and quantitative researchers.

Quantitative Research

Quantitative approaches are more closely tied than qualitative approaches to the positivist roots of modern-era research. Most researchers, however, do take the issue of human fallibility seriously, thereby disallowing a belief in the ability to achieve complete objectivity. The stance on objectivity has been rewritten to make it a goal toward which to strive, described by Gersten (2013) as the researcher being an "objective-as-possible designer and implementer" (p. 141).

Consequently, quantitative researchers consider objectivity as an important aspect of their work. How can they reduce partiality, lessen the impact of predispositions, and achieve a more accurate measure of the phenomenon at hand? In the words of researchers in describing a postpositivist position: "It is still possible for a field of research that is externally influenced by values to operate internally in a relatively objective manner (indeed it is crucial for the scientific enterprise that it does so)" (Phillips & Burbules, 2000, p. 53).

Quantitative researchers work toward being objective through many strategies, which can be understood as (1) removing the partiality assumed of people and (2) reducing the personal stakes in order to be unbiased. We will explain forms of these strategies in what follows.

Partiality is countered through the careful development and use of research instruments. It is common for research instruments such as surveys, child assessments, or observation tools to undergo lengthy development to ensure they 'do what they are intended to do' without systematic bias. We will discuss more about this in relation to reliability and validity in the next sections. For now it is important to understand that through the use of research instruments, quantitative researchers strive to operate more objectively—the instrument reduces the influence of a subjective individual researcher when it is used carefully and as it was designed to be used. Data collection flows through an instrument designed to operate in similar and objective ways whenever used.

To illustrate from the Piasta et al. (2012) study, the researchers adapted and used two teacher surveys that had been developed for studies conducted in 1985 and 1993. It is not uncommon for instruments to have a long period of use and also to be adapted along the way; often earlier research has established that the instruments operate in objective ways. Additionally, in this study, classroom videotapes submitted by teachers were coded for the presence of clearly defined teaching strategies by trained research staff, who watched 30 seconds of tape and then recorded whether the strategies were used. This systematic coding system and the training to use it allowed the research team to increase objectivity.

Another way to strive toward objectivity is to reduce the stakes for those involved in research. For example, many research decisions are made before data collection begins, and the analyses to be performed follow the questions that frame the study. The idea is that researchers will not examine the data looking for what strikes them or conduct analyses until something 'turns up.' Decisions made before data are collected are regarded as more objective in nature. As another example, data collectors may not know which children experienced an intervention and which ones did not, so that they are not inclined to act differently when assessing them. This is referred to as being 'blinded.' Quantitative researchers may not reveal much about the purposes of their study when recruiting and enrolling participants, so that the participants do not tailor their responses or behavior toward what they believe the researcher wants to see. In all of these ways, researchers are in effect detaching themselves, their team members, or their participants from becoming invested in a particular end point for the study. In an example from the Piasta et al. (2012) study, transcripts of classroom videos submitted by teachers were "checked for accuracy by an independent . . . transcriber after initial transcription" (p. 393). By having a check on the initial transcription that was performed by research staff, the researchers hoped to ensure the staff did not let their knowledge of the study impact the transcription of often-complex and messy classroom conversations.

Qualitative Research

In early anthropological studies, the notion of the objective researcher sent to study and describe the cultural practices of 'exotic' populations reigned supreme. It was largely believed that the social scientist, trained in traditional methods of ethnography (observation of phenomena with detailed field notes, interviews of participants/informants, and collection and cataloging of cultural artifacts being key methods), could objectively catalog and accurately describe the cultural practices of the mythical 'other.' However, over time in this discipline, the postmodern interpretive turn of research (Howe & Moses, 1999) has firmly turned the possibility of objectivity on its proverbial head. Trends in qualitative research in education have mirrored this same journey.

Rather than attempting to 'prove' or 'increase' objectivity, there has been a movement in qualitative research to rigorously consider, examine, and explain the perspectives, worldviews, and points of identity from which a researcher's work derives. This pushes qualitative researchers to address, navigate, and attend to the ways that these frame and influence the research endeavor. Qualitative researchers try to engage with and acknowledge exactly the ways in which who they are influences what they do. In many reports of research, the researcher will not only explain his/her perspectives and frames of reference but will also engage in discussion of the limitations that these perspectives bring to the study. Qualitative researchers do not develop tools of data collection in order to increase objectivity; rather, the researcher him/herself *is* the tool, and objectivity is not necessarily a goal.

Two approaches are used in qualitative research to address researcher subjectivity, 'positionality' and acknowledgment of 'insider/outsider' perspectives. Positionality refers to explaining social and cultural positions that one holds and embodies as a human being. Researchers often interrogate the social structures (institutions, ideologies, power, oppression) that have created the possibilities for their positions and consider them in relationship to the project at hand. The insider/outsider perspective refers to one's position in relationship to the group under study. Might the researcher be considered to be a member of the group (an insider), or is the researcher sufficiently unfamiliar with the activities of the group to be considered an outsider? The researcher must consider how this relationship impacts the assumptions, perceptions, and interpretations of his/her research agenda.

It is the case that within a manuscript, researchers will have more or less space to report on these processes, depending on page limitations. When qualitative folks have more space (i.e., when they are presenting a book-length treatise of their study), it is not uncommon for entire chapters to be devoted to discussions of researcher identity and relationship to the context of the study and to the study participants. A wonderful example of this is in Shirley Brice Heath's book, *Ways With Words: Language, Life, and Work in Communities and Classrooms* (1983), in which Heath provided in-depth discussions of her relationships with the communities she studied and the ways that this shaped the project.

In the Souto-Manning (2014) research example, Souto-Manning described her relationship to the teacher in the classroom in which she conducted her data collection. She noted that she was the facilitator for "the inquiry-to-action culture circle meetings in which [the teacher] participated" (p. 615). Souto-Manning described the kinds of inquiry processes in which this group engaged and the kinds of insights and discussions that occurred. From this, the reader can make clear inferences about some of Souto-Manning's social positions and things that she values and believes in. For instance, she indicated that she based the culture circles on the work of Paolo Freire, which set her in a particular theoretical camp in relationship to her beliefs about teaching and learning.

Forms of Data

We have mentioned previously that qualitative data is textual while quantitative data is numerical. In the upcoming chapters, we will discuss data collection in more detail. Next, we make some distinctions about how the forms of data are generated for a study.

Quantitative Research

It is important to remember that while a quantitative study presents data in numerical form, the study begins with concepts that are defined and expressed with words. From there the researcher devises ways to measure what is of interest, thus translating the concept into numbers. For instance, Piasta et al. (2012) were interested in several pieces of information about the teachers in their study. They recorded how many years of experience individual teachers had. This is a straightforward example of how a concept (experience) is measured in a numerical way (years). They also recorded the teachers' highest level of education. This is a readily understandable example to most of us: Did a teacher have a high school diploma or an associate's degree? A bachelor's degree or perhaps a master's degree? In order to measure educational level, the researchers would have assigned a number to each of these levels, such as a one for a high school diploma, a two for an associate's degree, a three for a bachelor's degree, and so on. In this particular study, the researchers did not describe this coding scheme, but because the study is quantitative, readers know that these levels of educational experience have to be represented with numbers that make sense. In this case, higher numbers mean a higher level of education. A characteristic such as gender is rendered into numerical form by assigning a number to children's gender. Then the information can be used in statistical analyses.

The researchers also used two attitude surveys (Piasta et al., 2012). One measured teachers' self-efficacy based upon the teachers' responses to 20 questions. The researchers named four focal areas within which the questions were clustered: discipline, instruction, positive environment, and school/classroom decision making. To measure the concept of self-efficacy, the teachers rated each item on a five-point Likert-scale, where 1 corresponded to "no feelings of efficacy" and 5 corresponded to "very strong feelings of efficacy" and the numbers in between could be used for responses in the middle of this continuum. The numeral used in analyses was the average score of all 20 items.

In sum, in order to understand quantitative research, one must first understand the concept being measured, for instance, self-efficacy. The reader also has to understand how that concept was used by the researchers. In this study, the researchers looked at teachers' sense of effectiveness in relation to several aspects of teaching. Then one has to understand how the measurement works, as in, what does a higher number indicate? A lower number? This translation from concept to measurement to score is a crucial part of quantitative research.

Qualitative Research

The goal of qualitative research is to understand the how and why of human and social phenomena and human decision making. Quantitative data takes the forms of careful observation and documentation of the actual phenomena within the social and cultural contexts in which it is occurring. Qualitative projects often involve a large corpus of data of varying kinds. Furthermore, copious amounts of time spent collecting and analyzing data are a key feature of this work.

Given the caveat and desire of design consistency within the project, as described earlier, the kinds of data and the methods of collection are shaped by the theoretical approach to the study, the kinds of questions being asked, and the choice of an appropriate context in which to study a particular phenomenon or group of people. The varying paradigms of qualitative research employ and subscribe to different methods and methodologies and rely on different kinds of data to varying degrees. The goal in qualitative research is to collect enough data to garner an understanding of and be able to have an evidentiary interpretation of what is under study. It is the case that the types of data that qualitative researchers collect are fairly similar across types of projects. We will elaborate upon the uses of the various types of data in a later chapter, but for the overview purposes here, consider the following list with an example (where applicable) from the Souto-Manning exemplar study:

Direct observations and field notes/reports: Souto-Manning (2014) described how she "visited Ms. Jill's classroom for a minimum of 5 hours each week, taking notes, audio recording classroom and playground interactions, and collecting, artifacts" (p. 614). The work extended over a period of 9 months.

Interviews: Souto-Manning (2014) described her interviews with the teacher in the classroom in which she conducted her study. She justified these interviews as a form of evidence for her project by noting the importance of developing a trusting relationship with this teacher and developing a 'safe space' for the teacher to try out new ideas and understandings, and that allowed the teacher "to open up and to share her uncertainties" (p. 615). This kind of data collection is consistent with Souto-Manning's purpose to explore conflict in classrooms and to examine how conflict influences power relationships therein.

Collection of artifacts: Souto-Manning (2014) reported that she collected artifacts from both the teacher and the children in her study. One of the artifacts she gathered from the teacher was the writings that the teacher produced in the 'inquiry to action culture circle' that Souto-Manning facilitated. She also reported collecting 'classroom artifacts' to round out the evidence of her observations and interpretations of the happenings in the classroom.

Defining Trustworthiness and Rigor

Scientific research is associated with the word 'rigor.' It is expected that researchers work carefully and follow common procedures to ensure their work is precise and thorough, leading to results (in quantitative research) and interpretations (in qualitative research) that can be trusted. Because of the differences in data sources, qualitative and quantitative researchers have different ways to achieve the goal of rigorous investigations.

Quantitative Research

Remembering that measurement (the translation of a phenomenon into a numerical score) is central in quantitative research is key to understanding how rigor is approached within this paradigm. In this section, we will explain how instruments are perceived as valid and reliable.

Instruments should measure what we design or want them to measure. This is at the heart of the concept of validity. The question here is how 'accurate' an instrument might be. Researchers approach validity from several perspectives. As we describe each, we will refer to examples from Soukakou (2012). Soukakou's paper addressed her development of an observation instrument (the Inclusive Classroom Profile—ICP) to assess what happens in inclusive classrooms in relation to the developmental needs of young children who have disabilities.

Once Soukakou (2012) wrote items for the instrument, she asked several content experts to review them. They provided their evaluation of the substance of the items, as well as a rating on how important they thought each item was to the purposes of the instrument. This is referred to as content validity. Do experts in the field regard the instrument as including what it should and representing the important content well?

Next Soukakou (2012) used the ICP in 45 inclusive classrooms, along with three other classroom observation instruments. The other instruments had been previously established as appropriate measures to assess classroom environments, curriculum, and teacher–child interactions. All had been used previously in published research, although not in a particular relationship to inclusive settings. Soukakou used the data from her observations to compare the ICP scores to the other instrument scores, an appraisal of construct validity. Think of a construct as similar to the underlying concept being measured. Soukakou's theory was that there should be a pattern of relationships among the ICP and the other instruments. If the constructs, or concepts, are more similar, the relationship should be stronger. If they are more different, there should be less of a relationship between the ICP and another instrument. The former—looking at relationships expected to be stronger—is referred to as convergent validity. The latter—looking at the relationships expected to be weaker—is called discriminant validity. Soukakou concluded after finding the expected patterns, "the ICP correlated higher with measures that were conceptually 'closer' to its content, while it was more weakly correlated with items that were conceptually 'distant' to the ICP constructs" (p. 485).

In addition to construct validity, there are other types of validity to be aware of and consider. To assess concurrent validity, the researcher examines how a new measure works in relation to a previously developed measure of the same phenomenon. Perhaps the new measure is cheaper to administer or quicker to use, but researchers would want the new instrument to 'behave' similarly to the older one, to be as accurate in measuring the construct. In predictive validity, the researcher examines if the new measure predicts outcomes as would be expected theoretically. For example, if Soukakou believed that a higher score on the ICP should result in children with disabilities doing better, she could compare ICP scores to outcome measures for the children in the classrooms being observed. In sum, validity is about how accurately an instrument measures what it is intended to measure.

The other half of the equation for quantitative researchers is reliability. The focus here is on consistency in the scores obtained for an instrument. Researchers expect and need to measure phenomena with dependability and stability.

Soukakou (2012) used two forms of reliability in her study. The first was interrater agreement. Researchers expect that who the data collector is should not affect the score on an instrument—that different raters or data collectors achieve roughly the same scores. On the observational instruments used by Soukakou, observers were trained until they achieved scores on the instruments that were sufficiently close to what is considered the 'standard' score by expert users of the instrument. This is done before any data are collected for a study. Sometimes researchers will do a check on a percentage of measures during data collection to ensure that data collectors have not veered away from using the scoring protocols as they are intended to be used. If researchers cannot reach reliability when their instruments are used, their results will not have much worth.

The second form of reliability used by Soukakou (2012) was internal consistency. When researchers combine several items on an observational instrument or a survey to result in one average score, they want all the items to 'hang together,' indicating that they are all aspects of the same construct. On the ICP, Soukakou examined how the items were related among themselves in consideration of how they contributed to the overall construct of program quality for children with disabilities. The higher the number reported for this measure (Cronbach's alpha, α), the more consistent the items are with each other.

Another form of reliability not utilized by Soukakou is test-retest reliability. When a direct assessment of individuals is used, the researcher wants to know that the individual would score close to the same in a reasonable amount of time (not too long, so there is no further growth or development). In conclusion, assessments of reliability help assure readers that the researcher's instruments operate consistently.

Qualitative Research

Because the findings from qualitative research specifically focus on interpretation of data rather than on "objective" measurement, it is not uncommon for qualitative research to be perceived as lacking in rigor. There is always a story to be told in the qualitative approach. Researchers directly address postmodern and critical ideas of objectivity where that story draws on the researchers' and participants' interpretations of phenomena and context (time, place, people) matters. So in qualitative research the burden is on the researcher to present enough evidence of the claims s/he is making about the data that the reader can believe and trust that those claims make sense.

One of the major differences between qualitative and quantitative research in this area is the idea and meaning of 'truth.' Quantitative researchers tend to be searching for a larger objective and universal 'Truth' and, thus, the focus on researcher objectivity is paramount to that endeavor. Qualitative researchers tend to focus more on the situated and local nature of truth where a variety of explanations and interpretations can all be 'true' depending on perspectives, worldviews, and experiences of both the researcher and the study participants. This makes it tricky at times, and the challenge is to support the reader to understand how the claims can be 'true' in a context that may actually be more or less familiar to the reader.

We rely on the notion of *verisimilitude*—or, simply put, "truthiness." Important questions include: What is the level of believability of the story that the researcher presents or the claims that s/he makes? How likely is it that the story or claims could be true based on the context and the participants involved? (Keeping in mind, of course, that the reader of the study comes to the reading with his/her own perspectives.) Does the researcher convince the reader of his/her expertise to interpret the data of the study? (Note that this relates to the earlier discussion of positionality.) Does the researcher present enough evidence from the data so as to convince the reader of the verisimilitude of the finding and interpretations?

This striving for believability and truthiness can take a good bit of effort and description, and thus qualitative projects and write-ups tend to be longer and include a great deal of detail. Many qualitative researchers have been stymied by page limits of the journals in which they publish their work. And many qualitative researchers have struggled with peer reviewers who strain to believe the claims that the researcher is making because the researcher cannot present enough of the data in the space allotted. So too, a good measure of believability in a qualitative study rests on the perceived rigor and consistency of the data analysis, which requires manuscript space to explain.

While we will go into more depth about qualitative data analysis in Chapter 6, it is important to mention it here because part of 'rigor' and believability of a study also has to do with convincing the reader that the analysis is sound and reasonable. A technique often used in qualitative research is called 'triangulation,' where once a claim is made, that claim can be considered more 'true' if there are three sources of evidence from different kinds of data for that claim. For example, the researcher might have observed evidence for the claim, heard evidence for it in an interview, and gleaned evidence from an artifact.

Returning to the Souto-Manning (2014) example, she presented a very brief vignette of young children in classroom talking about 'poop' and 'stink.' This vignette was drawn from her classroom observations and field notes. She ultimately made the claim that these kinds of conversations can be considered as in conflict with the official curriculum and that these places of conflict can be productively used as learning tools, both in pushing against that official curriculum and in "honoring the breathtaking linguistic and cultural diversity present in today's classrooms" (p. 612). She used data from her interviews with the classroom teacher to provide the evidence that the teacher initially viewed these kinds of topics as inappropriate fodder for the official curriculum. And then she presented more observational data to tell the story of how the teacher allowed the topics to come into the classroom and the subsequent learning that took place. She also used data from the teacher's participation in a teacher learning group to substantiate the ways that the teacher struggled with and ultimately came to differently understand points of conflict in an early childhood classroom.

Throughout the manuscript, Souto-Manning (2014) made sure to reference and explain the amount of time she spent in the classroom and the various types of data that she collected—"nine months of ethnographic work . . . through observations, informal conversations, interviews, and collection of artifacts" (p. 613). In this way, she established her researcher credibility in this setting. In this particular example, while Souto-Manning briefly described her method of data analysis (i.e., writing analytic narratives based in her data), she spent a great deal more time in telling the story of the classroom, presenting her findings, and providing her interpretations. This kind of give and take between brief explanations of data analysis and longer presentations of findings and interpretations are often evident in a journal manuscript, whereas in a book, there is likely a full chapter to explain the data analysis.

Making Meaning: Within the Study and Beyond

The closing sections of a research report typically help the reader to understand what the results or findings mean in a larger context and/or in light of the extant research. Often beginning with a summary or discussion of the findings, researchers then use these sections to consider the meaning of the study, discussion of potential limitations of the study, implications for practice, and suggestions for further research.

Quantitative Research

The discussion section of the report of a quantitative study is typically written around a set of topics: a summary of the findings, a discussion of how the findings fit with previous research, implications of the findings, limitations of this particular study, and directions for future research. Researchers vary tremendously in regard to how much attention they pay to each section. In addition, while the sections previous to the discussion have tended to follow long-standing conventions for the presentation of information, the discussion section has often been less prescribed. For example, in the fifth edition (American Psychological Association, 2001) of the *Publication Manual of the American Psychological Association* (APA), the guidelines were not very specific: "You are free to examine, interpret, and qualify the results as well as to draw inferences from them" (p. 26). Here one can spot the difficulties of the quest to be objective. In our experience reviewing manuscripts for potential publication, we have found it not so unusual for researchers to let go of some constraints, leading to concerns that the discussion goes beyond the actual results. This is one reason we do not want students to revert to the discussion section to get to a quick summary of a study; they are then taking the researcher's interpretations for granted rather than examining whether those interpretations appear founded.

In the most recent edition of the APA guidelines, the wording of the quoted sentence has changed: "Here you will examine, interpret, and qualify the results and draw inferences and conclusions from them" (American Psychological Association, 2010, p. 35). Note that the wording "you are free" has been removed. In addition, there is much more prescribed in this latest edition in regard to what researchers should include in the discussion section. Researchers are further cautioned, "This concluding section may be brief or extensive provided that it is tightly reasoned, self-contained, and *not overstated*" (American Psychological Association, 2010, p. 36, emphasis our own). This is an example of how professional associations are attempting to discourage researchers from taking too much license when interpreting their results.

In the Piasta et al. (2012) paper, the discussion section is rather extensive. The researchers are cautious in their wording. Many times results are discussed with wording such as "might reflect," "it might be," "it is possible," and "suggesting that." It seems clear that the authors are trying to avoid overstatements. The authors also discuss four limitations of the study. For the reader, it may feel that a story was being created by the researcher's work and then at the last minute revised to 'well, but . . .' Part of the mindset of many quantitative researchers is that results are somewhat tentative and might be revised upon further study. Remember, though, that there are a variety of stances, and in some studies the researchers appear quite sure of the meaning and importance of the study and less expansive about possible limitations.

One of the long-standing assumptions of quantitative research is that it allows researchers to make generalizations to other groups. In fact, the statistical analyses operate with the notion that the sample of participants for a study is a subgroup of a larger population of individuals. The question at hand is: in what other situations might we expect to find the same results? Although this is an assumption of the paradigm, some researchers do not directly address this question, and it is up to the reader to consider. Knowing quite a bit about the particular sample of participants and features of their context is essential to making any educated speculations about how far generalizations might be made.

In the Piasta et al. (2012) paper, we do find attention to the question of generalizability. Noting that the sample consisted of teachers and children in classrooms targeted for particular children (e.g., living in poverty), the researchers noted, "It is unclear whether findings would generalize outside of these settings—for instance, in home-based programs or for-profit private day cares—and to children who are not eligible for these subsidized programs" (p. 398). Without saying so directly, the researchers appear to assume that the findings would generalize to similar programs with targeted enrollment policies based upon poverty status.

Qualitative Research

Quantitative research studies are specifically designed around the goal and purpose of explaining social phenomena in such a way that that explanation can be used to predict what will happen in other situations and with other groups of people. The ideas of prediction and generalizability are actually antithetical to the goals and aims of qualitative researchers. In qualitative research, the context and local situation are important to understanding how and why things happen. As a consequence, qualitative researchers are uncomfortable suggesting that the occurrence in one time, space, and context could be applied to another situation or phenomenon in a predictive manner.

Now, that is not to say that qualitative researchers do not desire to help readers consider phenomena in ways that will be helpful (or disruptive) or applicable to their own or other situations. Qualitative researchers seek to provide a variety of interpretations to help readers consider their issues or phenomena in a multitude of ways, stemming from the basic belief that knowledge and understanding are local, situated, and contextualized. As we learned in Chapter 2, different paradigms across qualitative research have different aims and goals. These range from providing new and enhanced interpretations to providing an alternative (critical) lens to elucidate and push on power structures to complete deconstruction of the theories behind how and why things are the way they are. However, while a qualitative researcher desires to provide a reader with a new way to think or a new way to act in or on the world, s/he in no way would suggest that it could be predicted what that would look like, as it would involve different actors with different experiences in different contexts. This illustrates the generative nature of qualitative research.

When a qualitative researcher discusses what his/her study means in education (or in the world), that discussion should be consistent with the larger theoretical framing of the study and the aims of the interpretation at hand. To return to the Souto-Manning (2014) example, her goal was to apply the lens of conflict theory to bring the reader to an alternative understanding of how conflict can be applied to and used in the early childhood classroom. In addition, she wanted to use conflict theory as a means to disrupt the official curriculum in order to authentically connect to the diverse cultural and linguistic assets the children bring to school. After she carefully laid out the story of the children and the teacher as they embarked on the new way of considering and accepting conflict in their classroom, she ended the paper with a section called, "So What? Implications and Invitations" (p. 629). Her discussion centered on how the story that she provided could be used to reconsider how people think about, understand, and enact the notion of the 'ideal' early childhood classroom—consistent with her goal of disrupting the larger dominant narrative that can ultimately be harmful for some children. She did not suggest that what happened in the classroom that she studied could or should be reproduced but rather invited readers to reconsider their own policies and practices through an alternative lens with the potential for transformation.

Many qualitative researchers will discuss *potential* implications of their work for other similar settings or situations. Souto-Manning (2014) invited preschool teachers to reconsider how conflict is addressed and used in their own classrooms. They will often offer ideas for other ways that their study could be considered or suggest areas for further research. It is frequently the case that a good qualitative study will generate more questions than answers—especially given that 'answers' are not really the goals of the research in the first place! And sometimes, because qualitative research provides insight into particulars, it can provide fodder for quantitative colleagues to identify potential trends occurring that could benefit from study from a broader and larger vantage point.

Summary

Our discussion has been long, and there is much information to digest here. By contrasting the qualitative and quantitative paradigms, we have attempted to uncover key beliefs that work to take researchers in each paradigm in different directions. We urge readers who may feel overwhelmed to take a deep breath and continue reading forward. As more information is added, frequently the picture being drawn becomes clearer. It may also help to review this chapter following our in-depth discussion of quantitative and qualitative methodologies.

A Deeper Look

To this point we have discussed varied approaches to research separately via the quantitative and qualitative paradigms. Yet, as usual in the 'real world,' distinctions, boundaries, and definitions are rarely so clear cut. Among researchers, there are varied perspectives about the existence of distinctions and the importance of differences. In addition, there are varying levels of advocacy for utilizing multiple, or mixed, methods within a single study, utilizing both qualitative and quantitative data.

Determining the Place of Paradigms

Before we take up the topic of multiple methods, we want to briefly explore how the research paradigms have been privileged across time. As we described in Chapter 1, the quantitative methods of psychology have greatly impacted educational research. Throughout history, quantitative methods have been viewed as undertaking to deliver what is needed to solve issues in education, as noted by Rudolph (2014), "In the face of complex and persistent educational problems, they [quantitative methods] seem to promise objective results, uniform solutions, and standardized interventions less prone to ideological distortion" (p. 16). Thus, as qualitative methods first secured a foothold among researchers, the identity of this group was as a "highly suspect newcomer" (Howe & Eisenhart, 1990, p. 2).

As qualitative research gained traction, researchers from both paradigms advocated passionately for the value of their perspective and methods. Sometimes the advocacy moved into critique of the other paradigm, instigating the expression 'paradigm wars.' Those operating from a quantitative base advocated for the strength of traditional, objective scientific methods for establishing cause–effect relationships and solving educational problems. They criticized qualitative methods for providing little in the way of explanation, being too relativistic in their orientation, and lacking in 'scientific rigor.' Those operating from a qualitative approach advocated for the richness of their data for understanding the complexity of human situations. They criticized quantitative methods as bringing a limited conceptualization of methods borrowed from the natural sciences that was not adequate for the social sciences, providing limited insight into complex situations and individual perspectives, and protecting existing power differentials in social structures (Gage, 1989).

Those who identified as interested in the problems best served with qualitative designs were dealt a difficult blow in the early years of the 21st century. At that point, federal education policy, specifically No Child Left Behind, included a definition of 'scientifically based research' that greatly narrowed its scope to quantitative designs. In addition, the What Works

Clearinghouse privileged evidence from experimental research in its evaluation of curriculum effectiveness. For qualitative researchers, the effect was to separate their work from what was privileged as 'scientifically based.' Ongoing debate resulted in some changes, but for many, the impact was felt as a devaluing of their research perspectives (Eisenhart & Towne, 2003). In trying to reduce the impact of these policies on the field, the National Research Council published a position statement, *Scientific Research in Education* (National Research Council, 2002), derived from the input of researchers rather than policy makers. In this statement there were attempts (viewed by some as not effective) to define 'scientific research' in broader ways that encompassed qualitative perspectives.

Several years previous to these events, as the use of qualitative methods rose, Howe (1988) declared that positivism "*has* fallen" (emphasis in original). Clearly, our description of the ascendency of quantitative methods in subsequent federal policy, epitomized by the experimental study, alters that conclusion. Interestingly, in that same paper, Howe described how at the turn of the 20th century there was a surge of support for positivism in psychology, and as a result, "any research methodology that failed to measure up was dismissed as unscientific" (Howe, 1988, p. 13) Thus, there have been waves of support for the paradigms representing quantitative and for qualitative methods since the beginning of the 20th century. The support for quantitative methods has been so strong at times that the word 'science' could be denied association with nonquantitative methods. The various ways in which paradigms have been privileged, or not, are an important part of the background story about research.

Mixed (Multiple) Methods

Within the last couple of decades, there has been increasing enthusiasm for the use of mixed, or multiple, methods within single studies. Johnson and Onweugbuzie (2004) offered a formal definition of this work: "the class of research where the researcher mixes or combines quantitative and qualitative research techniques, methods, approaches, concepts or language into a single study" (p. 17). Thus, mixed-methods research can range in how researchers attempt to create these hybrids that draw in various ways upon both research traditions (for example, combining methods and combining concepts are different from each other).

While there are many approaches to mixed-methods research, there are also many points of view regarding how it fits in the bigger picture. We refer you to Chapter 2, in which we discussed the philosophical roots of research. Some researchers who support mixed-methods research draw from the pragmatic approach we presented there. For them, the task of the researcher is to identify the most appropriate research approach for answering the question of interest. Approaches are neither weaker or stronger or more or less fitting in their assumptions about ontology and epistemology. Rather, what works for the research question is what is appropriate for the researcher.

When mixed methods are utilized, there are two dimensions along which the research designs might vary. One is the timing of the various methods and the other is the relative emphasis of each (Johnson & Onweugbuzie, 2004). Sometimes both qualitative and quantitative approaches are used within a single study. This would be designs with simultaneous data generation approaches addressing multiple questions. Other researchers might use a sequential design approach within a group of studies. Thus, they might begin with either a quantitative or a qualitative design and generate data in connection with one or more questions. The next phase of the research shifts to the other type of research design to continue the process of inquiry toward other forms of data (Johnson & Onweugbuzie, 2004).

In regard to relative emphasis, in some studies, the questions being answered through the two methodological approaches are relatively equal in status in the study (or studies, if this is an example of sequential use of mixed methods). In other studies, one methodological approach is dominant, and the other is utilized to generate supporting data but functions more obviously as a 'secondary partner' to the study's purposes (Johnson & Onweugbuzie, 2004).

It should be clear that the use of mixed methods requires a broad skill set from both researchers and consumers. One cannot be adept within a single paradigm to do this work well; for this reason, we believe that the strongest mixed-methods research comes from teams in which experts within each paradigm contribute to the study. Currently interest in this form of research is strong. One pitfall is the generation of studies in which the additional, nondominant methodology functions as window dressing, not having a reasoned place in contributing to answering the research questions. Instead, it may be added to the study to attract attention at a time in which mixed methods are popular. The onus is on the consumer to consider the effectiveness of the methodology—did the mixing of methods result in a coherent investigation?

For some, mixed-methods studies make a lot of sense, and they can step into the hybrid space rather easily. For others, navigating this is more difficult. When one's position is deeply tied to the underlying epistemology, it is different (with, of course, the exception of pragmatism). In a paper published before the current interest in mixed methods, Hatch (1985) proposed that some qualitative and quantitative researchers see "quite different worlds" based upon their "essential assumptions about how the world works" (pp. 162–163). He cautioned that an approach focused on the utility of the two approaches ignored the basic underlying philosophical differences.

While not denying the possibility of high-quality mixed-methods research, Phillips (2009) cautioned that some methods do not "sit easily with each other" (p. 185). When coteaching a research course, two of us operating with different methodological expertise (Jennifer and Nancy) would often somewhat jokingly ask each other, "Well, why would you ask that question?" This further illustrates the point that mixed methods present several challenges.

It seems appropriate to end this chapter with a reminder that all forms of research can be done wonderfully, and all can be done poorly. Both single-methods studies and mixed-methods studies must be carefully evaluated by the consumer. In the next set of chapters, we will explain the basic methods used by qualitative and quantitative researchers to design studies and analyze data, essential knowledge for being a judicious consumer.

5

QUALITATIVE RESEARCH
Framing the Study

In the next four chapters, we will separate out the qualitative and quantitative research paradigms in order to closely examine the key methods and terms of each. This will help readers understand the differing approaches in the chapters from the second half of the book as we compare and contrast the various ways that researchers ask questions and help us understand the field of early childhood education.

In Chapters 5 and 6, we will discuss the qualitative approach to research. In this chapter, we describe how a study is conceptualized and designed, how research questions are developed, and the important relationships in qualitative research between the theoretical perspectives employed in the study and the methods used to address the questions proposed. We will discuss basic aims for qualitative studies, for example answering questions such as "How does this happen in practice?" "What are the experiences of children in this context?" and "How can I more fully understand this and what it means to the people involved?" We will also present information on reading a piece of professional literature, here beginning with a focus on the opening sections.

Qualitative research as "naturalistic inquiry" is "discovery-oriented" (Guba, 1978, p. 1), whereas Patton (2015) explains, there is minimal "investigator manipulation of the study setting," and there are no "prior constraints on what the outcomes of the research will be" (p. 48). Because the goal of qualitative research is to interpret, explain, deeply understand, and reframe phenomena, it is a much less standardized enterprise than quantitative research. Qualitative research certainly employs standards for quality and rigor, and we can identify basic tenets of study design and implementation. However, the interpretive goal means that there are almost endless ways to conceive of and design a study to further our understandings of phenomena. Our goal here is not to be all encompassing but rather to lay out the range of possibilities and give enough insight that the reader is able to appraise the quality, usefulness, and trustworthiness of any qualitative project in early childhood education.

As we discuss the concepts and ideas of this chapter and the next, we will draw upon three studies as examples. We have chosen studies that draw from the variety of theoretical perspectives as outlined in Chapter 2 to represent the range of paradigms within qualitative research. As we will explore more in the second half of the book, all early childhood research projects, regardless of paradigm, focus on the various elements of the field of early childhood. For instance, researchers can study the activities of children, teachers and teachers' approaches to their work, curriculum and instructional strategies, or policies or policy implementation. For this chapter, we have chosen studies that focus on teachers—how they enacted curriculum, how elements of their identities shaped their work, and how a standard professional quality of the early childhood teacher might be reconceptualized to support change or new possibility.

First, an article by Graue, Whyte, and Karabon (2015) represents the constructivist paradigm. The authors employed a theory of teaching as improvisation, in which teachers "actively respond to children's diverse intellectual, social, and emotional experiences and needs; taking multiple bodies of knowledge into moment-to-moment interactions with children" (p. 14). Through improvisation—teachers used "their knowledge of children inside and outside the classroom as a source for teaching" (p. 14)—these authors argued that teachers might craft "individually tailored learning experiences" (p. 14) that supported young children to connect with curriculum and learning in the classroom in ways that were culturally responsive. They studied the cases of two teachers in their individual kindergarten classrooms. The teachers had participated in a professional development series that was "designed to promote culturally and developmentally responsive early mathematics teaching" (p. 15). They showed via comparison how each teacher was able to use improvisation (or not), giving specific vignettes from each classroom that provided examples of when improvisation was used effectively to help the children connect to the curriculum, and also demonstrated missed opportunities. They provided detailed descriptions of the teaching practices of each teacher, providing interpretive categories for the approaches of each teacher.

The authors ultimately argued that improvisation can be a productive teaching strategy, "providing a space that creates new knowledge by engaging the familiar in unfamiliar ways" (p. 20). They also made an argument against the scripted or prescribed curricula that can be found in early childhood classrooms, given the potential of improvisation to help young children make deeper and more productive connections between home practices and school practices to support learning.

Representing the transformative/emancipatory paradigm, we use an article by Adair (2014). Here Adair used critical race theory (which we will explain in more detail later in the chapter) to examine how 'whiteness' operated to shape the ways that preschool teachers discussed, approached and worked with children from immigrant families. She examined interviews from more than 50 preschool teachers from sites across the United States, providing categories and descriptions of the kinds of reactions the teachers were having to the immigrant families and children in their classrooms. She compared and contrasted the conversations of white teachers and teachers of color. She demonstrated the ways that her construct of whiteness manifested itself in the teacher interviews, making further connections to the potential of the teachers' beliefs and attitudes to impact the educational opportunities the teachers provided to the children. Adair concluded that the construct of whiteness operated in ways that presented obstacles for the ability of teachers to positively engage with the immigrant families in their settings. Her descriptions also provide alternative stories and scripts that teachers could try to employ in order to work more effectively with diverse groups of children.

The third article represents the postmodern paradigm and is by Madrid, Baldwin, and Frye (2013). In this article, using poststructural analysis, the researchers explored and deconstructed the idea of emotion in the early childhood classroom. They make the case that the idea of emotion has dominant meanings as socially constructed by the world of the 'good' early childhood teacher, in particular that teachers who are professional are not emotional. They argued that this could be a limiting (and potentially oppressive) way to view emotion in the early childhood classroom. Using the case study of a classroom, the researchers shared three vignettes that showed how "the teacher's discomfort and the resulting struggle and ambivalence she encountered as new information about children's social worlds disrupted her prior beliefs, values, and feelings" (p. 274). The authors concluded that a reframing and embrace of emotional discomfort has the potential to support productive reflection and dialogue. They suggested that by embracing the "emotional complexities" of early childhood, teachers can "draw upon alternative pedagogies and transform taken-for-granted assumptions" (p. 289) to reflect upon and enhance classroom practice.

Study Design and Context

In basic terms, a qualitative researcher must lay out how s/he intends to carry out the study or inquiry of interest. Designing a qualitative research project is a very personal endeavor, especially since the researcher will be engaged with the people involved as participants (Rhedding-Jones, 2007). And given that qualitative research focuses on the hows and whys of human interactions and experiences, that study must take place in a particular context. It seems obvious to state then that context and study design in qualitative research are intimately intertwined. Here we put forth some basic considerations regarding these two constructs, and then we provide more details regarding these within our example studies.

Given the range of possibilities in the study of human experience, designing a qualitative project can be considered an art. Janesick (1998) uses the metaphor of art in describing how researchers go about conceiving of and crafting an inquiry project:

> [T]he qualitative researcher is very much like an artist at various stages in the design process, in terms of situating and recontextualizing the research project within the shared experience of the researcher and the participants in the study . . . art forces us to think about how human beings are related to each other in their respective worlds . . . the qualitative researcher, as designer of a project, recognizes the potential of design. The design serves as a foundation for the understanding of the participants' worlds and the meaning of shared experience between the researcher and participants in a given social context.
>
> (p. 37)

All qualitative research begins with an area of interest on the part of the researcher, where the researcher is compelled to dig deeper, find out more, and get to the details of social interactions. There is often a great deal of passion on the part of the researcher around the topic or area of interest. And, as we shall discuss in more detail, the researcher will consistently need to address and deal with bias that always is the foil to deep interest in a context or topic.

The complexity of any situation or setting means that there might be any number of questions or areas of inquiry that are possible within any context. And the goal for qualitative researchers is not to reduce that complexity but rather to embrace and engage with it. Qualitative researchers will often begin with a larger, overarching question and make basic initial design decisions based on that question or set of interests. Unlike quantitative research, in which the design of the study must be conceived of beforehand, study design in qualitative research occurs ahead of the study, during the study, and can accommodate changes after data is collected as well. In reporting on a qualitative project, it is important that the researcher carefully explain the study design, since the research process will shape the eventual outcomes or findings that are reported. This is very different from quantitative work in which efforts are made such that the research process itself will not affect the outcome of the study. Since the study design can and does vary, the logic of the design must be evident in order to enhance the trustworthiness of the project.

There are several basic study designs that qualitative researchers could use. Again, the options we discuss here are not formulaic in nature, though we can offer some basic parameters for different study designs. The important part of the study design is that it follows the threads of consistency of the project. Essentially the study design has to do with the number of participants involved and the level of analysis that the researcher is attempting. (We will explain this in more detail in what follows.) The researcher may study an individual or individuals within a setting. The researcher may study a group of people with the goal of understanding group

50

norms and culture. The researcher may study people within a larger structure with the goal of understanding how and why that structure shapes the behaviors of the people within.

In quantitative work, researchers attempt to study a 'sample' of the population such that that sample would be representative of a larger population and, thus, give the results of the study predictive value. Qualitative researchers, on the other hand, study 'cases' of situations and phenomena in order to provide rich and detailed examples of what may be happening. And the way that a 'case of something' may be constituted in qualitative research is quite varied. Patton (2015) notes that "cases can be empirical units" (p. 259), which in early childhood education might be individuals (children, teachers, child care directors), families, or organizations (Head Start site, child care center, school). According to Patton (p. 259), cases might be "theoretical constructs" which could be resilience (in children), quality (of child care), or life in kindergarten, for instance. Cases can be "physically real" (death of children in foster care), "socially constructed" (whiteness, improvisation in teaching), or "historical/political" (history of Head Start). Cases can be in-depth study of one setting or individual, or they can be studies of several cases within a setting that are then compared and contrasted.

With all of this to consider, we now turn to the beginning sections of qualitative pieces to help a reader situate a study, become familiar with the kinds of questions qualitative researchers ask, and understand the importance of theoretical perspective in qualitative research. Here is a good place to remind readers that one of the standards of quality for qualitative work is that there is an internal consistency that is evident in the work and that has guided the process of the researcher. The researcher views the world from a particular vantage point and with a working set of theories about how the world operates. This 'theoretical perspective' should be evident and explicit in the research report. The kinds of questions being asked should make sense in light of this theoretical perspective. Then the methods chosen for data collection and analysis will also be consistent. We will detail and explicate further as we work through the parts of a research report.

In what follows and in the next chapter we walk through typically what one will see in an article-length presentation of qualitative research. However, it is very important to point out that for qualitative research, this is not to be seen as formulaic. We will see later in the quantitative chapters that there is a basic format and expected sections that indicate the quality of the study when research is reported. Qualitative researchers, on the other hand, are in the business of interpretation and deconstruction. It is often the case that research reports are written and presented in ways that are meant to purposefully disrupt convention and show the possibilities of alternative, new, or oppositional understandings of the world. This can also make for some dense reading for the student of qualitative research! Qualitative projects can be messy and ambiguous. They are invariably as complex as the phenomena under study, making explaining findings and drawing conclusions quite challenging. Internal consistency of any project is one hallmark of quality that the reader should be able to appraise regardless of methods or presentation style and regardless of whether the reader likes or agrees with the findings of the study.

Phenomena Under Study/Purpose of the Study/Research Question(s)

Recall from an earlier chapter that the goals of qualitative research are not rooted in prediction or generalization. The goals of qualitative research projects are varied and include: to understand phenomena more deeply; to interpret a situation or set of behaviors differently; to explain phenomena in order to expose and/or disrupt norms and power relationships; or to understand the perspectives, desires, or intentions of the people being studied. It makes sense, then, that the questions asked and the purposes for a study can be as individual as the researcher and the context and participants of the study itself. As we will continually mention throughout Chapters 5 and 6, the reader should look for the chains of internal consistency that must work across a qualitative study so that the approach (or theoretical framing) of the study matches with the kinds of questions asked, connects to the context of the study, makes sense given the data collected and the analysis completed, and is consistent with the kinds of conclusions that are drawn from the analysis and the interpretation.

Phenomena Under Study

A study introduction should give the reader a clear idea of what it is that the researcher is studying and attempting to interpret and explain. (This will also be connected to the context of the study, and the context needs to be appropriate to the type of phenomena under inquiry—but more on that later.) Similar phenomena can be studied across the paradigms of qualitative research, but each examination will have different purposes. It is worth noting here that it is possible to see, across a particular researcher's body of work, data from the same project—or even the same data—analyzed from varying frameworks to produce new or alternative interpretations.

It may be helpful for the reader to ascertain the level of analysis (individual, group, or structure) of the study in order to understand what the researcher is attempting to do. Very generally speaking, there are three levels of analysis apparent across all the paradigms of qualitative research. These levels of analysis can and do share types of data collection and methods of analysis. The reader should discern if what is being studied is:

Phenomenological: The researcher is attempting to explain and help the reader understand the phenomena or experience from the perspective of the individual(s) under study. How do the individual(s) in a setting or context experience the situation under study? What are their perspectives and views?

Ethnographic: The researcher is providing insight into the experiences, norms, beliefs, and/ or the ways of being a part of a group of people. Here the researcher may describe the actions of individuals within the group, and this is in relationship to the established group norms. Why do people act in the ways they do in certain contexts? How can one explain the decisions or behaviors of members of a group?

Structural: The researcher is exposing or illuminating the societal institutions or social structures that shape the choices that people make, the ways that people think, or how people behave. The researcher may describe how individuals or groups within the social structure under examination act or think, and this is specifically in relationship to the structure. How does social class (for instance) shape the educational experiences of children?

These categories are basic and for purposes of illustration. Given the complexities of social/ cultural actions and occurrences, there can be a combination of these going on in any given study. And, in the human experience, one level (individual, group, societal) has implications for the others. Sometimes a researcher will explicitly state the level of analysis of the study, but not always.

The embrace of complexity in qualitative research generally means that the corpus of data for most qualitative projects is quite extensive. It is not uncommon for the researcher to write about a small component of what was actually studied in a larger project. Qualitative researchers are often stymied by the page limits of journals, making it necessary to choose a small part of a project about which to write. It is also quite common for researchers to use the same corpus of data across several papers, slicing the data slightly differently for different audiences or to focus on a different interpretation of or lens for the data. Different from quantitative projects, in which it is unacceptable to 'fish' the data for outcomes that were not planned for ahead of time, it is very likely that in the course of a qualitative project new and unexpected questions will arise. Reinterpretation of data is common and encouraged.

Making a determination of *what* is being studied (the actions/behaviors of teachers or children in a classroom, the thoughts or approaches of teachers to their work, etc.) is the first part of the thread to ascertain. Understanding the level of analysis and what was actually studied should lead the reader to a discussion of why it was important to study that particular phenomenon.

Turning to our three example studies, Madrid, Baldwin, and Frye (2013) point out for the reader and state straightaway in the abstract that for 6 months they studied emotion in a preschool classroom. Both in the abstract and at the end of the section titled "Introduction" (p. 644), Adair (2014) makes it clear that the paper is based on in-depth interviews of more than 50 preschool teachers—interviews that were part of a larger project called the Children Crossing Borders Study. For Graue et al. (2015), it takes a bit more digging to get a clear picture of what they studied. In the abstract and at the end of the Introduction section, they note that data was taken from a mathematics-focused professional development for teachers. In the Methods section, they note that the data for this paper was taken from the larger 4-Year-Old Kindergarten Professional Development Project, which was designed to support "culturally and developmentally responsive early mathematics teaching with a group of public preK teachers" (p. 15). Then the Methods section goes on to detail who participated and what data was collected.

It is important to note here that quality of the project is not necessarily determined by writing or presentation style of the researchers. We will turn next to the purpose of the study, and depending on what that is, the presentation style may be more intricate. Again, the apparent threads of consistency are a good marker of quality in qualitative projects, even though there is not a strict formula for presenting data. So the fact that the reader needs to dig a bit more in the Graue et al. (2015) piece should not be viewed as problematic. As we shall see, they are applying a particular and complex theoretical lens to their data analysis, and this is the focus of their project rather than the specific activities of the participants.

Purpose of the Study

Especially since it is the case that the same study data can be used for different purposes, describing the intended purpose of both the study in general and of the particular report of research is important. This discussion can most often be found in the introduction, and there may be a specific section that indicates the purpose of the study or the specific research questions. There will likely be some accounting of why this study is important or significant and how it helps us understand a phenomenon more deeply, more complexly, or in a different way. Also, there may be discussion of why it is important that the data or a particular phenomenon be examined from the indicated interpretive framework. If the purpose is not explicitly stated, it may be inferred from the review of the literature, or sometimes the purpose is made most evident when the researcher discusses the research methods of the project. Whether specifically stated or not, the purpose of the study will be elaborated upon and justified within the review of literature associated with the study.

The Graue et al. (2015) study is a good example of a research report (in this case a journal article) that takes a smaller slice of a larger project, giving a particular purpose to the part of the study upon which they report. They use a particular lens of interpretation to analyze teachers' responses to and uptake of a professional development series. So while what they *study* is the teachers' reactions to the professional development and how the teachers enact the practices in their classrooms, here they interpret those activities through the lens of 'improvisation.' They lay out the purpose for this report in the Introduction section of the manuscript. They note how early childhood curriculum has become more and more standardized despite "a growing body of research on classroom quality [that] highlights instructional practices that are contingent on children's knowledge, experiences, and resources" (p. 14). This requires an ability on the part of a teacher to be very responsive to the individual needs of children in ways that are not captured in standardized curricula. They specifically explain:

> In this paper we explore an effort to rethink pedagogical decision-making and responsivity with a group of public prekindergarten (preK) teachers working in a context of curriculum escalation and commitment to play-based pedagogy. Through a professional development (PD) program designed to support developmentally and culturally responsive early mathematics, we examine how teachers took up the idea of engaging 4 year olds in mathematics in a way that married content knowledge and home practices. We use the notion of improvisation to describe how teachers can build on diverse information to enrich their educational interactions with children.
>
> (p. 14)

These authors are using a particular lens to interpret and reinterpret teachers' practices such that teaching practices can be improved and become more supportive for individual children.

Research Questions

Given the wide range of purposes and the goal of interpretation and understanding of qualitative research, it is challenging to categorize the types of questions that a qualitative researcher might ask. What we can say is that questions in qualitative research definitely do not put forth a hypothesis or any presumed outcome as in quantitative research—though they do enter a project with theoretical approaches and assumptions in mind. As mentioned, researchers often begin with a larger or overarching area of interest. Once a study is designed and a context for the research is determined, subquestions may be developed that connect more specifically to the setting of the project.

However, as we discussed earlier, there are differing paradigms within qualitative research, and the types of questions that interest any given researcher also stem from that researcher's view of the world (theoretical perspective) and the unit/level of analysis that the researcher seeks to undertake in a project. In some approaches to qualitative research (grounded theory in particular), there is actually a caution about developing research questions at all before collecting data, as the questions and theories are expected to arise from the researcher experiencing the phenomena. Agee (2009) suggests that the initial questions posed in a qualitative project can serve as a plan for the research and represent a beginning point for the project and can evolve. Agee notes, "First iterations of questions are tentative and exploratory but give researchers a tool for articulating the primary focus of the study" (p. 433).

Sometimes the research questions in a study are stated explicitly as questions, and these are often found at the beginning or end of the introduction. Other times the researcher will express the goals of the research in statement or narrative form. Turning to our three example studies, for Graue et al. (2015), the research statement/questions are found at the end of the introduction. They noted that the goals for this presentation of their project were to:

> deepen our understandings of the role improvisation plays in an early childhood classroom we address the question: How do teachers and children take up the resources that they bring into the classroom in improvisational practice?
>
> (p. 14)

Note that this is a mix of a statement and a question.

In the Adair (2014) piece, it is also the case that a particular theoretical lens is being applied and is driving the data analysis using data from a larger project. The goals of this particular presentation of the research are stated in narrative rather than as a specific question. The study purpose is highlighted in the abstract:

> *This article* examines whiteness at the intersection of immigration and early child-hood education as it was made visible during interviews with 50 preschool teachers in five US cities as part of the Children Crossing Borders (CCB) study.
>
> (p. 643, emphasis ours)

Then again at the end of the Introduction section, Adair reiterates her use of the interview data, further explaining her goals for this piece and detailing the particular way she is applying the chosen theoretical framework:

> I detail how preschool teachers new to immigration drew heavily upon a perspec-tive of whiteness . . . to make sense of the changes they were seeing in their schools and neighborhoods. Our discussion, however, is not just about whiteness in terms of its powerful positioning of the Other but also its potential for contradiction and complication when teachers have the opportunity to wrestle with situations that put whiteness at odds with good early childhood pedagogy or their strong desires to be caring teachers.
>
> (p. 644)

Madrid et al. (2013) include a section specifically titled "Purpose of Study" (p. 276) and include the research questions at the end of this section. These authors note:

> The first question guided the larger ethnographic study with the second question guiding just this particular data analysis: (1) What are the emotions that exist in the daily life of this preschool classroom? (2) How did the graduate online course and the children's play themes affect the teacher's emotion and classroom practice?
>
> (p. 277)

As we are sure the readers are beginning to see, it is challenging in qualitative research to isolate and discuss the various parts of a research presentation, since each part is interconnected and dependent upon other parts. The threads of consistency only make sense when the whole comes together. Indeed, when Janesick (1998) describes qualitative research design, she uses the metaphor of choreographing dance in which all of the various parts and movements come together to make a cohesive whole—and attention to each of the movements is necessary but will not make sense in the absence of placing it within the whole. Next we discuss the theoreti-cal framing of a study, which should help the reader contextualize the study within an approach to how the world works and then also within the appropriate body of literature.

Theoretical Framing and Review of Literature

One of the defining characteristics of the qualitative paradigm is that researchers embrace the fact that all research is ideologically driven—meaning that the researcher's frames of reference, beliefs, and ways of understanding the world will, in fact, bias the research. There is no attempt in qualitative research to suggest that any research project is value free. And given the multiplicity of paradigms that constitute the larger qualitative paradigm, there are a wide variety of theoretical perspectives that a researcher can employ in designing a study and analyzing the data.

Given this, it is important that in a presentation of research, the author discuss and explain the perspectives and worldviews upon which s/he draws and the theoretical framework that s/he has employed. While we have mentioned it previously, it is worth reiterating here that in qualitative research, literally the same body of data (or parts of) could be analyzed from different kinds of theoretical perspectives within the qualitative paradigm, and different kinds of findings or new understandings could be derived. It is incumbent upon the authors of a study to make it clear for the reader how these perspectives have shaped the research questions, the design of the project, the findings that emerged, and the conclusions that were drawn.

Here it makes sense to define one of the uniting themes of qualitative research, which is the idea of contextualization. While we have made it clear that the context of any qualitative research project is a centralizing force of the project, contextualization is the process through which meaning is assigned to a phenomenon via the context in which it occurs. Also, meaning can be assigned to a context via the way that a phenomenon plays out. The context of a project is literally the place, space, and participants from where and whom data are collected. The researcher will interpret and give meaning to the space, place, and phenomena observed by placing his/her analysis of the data collected within the larger theoretical framing of the study—contextualizing the analysis within a larger body of research or literature. Similarly, a theoretical perspective can gain meaning in the practical world via contextualization within the activities or interactions of the phenomena being studied.

We help the reader make sense of this now by taking a closer look at the sections of a research presentation in which the theoretical framing of the study is detailed and the study is placed within the larger body of literature related to the topic of the project.

Theoretical Framing

It is often the case that there will be a section explicitly labeled 'Theoretical Framing.' If there is not, the reader should be able to ascertain the author's perspectives via the introduction to the study and through the review of the literature that is related to the justification of the study. Since the threads of consistency of the project should be in play, it can also be the case that the theoretical framing is a part of the discussion of the methodology of the study. As we will detail in the next chapter, the methods of data collection and analysis should make sense given the theoretical framing of the study.

The explanation of the theoretical framing can occur on several levels. The author may situate him/herself socially and culturally as a means to situate or contextualize the origins of the theoretical approaches s/he takes. This may be more or less important depending on the purposes of the study. For instance, it may be quite pertinent that a research study about the play interactions of children of Indigenous origin be conducted by a researcher who is also of Indigenous origins. There is no right or wrong way to do this—a non-Indigenous researcher can also research this topic—but that social positioning might need attention, with the researcher explaining how they dealt with bias or acknowledged ideology.

If the data is taken from a larger study—which it often is—then the researcher may explain the purposes and theoretical framing of the larger study. Then the researcher will further explain the theoretical framing that is particular to the part of the study upon which s/he is reporting. In Adair's (2014) case, the larger study (which is a fairly well-known study) she notes is the Children Crossing Borders study, and Adair devotes a section of the paper (pp. 646–647) to describing that work—providing the contextualization of the slice she takes in her paper. This gives the reader an idea of what kinds of data were collected and what the purposes were for the larger study.

Adair very explicitly explains that she chose some of the data (interviews about immigration and immigrant families from preschool teachers in a variety of U.S. settings) from this larger project and has analyzed it from the theoretical perspective of critical race theory (CRT) (p. 643) and has used "post structural analyses" (p. 643) to generate the findings. This means that Adair believes that sociocultural constructions of race structure the lives and realities of people, with whiteness being a dominant force—and that this enhances the lives of some and marginalizes others. Rather than take this as 'normal,' Adair believes that we need to expose and deconstruct these power structures thus making spaces for a multitude of possibilities for reality—that is, the valuing and uplifting of a diversity of ways of being, in this case based on race. CRT also deals with issues of power and dominant culture ideology. By using poststructural analysis, Adair also believes that individuals have agency within and can change these structures. This means that she will look to see how, in this case, whiteness might be operating and where the opportunities for change could occur. If the threads of consistency hold, we will see then how the methods she chooses to analyze the data fit with this framing of the world.

Review of the Literature

The review of literature in a qualitative study serves the basic purpose of making the case for why the current study is necessary to be conducted in the particular way that the researcher has planned. If the reader has figured out the basic purpose of the study, a perfectly legitimate set of questions are "And? So what? Why do we care?" The review of literature should provide these answers. These sections will provide the justification for deeper examination of the phenomena and for the particular design of the study. The researcher will use existing literature to help the reader understand what other related research has been conducted and where there are gaps in our knowledge or views. The extant literature may also be used to demonstrate how or why a more nuanced or alternative understanding of what the researcher is studying is necessary to promote productive change, disruptions of power relationships, or problematizing of what is seen as the norm.

Writing a good review of extant literature is a skill, and not an easy one at that. The reader should definitely be thankful if the author is able to wade through what is usually a huge body of available research and provide a logical roadmap for the reader of why the current study is important to undertake based on what has and has not been discovered before. Let's take a look at the Madrid et al. (2013) piece to see how they make the case for their study of emotion in the early childhood classroom.

These authors state early on that they conducted a 6-month ethnographic study of emotion in a preschool classroom while the teacher in the classroom was also taking a graduate class on the sociology of childhood. The goal of the larger study was to understand "what emotions 'do' in the everyday life of one preschool classroom" (p. 276). They also note that they analyzed this data "using feminist and poststructuralist accounts" (p. 276). With just this information, the reader needs more information about why we need to study emotion in a classroom. What has been studied already about this topic? Why is this particular theoretical approach and set of methods important?

In the section "Learning How to Feel, as a Professional" (pp. 275–276) these authors note the complexity of emotion in teaching and make the case that this has not been sufficiently studied. Further, they point out the contradiction that in a largely female profession, teachers are told that emotion should not be a part of their professional decision making. And yet, in the casting of the 'good' preschool teacher, the "dominant discourse of emotion . . . revolves around pedagogy of 'maternal' emotions such as gentleness, love, and care" (p. 275). They cite several studies of emotion in early childhood teaching showing how this complexity has not been adequately captured. They go on to further explain that emotion in teaching can also emerge in the form of "guilt, stress, frustration, and worry" (p. 275) and that these are "pushed underground" (p. 275). Thus, professionals are rarely being provided "any opportunities for difficult feeling to be examined and discussed in the workplace" (p. 275). The authors make the case that "there is a resultant need to understand how teachers use their emotions to moderate and modulate their work and the importance this may have for teachers and children's overall well-being" (p. 275).

Further, in the review of the literature, the authors also make the case that the feminist and poststructural approach to teacher emotion is a necessary and previously unaccounted-for stance. They review literature from outside of education to make the case that emotion is not static and is "socially and culturally situated and embedded" (p. 276). The feminist approach means that they believe that socially and culturally constructed ways of being female that are considered 'normal' structure the lives and decision making of people in ways that can be harmful or oppressive. The authors make the case that we must expose this and find ways to push upon this power structure to reimagine our ideas of 'normal.' The poststructural means that they believe that human behavior is not wholly determined by these structures, and they are examining the ways that humans (the preschool teacher in this case) act in ways that go against the culturally defined norms. They note, "Identifying emotion from this perspective is necessary because it open up the possibility of transformation. Emotion, rather than intellect alone, becomes the space in which teachers can act to constitute their identities and classroom practices" (p. 276).

Madrid et al. (2013) have made the case for why they will interpret their data in the ways that follow. Their theoretical perspective and the situating in the larger body of research should give clues to the reader about what to expect from the data collection and data analysis methods. The reader can also expect that the findings will provide details and deeper understandings of how emotions operated for this teacher in her pedagogical decision making. We do not know what will be found, but we do know that a more nuanced understanding will be put forth.

Now that the reader has a good understanding of the beginning steps of qualitative study design and the importance of the initial framing of a study, the next chapter delves into the nuts and bolts of qualitative projects—methodology, methods of data collection and analysis, and reporting of the findings of the project.

Reading and Understanding a Qualitative Study

Phenomena Under Study/Purpose of the Study/Research Question(s)

Task: *Determine what the phenomenon under study is. What did the researcher actually study?*

Look for: This is often explained up front in the abstract or at the end of the introduction.

Task: *Figure out why the researcher is undertaking the study. This should help you further determine what the study is attempting to explain, deconstruct, more fully understand, or reframe.*

Look for: The study introduction should provide an accounting of why this study is important and why using the indicated interpretive framework is important. How will this study help us understand the phenomenon in question more deeply, more critically, or in a different way? The actual research question is most often explicitly stated, but not always. One can often find the research question(s) at the end of the introduction, but they may also be found within or at the end of the review of literature.

Theoretical Framing/Review of the Literature

Task: *Determine the theory or theories from which the researcher is drawing to examine, interpret, or differently explain the phenomena under study.*

Look for: The theoretical framing of the study is often explicitly stated and discussed. This most often will occur within the review of the relevant literature. Explanation of this sometimes also happens at the beginning of the Methods section. For some studies, the theoretical framing is implicit and can be inferred from the works cited or from how the review of the literature is discussed.

Task: *Map out how the study is framed within the literature base.*

Look for: To begin to build your understanding of the literature review, look for the headers used to identify topics. Read the topic and concluding sentences of sections or paragraphs carefully to set up your understanding of main points. Examine how the researcher set the stage for this study by describing what has been found in previous research and how this study addresses gaps, provides alternative interpretations, deconstructs mainstream or canonical ideas, or helps us understand something more deeply.

6

ANALYZING AND REPORTING FINDINGS IN QUALITATIVE RESEARCH

In this chapter, we describe the primary data sources and methodological and analytic strategies used in qualitative research. Readers will gain an understanding of how qualitative researchers approach the process of interpreting data, including the use of descriptive and interpretive coding schemes, organization of data, and eliciting meaning from the data. We will also present information on understanding the presentation and discussion of research findings in the professional literature. We begin with a discussion of quality and rigor in qualitative methods and projects.

Keeping in mind the threads of consistency that are an important feature of a good qualitative study, one thing for the reader to consider is that there is no right or better method for data collection and analysis in qualitative research. The goal of the qualitative researcher is to tell the story of what is occurring in the setting—to understand the actual experiences of the people involved. The types of data collected and the ways that the data are analyzed should make sense in light of the theoretical framing and stated perspectives of the researcher and should have a logical flow from the types of questions that are being asked or the goals of the project. And the story that is finally reported should flow from and make sense given the framing of the project and the data that was collected. That is not to say that from a qualitative project unexpected findings will not emerge. Indeed, most qualitative research is designed specifically to gain alternative perspectives or to expose what has beforehand been invisible. However, the threads of consistency also support the believability of the findings and the trustworthiness of the interpretations. The researcher might not find what s/he was looking for and certainly will find things that s/he was not looking for. But the project must be designed and the findings reported in ways that the reader can trust in what is being reported.

This brings us to the important issues in qualitative research of trustworthiness and believability, which are related to the quality and rigor of a project (Loh, 2013). In quantitative projects, one would consider the concepts of validity and reliability that are expressly designed into a research project ahead of time. For the qualitative researcher, trustworthiness and believability must flow through and be carefully considered throughout the whole process of the research project and are particularly important in choosing and implementing the data collection and analysis methods. Qualitative researchers often turn to the concept of verisimilitude, which the American Heritage Dictionary defines as "the appearance or semblance of truth; likelihood; probability." In order for findings of a qualitative project to carry this characteristic, many would argue that there needs to be evidence of care, thoughtfulness, and rigor taken with the data analysis and the interpretations. And this is of course all up for interpretation by the reader.

One way that qualitative researchers attain verisimilitude (and quality and rigor) is through what is called triangulation of data, where the researcher uses several kinds of data to provide evidence for the claims that a researcher might make. Janesick (1998, citing Denzin, 1978) explains five types of triangulation:

1 *data triangulation:* using a variety of data sources
2 *investigator triangulation:* using different researchers or evaluators to examine data
3 *theory triangulation:* using multiple perspectives to interpret a single data set
4 *methodological triangulation:* using multiple methods to study a single phenomenon
5 *interdisciplinary triangulation:* using other disciplinary perspectives to inform research processes. (pp. 46–47)

With this in mind, we turn back now to the sections of a research report and to our exemplar studies. Recall that Graue, Whyte, and Karabon (2015) examined how kindergarten teachers used improvisation in their teaching of mathematics. Adair (2014) examined how whiteness shaped the ways that white preschool teachers understood the issues of immigrant families. Madrid, Baldwin, and Frye (2013) studied how emotion played out in the teaching practices and classroom activities of one preschool teacher.

Data Sources and Methods of Data Collection

As mentioned in an earlier chapter, it is the case in qualitative research that the researcher is considered the 'tool' of data collection and analysis. In quantitative methods, there is always a search for the objective tools of research—validated surveys, ever-more-powerful statistical analysis methods, assessment and measurement instruments, and so forth. The goals in this research paradigm are to support the researcher to act as objectively as possible, and the tools are designed to ensure that rigor and objectivity. On the other hand, qualitative researchers (particularly in postmodern times) seek to explain the phenomenon under study from the perspectives of those participating in the project and to pose a description and an interpretation of what, how, and why something is happening, how relationships carry out, and why people behave in the ways they do. The goal of quantitative research is to prove, predict, and create universal reality, while qualitative research seeks to describe and deepen understandings of the reality as experienced by the participants of the study.

This puts a great deal of responsibility on the qualitative researcher to collect data that allow him/her to obtain a picture of phenomena that is as close to the actual happening as possible. And, since interpretation is key, the ability to make accurate or appropriate interpretations is predicated on having a high-quality data set that provides enough information that the interpretations are believable. Following are key considerations and key methods of data collection.

Time in the Setting

Time is a very important factor in the design of a qualitative project. The researcher will be spending a great deal of time in the research setting and with the research participants in the effort to be able to tell the story of the phenomena in a comprehensive and trustworthy manner. The researcher must spend enough time in a setting and enough time with the study participants to be able to gain their perspectives and to understand the hows and whys of what is going on. There is no prescription for how much time is enough time, but it is evident in research findings when the time spent is not enough.

Projects can also be a point in time in nature or can be longitudinal (data collected over a longer period of time), and this is part of the study design we discussed in Chapter 5. For example, a researcher may study how a policy is initially implemented in a child care center and may spend only a few weeks at the site collecting data. Or a researcher may want to see how the policy implementation takes place and evolves over a longer period of time and study how that happens in the daycare center over the course of a year. Ethnographic research in which the researcher is trying to explain the behaviors and norms of a group may take place over years. For example, referring to Heath's *Ways With Words* (1983), she spent the better part of a decade living in the three communities she studied, collecting data, and coming to understand the literacy practices of the three groups.

The research design must include spending enough time and care, particularly at the onset of a project, so that trust and rapport can be established with the participants. In a research report, the author may talk explicitly about this process, particularly if it is especially important to the kinds of data that were captured. In research in early childhood when children are involved, developing age-appropriate rapport and trust is particularly important. The researcher(s) is/are going to be collecting data within the lives and spaces of the participants. The participants need to feel comfortable sharing this space and need to trust that their stories will be considered and told in a thoughtful manner.

In a journal article–length presentation, of qualitative research, the author may simply explain how long was spent collecting data and what kinds of data were collected, but there may not be enough space for lengthier discussions of the study design issues that arose related to time in the setting. In many cases, the reader has to trust that the amount of time was appropriate, though if findings seem inappropriate or off in some way, it is not a bad idea to look to see if the amount of time spent seemed reasonable given what the researcher was studying.

To give examples, the Graue et al. (2015) study was a large-scale qualitative project funded by the National Science Foundation, which allowed for a large corpus of data to be collected and involved several researchers. The project spanned 4 years, and data was collected for three cohorts of prekindergarten teachers (55 total) as they participated in professional development sessions and graduate courses. The teachers took four graduate courses over 2 years, and data was collected from them. Additionally, a subset of these teachers was chosen for case studies, and researchers spent an additional 30 hours of time over 9 months collecting data in these classrooms.

Conversely, the Madrid et al. (2013) study was conducted by one of the authors in the classroom of one of the other authors. And the classroom teacher also took an online graduate class with the researcher, and data was also collected throughout the time of the course. The researcher spent 6 months collecting data in the preschool classroom and listed the children in the classroom as participants in her research.

As the reader can see, both larger-scale projects with teams of researchers and the model of the 'lone' researcher are appropriate for qualitative projects.

Context of the Study and Study Participants

The context of a qualitative project is very important, as it is the context that will provide connections and meaning to the phenomena being studied and thus to the findings of the project. For instance, if one desires to study play interactions among preschoolers (which could be studied for a variety of reasons), it will make key differences if those interactions are studied in children who attend a Head Start in a low-income urban neighborhood versus children in attendance in a home child care setting in a small town versus children in attendance in a private, high-tuition child care center in a wealthy suburb. Here the quantitative researcher would look to remove the influences of those contexts on the results of his/her study, seek to control the related variables, and attempt to ascertain results that could be generalized and predict behaviors across settings. The qualitative researcher, on the other hand, would seek to capture the details and nuances of the interactions within each of these settings. It is possible that a qualitative researcher might study play interactions in different contexts in order to compare, but a qualitative researcher might also find it equally compelling to deeply examine the interactions in just one setting. The important part of the research design is that there is careful thought about and rationale for the context of the study and then that there is careful consideration of how the context shapes what it is the researcher is seeing and interpreting.

Access to and entry into a site for the purposes of conducting qualitative research can be fraught. Qualitative researchers are trying to understand how and why people think and behave the ways that they do, which automatically sets up a situation in which trust, rapport, and relationship are a key part of the research process. There is an intimacy involved in qualitative data collection, which can raise a whole host of both methodological and ethical considerations for the researcher to grapple with throughout a project. In fact, a regular critique of this paradigm is that qualitative projects occur in settings of convenience for the researchers. This means that a setting for a project is chosen based on the ease of access to the setting on the part of the researcher. For example, the researcher who wants to study play interactions in preschoolers might choose a site either of a teacher already known to the researcher or in a school close to the researcher's university campus with whom the researcher already has an established relationship. This kind of 'convenience' decision can have its positives and its pitfalls.

Since a journal-length reporting of a project with large amounts of data can be constraining for a qualitative research report, there may not be ample space for deep descriptions of the context of the study and the participants therein. However, there must be enough of a description that the reader can understand what the situation is and why these participants were chosen as the 'case' for this phenomenon. Simply, the reader should determine what the context of the study is and who actually participated in the project. For the reader, this might be intertwined with the determination of purpose of the study that was discussed in Chapter 5. This information may be found in the introduction to the study and then is often explained in more detail in the section about study methods. The reader should also look for an explanation (even if brief) of why a particular setting and why the particular participants were chosen. And this should make sense in light of the indicated theoretical framing and the questions for the project. Further, if the project is a smaller part of a larger study or the data collected is from one part of a larger system, the researcher needs to provide enough information so the reader can make sense of the reporting.

The Graue et al. (2015) study is a good example of a much larger project from which a smaller slice of data was chosen for the study that they published. These authors carefully explain the contexts and participants from the larger study and then provide the details as to why the data from the particular participants was reported upon in this article. These researchers collected data over 4 years and across multiple settings. They carried out professional development sessions with kindergarten teachers and then also observed a subset of the teachers who participated in the professional development in their classrooms. For the particular research report here, they chose the specific case studies of two teachers.

Graue, Karabon, and Whyte provide broader explanation of who the participants in the larger study were, and this includes demographic information. They note that:

> A total of 55 teachers, across the 3 cohorts, elected to participate. The teachers ranged from first year novices to educators close to retirement, working in public schools, childcare centers, and Head Start. All of the teachers were white women with the exception of one white man and a Vietnamese-American woman adopted by a white middle class family as a child.

> (p. 16)

They then explain how they chose the case study teachers from this larger group. They called this group the "case study sample" (p. 16) and noted that these teachers were chosen so as to represent the "range of teaching contexts" (p. 16) present in the larger sample. They designed the sample to include "veterans and novice teachers in child care centers and elementary sites" (p. 16). They then go on to describe how and why they chose the two specific teachers' cases that are reported on in this particular journal article. They noted that they wanted to "provide in-depth portrayal of improvisation in action" (p. 16). The two teachers' cases they chose were "illustrative examples" (p. 16) of the phenomenon under study, and the two represented the "range of teacher improvisation from the larger data set" (p. 16). The reader can make sense of how and why the contexts and participants were chosen in light of the study design, questions, and theoretical framing of the study. Since improvisation is an act that occurs in interactions between or among people and is spontaneous given a particular context, the threads of consistency for this project are very apparent. This is not a phenomenon that could have been captured through a survey. It is a very particular kind of interaction that needed to be studied carefully in the context of classroom teaching, and the two teachers whose practices are highlighted in this report were chosen intentionally to provide illustration of the range of practices of the larger group of the study.

A final note here on participants is exemplified quite well in our Madrid et al. (2013) study. We have mentioned the importance of developing relationships with participants in qualitative studies in order to attain trust and a willingness for them to share their experiences with researchers and ultimately with a public audience. While this is always important, in some studies this relationship is more key to the study outcomes and thus is explained in more detail. In the Madrid, Baldwin, and Frye study, one of the authors is the researcher and one of the authors is the teacher who was studied. In addition, the teacher was also taking a graduate class with the researcher and therefore was her student. This made the research process more complex, and it was important for them to explain how they navigated that relationship across the research process, not simply at the beginning when designing the study. Studies like these make for interesting fodder to consider ethics and how the design and questions of a research project need to be considered throughout the project. To explain, the authors noted, "This space was navigated carefully and thoughtfully by remaining mindful of my goals, paying attention to my own subjectivity, and being respectful of her classroom space and our research relationship" (p. 279). They also note the connection to this approach to their feminist theoretical framing, making the threads of consistency of the project apparent.

Key Methods of Data Collection

Here we provide a more detailed yet still summary-driven overview of the kinds of methods of data collection that a qualitative researcher may use. Again, recall that the kinds of data being collected should make sense given the questions being addressed, the theoretical framing that the researcher has indicated, and the type of context that is under study. Qualitative researchers are always on the lookout for new and better ways to collect data that will help them to more closely or accurately capture the actual happenings that they are studying. Technology has been incredibly useful in this endeavor. In what follows, we discuss some main types of data that are collected across qualitative projects.

Observation

Skilled observation of the phenomena under study is the foundation of much of qualitative research. Researchers will spend a great deal of time with people and in settings (e.g., classrooms) and carefully observe the happenings. It is important to qualitative researchers that the settings be as natural as possible. There is a great deal of what Patton (2015) calls 'folk wisdom' about observing in a setting, that the researcher must actually overcome in order to engage in the thorough and systematic observation required for rigorous qualitative work. Making any assumptions about what is going on in a setting must be avoided to the best of the observer's ability. Observation is more than simply going in and watching what is going on. The observer must carefully 'see' and capture in written (or in some cases video- or audio-recorded) form all of that which is occurring in a setting. And because there is so much possible to observe, this is where a good study design will help the observer focus the observations. However, the observer must also be open to noting the unexpected or to 'seeing' that which was not anticipated.

While observing, researchers employ various methods to capture what it is they are observing. More traditionally, the researcher will take written 'jottings' while observing and then write up more lengthy and descriptive memos and field note reports immediately following an observation. The idea is to capture as accurately and descriptively as possible what one is observing. Given the flurry of technological advances, researchers may also videotape and/or audiotape during an observation. Remote video observations are possible, as are observations of virtual behaviors.

Depending on the goals of the project, researchers will be involved in the settings with the participants to varying degrees while observing. This ranges from complete nonparticipatory observing to being a full participant-observer. In the research reporting, it is expected that the researcher will explain and justify the chosen level of involvement, the impact of that involvement on the participants, and the implications of this on the types of interpretations that are made.

Interviewing

Qualitative researchers spend time talking with their participants and others involved in the context of the study, asking questions, clarifying what they have observed, gaining insight and information, understanding background experiences, and checking their interpretations of the data. Interviews are a staple of qualitative work.

Interviews can take many forms from formal to informal, from scripted to semistructured to open ended (Strauss, 1987). Interviews can occur at any phase of a qualitative project and can serve a variety of purposes. They can be done with individuals or with groups of people. Sometimes researchers will interview participants individually and then also bring them together into groups to deepen the discussions. *Focus groups* can also be drawn together to obtain a representative interpretation of a phenomenon when individual interviews are not feasible. Interviews are very often recorded in some way and then later transcribed verbatim for use in data analysis. Often researchers will develop a pilot interview that s/he tries out with people outside of the possible participant pool to ensure that the questions are designed to capture the appropriate information. Questions are then revised as necessary.

The important part of interviews is that there is some logic to how they are conducted in relationship to the necessary consistencies and goals of the project. The decisions about what kinds of interviews are used, how often, and how in depth need to be explained and justified by the researcher. In a journal-length write-up of a study, it is rare to see the actual interview questions that were used, though one may see reference to the kinds of questions asked and to the larger goals of the interviews for the project.

Collection of Artifacts

Artifacts are often collected as a part of the data corpus in order to provide further evidence of the researchers' interpretations of the phenomena under study. Cultural artifacts can also provide insight into what participants value (or not), how they go about their lives, their relationships to/with the contexts in which they exist, and clues as to how a participant is experiencing or interpreting phenomena. In educational research, artifacts are often textual or graphic in nature and can include such things as notes, drawings, flyers from events, diary entries, emails, lists, artwork, posts from social media, photographs, course assignments, journals, and the like. If the study is of organizational structure, the supporting documents to the functioning of the organization may be collected and examined. This could be bylaw documents, policies and procedures documents, forms, evaluation materials, websites, and so on.

We turn here to the Adair (2014) piece to provide an example of how a researcher explains and justifies the types of data collected for a project. The data for this project was collected using some rather innovative techniques, and this author does a good job of explaining why they collected the types of data they did and how that particular data provided them a nuanced insight into the phenomena of study. In this write-up, the threads of consistency among the theoretical framing, the study questions, and the methods for data collection are clear.

For the larger project from which the data for this particular article was derived, a technique called "multivocal ethnography" (p. 646) was utilized. The purpose of the larger project was "to collaboratively understand and compare preschool teachers and immigrant parents' perspectives on preschool education" (p. 646). This larger project was quite large scale and, all told, the research team interviewed more than 200 preschool teachers in five countries as well as more than 300 immigrant parents. A subset of the interviews were used specifically to "compare the perspectives and ideas of immigrant parents and preschool teachers in the US on the early education of children of immigrants" (p. 646). The subset of participants for this part of the project included immigrant parents from nine countries and 50 preschool teachers from five locations in the United States. The author describes these five locations and gives explanation as to why these areas were chosen and how they were representative of the insights the researchers were trying to attain.

As mentioned, developing relationships and rapport with study participants so as to capture their thinking and perspectives as accurately as possible is a goal in qualitative research. The data from Adair's (2014) study is a good example of qualitative researchers collecting data on a large scale while developing innovative data collection techniques to address the rapport issue in the situation in which you have less time spent with individuals so as to be able to collect data over a larger pool. The multivocal ethnography used "film as a catalyst" to support participants to speak candidly "about ideas or concerns that may be uncomfortable to talk about such as immigration, parent–teacher relationships, language differences, cultural misunderstandings or discrimination" (p. 648). The team developed a film that showed "a typical day in a preschool that serve[d] mostly children of immigrants." The film showed characteristic activities, such as "children fighting over clothes in the dramatic play area, children laughing and singing with their teacher during group time, children painting in the art area, and teachers reading and acting out stories." The film also showed other activities that the researchers deemed less typical and included "bilingual teachers, Spanish and English words on the walls and children using a mix of languages in the classroom" (p. 648). For the larger project, teachers and parents viewed the film and then were interviewed, both individually and in focus groups, about the practices they saw in the film. For the analysis that Adair conducted, she used the focus group interviews of the teachers in the U.S. settings, and in the article she explains why in relationship to the goals and theoretical framing of her part of the analysis.

On page 649 of this piece, Adair also includes a section titled "Combining Multivocal Ethnography and CRT." Recall that CRT is critical race theory and is the stated theoretical framing of Adair's part of the analysis. In this section, Adair spends time explaining and helping the reader understand the connections among her theoretical framing, the data collection, and ultimately the ways that she analyzed the data. This is a good example of an author carefully highlighting for the reader the threads of consistency of the project. These kinds of sections are helpful to a reader to determine if the logic of the project is consistent and evident, and the explanation lends support to the believability of the findings. A reader may not agree with what the author ultimately finds; however, the quality of a project rests both on a solid study design and on the author's ability to narrate and articulate how and why the design and study process decisions were made.

Making Meaning of the Data—Analysis and Interpretation

So here the researcher sits with what can seem like mountains of data, and his/her job now is to tell the story about this data in a way that is representative of the participants' experiences of the phenomena. It can be a daunting task! Observation field narratives have been written up and organized. Audio recordings of interviews are transcribed verbatim. Video recordings are transcribed and perhaps cued or cut into episodes. Artifacts are cataloged and organized. The process of data analysis is the part during which the data gets interpreted and then converted into findings—into the story of what has occurred, according to the researcher.

Truth be told, there never is really a time when a qualitative researcher officially 'starts' data analysis. From the moment data collection begins, it is likely that preliminary analyses have also begun. Analysis of qualitative data is a time-consuming and detailed process and is a process that is as individual as the researcher and the design of the project. It is very nonlinear, and it will be difficult to describe here in a way that reflects what actually happens as data is analyzed. There is no checklist or recipe for how analysis goes, although most qualitative researchers can agree on some basic principles of rigor and quality. While a researcher can lay out a plan, as one gets into the data, twists and turns can occur that require different approaches or additional phases of analysis that were not planned. Data collection and data analysis in projects are often happening simultaneously. It can be the case that initial analyses occur that then suggest new or more in-depth data collection. As we have already seen, parts of a data corpus can be analyzed using a different lens than other parts. As Patton (2015) notes, "Direction can and will be offered, but the final destination remains unique for each inquirer, known only when—and if—arrived at" (p. 521). Despite this complexity, there are some basic processes and procedures that many researchers use that we will outline here.

In journal-length write-ups, it can be argued that explanation of data analyses often gets short shrift unless the researcher is using a particularly innovative or unusual process that requires more in-depth explanation. This occurs because explaining the analyses means describing a very detailed and messy process with many starts, fits, and unexpected turns of events. Yet the way the analyses proceeded is the hallmark of rigor and quality for the project. And if the methods for analyses are not explained, how the researchers arrived at the interpretations may not make sense to the reader. It is important for the reader to ascertain as much information as possible and for there to be a sense of trust that the analyses were carried out with open-mindedness, thoughtfulness, detail, and organization.

Identifying Patterns and Themes

Quite literally, beginning analyses are carried out by reading and organizing the data. In this phase researchers sometimes talk about this as a process of 'reducing' the data. For a qualitative researcher, this does not mean that one is trying to reduce the complexity of the information. But given the amount of data that is possible in a qualitative project, there has to be a means for the researcher to examine the data in manageable chunks or units. Oftentimes this will start with the researcher reading and rereading a set of interview transcripts to begin a process of identifying themes and patterns that arise. Careful notes are kept during this process, and in many cases the researcher will begin to write what are called descriptive memos so that s/he has a way to track emerging thoughts and ideas.

A common method utilized here is called 'constant comparison,' a process described by Glaser and Strauss (1967). This is a process whereby as the researcher begins to more closely examine a new piece of data (the next interview, for example), the new information is being compared to the thoughts and ideas generated from the last piece of data. As emerging themes and patterns come to light, this comparison process continues to confirm and disconfirm initial theories and interpretations.

As this initial analysis process carries forward, many researchers will use this phase to begin to develop a list of codes to be used for more detailed analysis. This phase also provides a structure for the next phases of analysis, which we describe shortly. The researcher is trying to create an evidence trail that supports the interpretations that s/he is making about the data and ultimately about what was observed. This provides credence for the scaffolds of believability of the analysis and interpretation. Throughout the whole process, the researcher makes claims about what was observed occurring and then provides data to buttress those claims.

Coding Data and Developing Categories

Coding of data is a fairly common method of qualitative analysis (though certainly not the only way to go about data organization). While the researcher is working through the initial identification of themes and patterns, s/he will begin to develop a list of codes that can be applied to help describe the data in greater detail. Coding is an organizing framework for the researcher to use as the analysis grows and becomes more complex. It is a way to mark common instances across a data set to see how similar occurrences might play out in different parts of the project. Saldaña (2013) describes a code as "a word or short phrase that symbolically assigns a summative, salient, essence capturing, and/or evocative attribute for a portion of language based or visual data" (p. 3).

Once the researcher develops the list of codes to be used—and this is via inductive analysis of the data—one process is to go through the data line by line and assign a code to words, phrases, and chunks of narrative to mark when one of these is an instance of something the researcher believes s/he is finding. So, for example, one code might be 'Race,' and anytime anyone talks about race or the situation has to do with race, the data chunk would be coded as such. This allows the researcher to go back to these instances as a group and further analyze and interpret what might be going on over the data set in relationship to that code. The descriptive codes can then also mark where further interpretation is required. So in the example of 'Race' the researcher may assign an additional analytic subcode that describes more specifically what the instance was referring to. Is the instance an example in which someone is talking about his/her own racial identity? How race operated in a certain situation? Racism?

There are many ways to approach and think about coding, and this is determined through the conceptual framework of the project. Some codes will be determined ahead of time (a priori), and other codes will emerge through the process of identifying themes and patterns and then will be applied to the rest of the data. Qualitative analyses are not usually complete after one time perusing the data. Oftentimes data is analyzed many times and potentially via different perspectives. Once coding is 'done,' then often researchers will begin to develop broader descriptive and analytic categories to frame what they are seeing in the data. For instance, in the Graue et al. (2015) piece, they briefly describe their coding process across a huge corpus of data (p. 16). They note that the two case studies chosen for more detailed discussion were illustrative of the range of improvisational moves made by the teachers they observed. While these authors did not have the space to describe this process in detail, the reader can infer that they developed categories of teachers and the kinds of improvisation strategies that the teachers used in order to know what the range was and then which teachers to choose to illustrate that range.

Writing Analytic Memos

Broadly, this is a process almost akin to journaling. As the researcher moves through the data analysis process, s/he might keep memos or write-ups about what s/he is seeing or ideas s/he is having about what is emerging from the data. This memo-ing process can occur throughout data collection and all throughout the analysis. In some cases, these memos are then organized and used as additional data. Sometimes researchers will use the codes and categories they developed and analyze the information in the memos. Sometimes the memos will be used as data triangulation to support claims the researcher is making. This process can be especially important when there is a team of researchers analyzing the data. A memo provides the breadcrumb trail that explains what the researcher was thinking about as s/he read through or coded data, and others can then use this either as a springboard for further analysis or as confirming/disconfirming evidence of emerging themes and patterns.

This memo process is very rarely described in detail in a journal-length reporting of research. However, it can be a very important part of the data analysis process. It is some of the 'behind-the-scenes' work that is not usually discussed but was likely an important organizing feature of the data analysis.

Within-Case and Across-Case Comparisons

Once data is coded, the researcher can begin to examine the ongoing analyses both within and across the data in the various 'cases' that may be a part of the data collection. How this might occur depends on the design of the study, of course. We use the Graue et al. (2015) article to provide an illustrative example of how this might have played out. It is important to note that the description of this level of analysis is not likely to appear in a journal article, so we summarize the process here to provide the example.

Data collected for this study included observation records of each of the professional development sessions that were held for the teachers, interviews of the teacher participants, and observation records of the classroom practices of the subset of teachers chosen for the more in-depth case studies. A within-case analysis might have been carried out as follows, beginning with the determination of 'teacher' as the case. All of the data related to one of the teachers was organized together. That teacher's activities and artifacts related to his/her participation and engagement with the professional development sessions were examined over time to suggest patterns, themes, and shifts in thinking related to the activities of the professional development sessions. Then s/he is also chosen as a case-study teacher, so his/her interviews and classroom observations were also examined over time. (All data has been coded by this time so that there is a structure to the in-case analysis.) A 'case' is then developed, in great detail, which describes this teacher in relationship to the questions of the study.

The across-case analysis could then proceed. A case as described above is developed for each of the teachers, and the further analysis ensues in which those cases are compared with each other given the established codes and categories. It is possible within this process that different categories emerge, and then the cases can be reanalyzed in light of those categories. Finally, the analysis proceeds to the point at which the researcher feels as though a reporting of the findings is valid. And findings can be drawn from various phases of a project. For the article we have used here, the findings reported are of the improvisation strategies of two of the case study teachers. A report could be generated simply about the professional development sessions. A report about the mathematics strategies of the teachers might be generated. The level of analysis for any report of findings can be varied—in this case it could be individual teachers to professional development sessions to teaching strategies. This is how and why qualitative analyses can be said to be generative. Good, detailed, and rigorous analysis should produce a variety of reportable findings.

As one can see, qualitative analysis is a completely iterative process. There is a great deal of back and forth. One can think of the process as an investigation in which the researcher is searching for evidence (both confirming and disconfirming) to support his/her conjectures about what is going on. Researchers talk about following leads, hitting dead ends, and 'breaks' in the analysis. Researchers have to be open to interpretations they did not expect and to find disconfirming evidence of things they did expect. The analyses themselves often end up producing more data than expected.

The range of data analysis methods and tools used across the three exemplar studies is a good representation of the variety of processes that are used. The Graue, Whyte, and Karabon and the Adair studies were both projects that gathered large amounts of data over longer periods of time. In both of these projects, a research team was employed to analyze the data to tell a variety of different stories about the data. No doubt that for both of these studies, the analyses took place in phases. Section 3.3 in the Graue, Whyte, and Karabon piece is titled "Data Collection and Analysis" (p. 16). Considering the scope of this project, it is interesting to note that only three paragraphs are devoted to describing the very complex and detailed analysis process that was undoubtedly undertaken. It is always up to the reader to determine if sufficient information has been provided that one can trust the analysis procedures.

In the Adair project, since her report was derived from a larger project, she not only describes a bit about the data analysis from the larger project, but she also spends time explaining how she framed her particular analysis of the data. As mentioned, she used a guiding theoretical framework of CRT to analyze a portion of the data from the larger project. Because the project used innovative techniques and because she applied a slightly different lens for this report, she spent more time explaining both how CRT was used in relationship with the multivocal ethnography and how that guided the data analysis. Two sections covering pages 648 to 649 ("Multivocal Ethnography" and "Combining Multivocal Ethnography and CRT") are devoted to explaining how she decided on the analysis processes that she did.

The Madrid, Baldwin, and Frye study represents a study on a smaller scale that was largely conducted by a single researcher. Nonetheless, the research generated a large corpus of data. In this case, the researcher applied a particular kind of data analysis process called Spradley's Developmental Research Sequence (p. 280). The authors devote a small section to explaining how the analysis proceeded. Since the project used ethnographic methods for data collection, the section helps the reader understand how and why this particular process of analysis was appropriate for the kinds of data and for the types of understandings that were being sought.

Findings and Discussion of Findings

This section of a journal article is where the researcher tells the story that has emerged from the data. Different from quantitative research in which 'results' of analysis are presented in numeric form, qualitative research is always narrative and gives details and description of the phenomena under study. Additionally, the researcher will provide his/her interpretations of what occurred—the 'so what' part of the explanation. It is always a balancing act for a qualitative researcher to include enough description and enough interpretation to make the 'story' believable.

From a consumer's perspective, this is usually the most interesting part of the article; however, the reader should be diligent in going through the steps described earlier to ensure that the story is accurate and believable and not just read the discussion section. Also, in this section(s) it is important that the researcher help the reader see how threads of consistency of the project have been drawn through the project. This means that it should be clear in the telling of the story how the theoretical framing generated the question that should now be apparent and connected to the findings.

In many cases, the findings narrative is organized around the themes or categories that came from the analysis. The researcher will explain what occurred in a part of the data collection (make a claim) and will provide evidence from the actual data to support the claim that is made. Quotations and data excerpts are common elements, and here is where qualitative researchers can struggle. One must provide enough data evidence so that the claim is believable or makes sense to the reader. Here also, the researcher may draw from extant literature to support claims, particularly in light of the theoretical framing of the study. Given page constraints, it is common for peer reviewers to want more data to support the claims. The author must do a very careful job of explaining how and why the evidence supports the claims being made. And there is never enough space to do this!

It can be the case that graphic representations (of various kinds) of the data are presented as a means to help the reader understand the way the researcher presented the interpretations of the phenomena. A graphic representation can be used as a way to present how the data was utilized to develop new theory, and it shows how a theory (generated from the data) might work on a larger scale in a more universal manner. (Though recall that for the most part, generalizability is not always a goal for the qualitative researcher.)

The Madrid et al. (2013) article illustrates the process of making claims, providing evidence, and providing interpretation. The section in this article is titled "Findings and Interpretations" (helpful!) and begins on page 280. The discussion is structured around the two themes that the researchers identified via their data analysis process regarding how emotion was playing out in the classroom they studied. These themes were *Toys from home & consumerism* and *Sassy girls: relational and physical aggression*. In each subsection, the authors follow a consistent pattern of making a claim from the data related to the theme (telling part of the story), providing data excerpts that provide examples of the claim (providing evidence), and then explaining to the reader how that data excerpt is an example of the claim that they are making (providing interpretation). Throughout, the authors also draw from outside literature to help explain to the reader why the claim is important and how the interpretation enhances or extends our current understanding of the phenomena.

In final sections of qualitative work, authors will often draw conclusions, explaining why and how the claims and interpretations presented are important or how they may be applied to other situations. Here the authors may suggest implications for their work. They also may discuss the limitations of their study. Finally, they may suggest how their study is a springboard for further research. It is the case that these sections are often shorter. The reader should look to see if the conclusions make sense in light of the data, are not overstated, and fit with the threads of consistency related to the original theoretical framing of the project. Madrid, Baldwin, and Frye draw the following conclusion:

> The emotional life of this teacher was associated with both knowing and not knowing as a teacher and learner. The study uncovered the discomfort associated with her

responses to children's play themes and issues of socially just classroom practices. It also made visible the teacher's willingness to get comfortable with uncomfortable emotions as a teacher and learner. Discomfort emerged as a dominant concern connected to Eleanor's struggle and ambivalence, which were associated with the tensions and contradictions that arose as she examined the children's social practices in relation to the graduate course content, with her discomfort often resting on "not knowing" what were "right" social practices for the children.

(p. 288)

They go on to note that understanding discomfort in the context of everyday classroom practices could serve as a "catalyst for transformation" (p. 288), suggesting avenues of further investigation.

So welcome to the messy, complex, and nonlinear world of qualitative research. We have attempted to provide an overview of the main approaches, methods, and processes of qualitative work. What we have provided here should not be considered an exhaustive treatment but, rather, as the basics to help a reader appraise the quality and believability of qualitative work.

Reading and Understanding a Qualitative Study

Methods: Context of the Study and Participants

Task: *Determine what the context of the study was and who participated in the research.*
Look for: Note the descriptions given of the participants in the research. How much does the researcher tell you about their backgrounds? What do you wish you knew that isn't reported? How sufficient does this group of participants seem (e.g., number involved, their local contexts)? How did the researcher find the participants and, if pertinent, group them (note: if this is not detailed, most likely it was a matter of convenience)?

Task: *Appraise the description of the context(s) of the study.*
Look for: Does the researcher give you enough information about the context? Remember that context is very important in qualitative research, so is there enough detail provided that the reader can understand how a phenomenon may play out? What is missing that leaves the reader with questions? Note that in some case study research, the context may be included in the description of the cases rather than in a separate section.

Task: *Determine the relationship between the researcher and the study participants.*
Look for: Does the researcher discuss this, and what might this relationship mean for the later interpretations of the phenomena? Do there seem to be any conflicts of interest or biases, and how does the researcher explain these? Was the researcher an outside observer or a participant observer? And if a participant, what was the level of participation, and does the researcher account for the impact of this participation on the outcomes of the study?

Methods: Data Collection

Task: *Identify the kinds of data that were collected and what methods were used for data collection.*

Look for: Does the data collected seem to be relevant to the questions asked? Does the data collected seem to fit within the theoretical framework and the purposes of the study? Is there enough data to provide evidence connected to the questions? How long did the researcher spend in a site or with the participants? How did the data collection process impact the relationships with the participants? Did the data collection methods change at all over the course of the study? Why? Look for explanations of triangulation of data in which various types of data are collected to provide evidence of later claims.

Methods: Data Analysis

Task: *Identify the methods that the researcher used to analyze the data in order to create the story or narrative that will later be told about the data.*

Look for: While there are some standard methods of analyzing data used in qualitative research, the methods are not standardized as in quantitative analysis. Especially in journal article–length presentations, the explanation of data analysis may not always reflect the complexity of what the researcher actually did. Does the researcher provide an adequate accounting of the methods used to analyze the data? Can the reader make sense of how the researcher may have come to the conclusions that the researcher later draws? Does the analysis seem to make sense given how the researcher has framed the study? Does the analysis engender enough evidence to support the claims that the researcher makes? The reader may have to read the findings and discussion of the study and then come back to the analysis to see if the analysis provided the evidence to make the researcher's explanations and interpretations plausible or reasonable.

Findings and Discussion of Findings

Task: *Appraise the story/narrative that the researcher tells that emerged from the researcher's analysis of the data.*

Look for: Study findings are written in narrative form and tell the story of the data as interpreted by the researcher. There may be descriptive tables or other visuals/ models included to enhance the reader's understanding of the story. Look for dialogue and data excerpts that support the claims that the researcher makes. Do the findings make sense given the kinds of data collected? Does the story provide insight into the research questions? Do the findings make sense within the theoretical framework proposed? Does the story provide insight into the phenomena in the ways that connect to the stated purpose of the study? Do the findings seem plausible given the types of data and analysis conducted?

Task: *Evaluate the researcher's discussion of the findings which indicates the 'so what' of the study.*

Look for: Are the claims made about the research consistent with the purposes of the study, the research questions, and the theoretical framing of the study? Do the findings presented support the claims that the researcher makes? Does the discussion adequately explain how the study enhances our understanding of the phenomena, reframes the phenomena, or pushes the reader to understand the phenomena from a different lens? The researcher may provide further discussion of the possible implications of the findings and/or the limitations of the study. Do these make sense given the kinds of data collected?

7

QUANTITATIVE RESEARCH
Study Questions and Methods

As we have just done with qualitative research, our aim in this chapter and the one to follow is to explain the basic principles of conducting research in the quantitative paradigm, including determining the research questions, enrolling a group of participants, deciding upon instruments and measures, collecting data, and analyzing the data. Along the way, we will add to the body of terms that are central to understanding the work of quantitative researchers.

As a reminder, quantitative studies are developed out of the existing literature. A researcher typically begins with an area of intellectual curiosity. At this point the researcher's role is to find out 'what we know' about this phenomenon, in other words, what has already been studied. The findings of previous research are of interest, of course. But researchers also look at how the studies were conducted—the types of instruments used, the particular group of participants involved, and so on. From there the researcher builds a new study to add another installment to the account of 'what we know.'

Importantly, in quantitative research most of the decisions about how the study will be conducted are determined at the outset of the process. This reflects the ideal of objectivity, in that the researcher is working along the lines of logic established by the study design rather than reacting to what happens along the way. Occasionally during the analysis of data, the researcher will make some decisions to conduct post-hoc analyses (defined as analyses conducted to follow-up the analyses that were planned at the start of the study). These are conducted based upon what was revealed during the planned analyses. However, there are two reasons this is done very cautiously. First, the more analyses conducted, the more likely the researcher will report a result that is deemed to be 'significant' but in fact is not. We will explain why this is the case in the next chapter, but for now remember that analyses are planned and conducted to be parsimonious—'more' is not 'better' in the case of statistical analysis. Second, and reflecting the ideal of objectivity, when researchers decide upon analyses based upon what the data looks like after the fact, there is skepticism about the findings. One colloquial term for this is 'fishing expedition.' The pattern found among the data might be spurious, or false. Now, the same can apply to a pattern found among data when answering a planned question and analysis. If so, the spurious finding is a result of finding something false while looking for that particular something. This is a consequence associated with research to which we will return in Chapter 8. In the first case, the fishing expedition, the spurious finding is a result of finding something while looking for *anything*. This process is contrary to the deductive logic associated with quantitative research that we explained in Chapter 4.

As we discuss concepts in this chapter and the next, we will draw upon three studies for examples. Here we briefly describe each study.

Denham, Bassett, Sirotkin, Brown, and Morris (2015) examined preschoolers' executive control in relation to the children's age, gender, and the level of their mothers' education (we will refer to this as the executive function study). They used two measures of executive control, cool executive control (orderly and flexible responses for shifting attention and focus) and hot executive control (regulation of emotional arousal and impulses). They hypothesized that older children, girls, and children from higher socioeconomic levels would score higher on these measures. Second, they examined how executive control was associated with teachers' reports on the children's social competence and adjustment in the classroom. They expected that cool executive control would be more highly related to children's classroom adjustment and hot executive control would be more highly related to children's social competence.

Sheridan et al. (2014) randomly assigned Head Start classrooms to participate, or not, in an intervention designed to engage families in understanding their children's development, forming goals for their children in partnership with program staff, and responding sensitively to engage their children in learning to meet goals (we will refer to this as the family engagement study). During the 2 years that children and families were participating in the program, the researchers collected data by periodically observing the parent and child as they played together in tasks set up by the researchers (e.g., book reading, puzzles, free play, and cleanup). They expected that as the intervention proceeded, the children whose families participated would show increases in learning-related behaviors (e.g., persistence, activity level, positive affect, distractibility) compared to children whose families did not participate. In addition, they tracked the family members' self-reported depression to examine if this had any influence on how the intervention impacted the children's learning-related behaviors.

Fisher and Ellis (1988) examined children's responses to poetry (we will refer to this as the poetry study). Children in 34 classrooms across four states (grades 1, 2, and 3) listened to recordings of poems and then were reread one of the poems by their teachers according to a schedule determined by the researchers. For each of eight reread poems the teachers asked the children why they liked or disliked the poem and transcribed their responses. The researchers were interested in what aspects of the literature were utilized by children in their responses. They coded the children's replies by noting the focus of attention (i.e., the structure of the writing, the ideas expressed or provoked, and the feelings evoked) and by distinguishing the content of the responses (e.g., knowledge, interpretation, application, judgment). The categorization process served to reduce the children's responses into numerical data, the number of times each type of response was utilized. This data was then analyzed to examine differences among the children's responses.

Determining Research Questions

The purposes of quantitative studies fall into a small number of major categories. Researchers' questions are descriptive, relational, comparative, or causal in nature.

Descriptive Questions and Purposes

Quantitative studies are invariably descriptive; in presenting numerical data, researchers are describing a phenomenon or characteristic. A small number of studies stop there, with the sole purpose being to describe the phenomenon of interest. The question at the heart of this research is along the lines of "How much of 'this' and 'that' do we see?" For example, Holmes, Holmes, and Watts (2012) were interested in how often teachers in kindergarten through third-grade classrooms used concrete materials in their vocabulary instruction. They observed vocabulary lessons, using a coding scheme that categorized teaching materials within a hierarchy that began at one end with oral description/definition of vocabulary and moved through written descriptions/definitions, visual representations, models, artifacts brought into the classroom, and real-world materials in their natural context. The data in this study is reported as the percentage of observations within each of the levels of the hierarchy in three different ways: in regard to the grade level, in regard to the content area of the lesson, and in regard to the schools' level within an accountability scheme (e.g., high performing, low performing, at risk of failing, etc.). It is possible to see on the tables in the paper that there are both differences and similarities in the percentages reported among various categories. But this is all we know from the study—that vocabulary teaching was approached differently, and sometimes not so differently, in regard to a continuum ranging from oral definitions to real-world materials when looking at different teaching contexts (Holmes et al., 2012). No further statistical analyses were performed to examine whether these differences might represent the random variation one would expect in any real-world phenomenon or might be more selective. An example of the latter (are differences selective?) would be using statistical analysis to determine if the teaching choices were related systematically to the children's age. The Holmes et al. study provides us with a window into classrooms, reflecting teaching strategies in use. But when we see differences, we are not able to determine if the differences are large enough that they might represent something systematically different for children of various grade levels or for lessons in different content areas.

Most often, quantitative researchers take that next step, which is where statistical analyses come into the picture. Still, in all of those studies, typically the discussion of the study's results, or findings, begins with descriptive data. Descriptions are offered to characterize the study's participants and to provide information about the data collected in the study, such as the average scores and the range of scores on instruments.

Relational Questions and Purposes

A large number of quantitative studies focus on the relations among variables (the pieces of information that are the object of the study). These relationships are referred to as correlations. The research questions might include:

- How strong is the relationship between this variable and that variable?
- How does a third variable affect the relationship between this variable and that one?
- How accurately can we predict a variable based upon knowing these other variables?

In Denham et al.'s (2015) executive function study, one of the research questions was relational in nature. Specifically, the researchers wanted to "describe associations of . . . [children's executive control] with teachers' reports on children's social competence and classroom adjustment" (p. 215). For example, were children rated as more socially competent if they scored higher on executive control? Denham et al. complicated the relationships they explored by looking first at how social competence was related to children's age, maternal education, and gender. Then they looked at how much more of the social competence ratings were related to an association with the executive control variables. We will return to this example and others we present in this chapter in Chapter 8 to examine how to read and understand the results of the analyses presented by the researchers.

It is important to note that the relationship that might be found between two variables using correlational analyses does not imply that one variable causes another. They simply are related in how they vary. For example, among children, height and weight tend to vary together—taller children tend to weigh more and shorter children tend to weigh less. The relationship is not perfect, certainly, and we did not use adults as our example because adult weight at any one point in height tends to vary even more than among children. But height does not cause weight. In correlational research, even if one of the variables comes temporally before the other variable, the first cannot be assumed to cause the second; it could be the case that another, unmeasured variable was involved. Therefore, a maxim to always keep in mind is 'correlation is not causation.' With a correlational analysis, we can say that one variable tends to 'go along with' another variable, and that if we know one variable, we can make predictions—with a limited certainty—about another variable.

Comparative Questions and Research

Just as prominent in the literature are studies in which the research questions focus on differences, or comparisons, among groups. The nature of this question is whether one might expect to see the differences found between or among groups by chance alone or whether that is unlikely, implying that something is operating to generate a difference.

Returning to the executive function study by Denham et al. (2015), one of the research purposes was to "evaluate differences in [executive control] according to child characteristics (age, socioeconomic risk status, and gender)" (p. 215). The researchers compared the scores of girls and boys and of children at different age levels to see if the group scores were selectively different from each other. Similarly, Fisher and Ellis (1988), in the poetry study, examined how the responses of children to poems differed across the three grade levels in their sample.

Knowing that groups are different does not tell us why they differ, only that they do differ in ways that appear systematic (not random). For example, in the executive function study, Denham et al. (2015) found that boys and girls differed on the measures of executive control, with girls scoring higher. But we cannot determine what led to these differences—Are girls naturally more inclined toward these skills? More likely to have been expected and supported to develop these skills? More rewarded for demonstrating the skills? Once again, causality cannot be assumed. The limits of the answers to these research questions are important to remember, particularly when existing groups are examined. In the case of existing groups, we do not always know what differences are occurring naturally that might impact the research findings.

Causal Questions and Research

As we have just described, many research questions cannot address causality. It is not surprising that researchers (and policy makers) do want to ask questions about whether one variable causes another. This type of research is more complex to undertake and so often more costly and difficult. It requires that the researcher is able to control variables (e.g., what is taught, how it is taught, to whom it is taught). For these reasons, it is not the major form of research within education, although many might wish for the type of answer that it appears this research could provide.

Causal questions, such as does an intervention lead to desired outcomes, are addressed through quasi-experimental and experimental research. In quasi-experimental studies, researchers use existing groups of individuals but work carefully to ensure that the individuals in one group (i.e., intervention group) are similar in key ways to the individuals in the other group (i.e., comparison group). To illustrate, Winter and Sass (2011) tested an intervention designed to prevent obesity and increase children's school readiness as assessed through their receptive language. They used four Head Start centers located within the same agency as the existing groups, with the intervention conducted in two of the four centers. Comparisons among the four centers were conducted to assure that they were similar. Thus, the researchers were able to state that the two groups of centers (intervention and comparison) did not differ systematically in regard to children's gender, age, ethnicity, and family income. Furthermore, all centers used the same curriculum.

The findings of a quasi-experimental study are generally regarded with some caution because of the use of existing groups wherein an unmeasured phenomenon might impact the outcome. Consider this case in regard to our exemplar study by Winter and Sass: the obesity prevention program involved parent education. We do not know if there were any systematic differences among the four centers in regard to the effectiveness of their general family engagement efforts that might have impacted the intervention. If, perhaps, one center had a very effective family engagement process that altered how families responded to the intervention, it could impact the study processes and findings if this center was one of the two intervention sites.

In a true experiment, random assignment helps ensure that groups are as comparable as possible and that factors vary at random within each group; participants have an equal chance of being in the treatment or control groups. Thus, there may be groups of children who vary similarly on several different demographic measures (e.g., gender, age, socioeconomic status), and both the intervention and control groups have teachers with a range of years of experience. Furthermore, the experiences the participants bring into the study are expected to vary in random rather than systematic ways.

It is very difficult, if not often impossible, in educational settings to randomly assign children to schools and even classrooms. Sometimes, then, classrooms are randomly assigned; to ensure that randomization has the desired effect, a number of classrooms must be included. If too few 'units' are randomized, the effects are more tenuous. Consider tossing a coin. If you toss it 50 times, you can reasonably expect about 50% of the tosses to come up heads. However, if you toss it only five times, you may reasonably come up with 80%, or even 100%, heads just by chance.

Sheridan et al. (2014) used a true experiment in the family engagement study or, as it is sometimes called, a randomized control trial. They examined an intervention designed for engaging families with their children's learning and development to support social-emotional and language/literacy skills. The researchers randomly assigned Head Start classrooms in 21 different buildings to either the treatment or control groups. These 21 research sites reflect a far more expansive and expensive study than the four centers that made up the quasi-experiment performed by Winter and Sass (2011). In each of the intervention buildings, the researchers had to ensure that the program was implemented as it had been intended, with teachers participating in training and carrying through with the intervention's features. The researchers then compared the outcomes between the two groups, intervention and control.

In sum, in this section we have described the major types of questions posed by quantitative researchers. Each type of question has its own set of possibilities and limits. Knowing what the questions and resulting answers mean is important to understanding the story of each piece of research, what it tells us, what is left unanswerable, and where we should exercise judicious caution in making meaning of the story.

Enrolling Participants

As researchers enroll participants in their studies, the resulting group is referred to as a sample. The use of statistical analyses typically requires a number of individuals to contribute data to the study. Indeed, a strong statistical analysis is dependent upon having a sufficient number of data points. Therefore, quantitative studies most often have more participants than qualitative studies, and often the difference is quite large.

In theory, the participants in a quantitative study represent some larger population of individuals. Remember that previously we have explained that quantitative researchers assume that the results of their study, using a sample, can be generalized to a larger group of individuals (the population). Of course, in order for this assumption to stand, the sample must adequately reflect key characteristics of the population. Researchers rarely define the link between their study sample and a larger population in their papers, so often this is a judgment the reader must make. Who is the larger population represented by this sample? Obviously, we might not generalize findings from a study using a sample of 3-year-old children to children who are 6-year-olds. Research done in the past has been criticized for using largely samples of white children while operating under the assumption that the findings could be generalized to children of all racial and ethnic backgrounds. Now the scientific community is more likely to acknowledge that unique factors of culture make these assumptions questionable. On the other hand, can we generalize a study of children attending Head Start (and thus meeting eligibility requirements concerning family income) to represent a population of all children who attend Head Start? We hope readers realize how fraught the issues are—how do we understand what larger group might be represented by a particular study sample? While researchers might address issues of generalizability in their papers, it is still up to individual readers to consider how far they might go in assuming that what was found for this particular sample within the study might apply to others with similar backgrounds.

In the ideal world of research, the sample is carefully chosen by the researcher. In reality, locating individuals, programs/schools, and/or families who are willing to participate in research is difficult. Research requires a willingness of the participants to open themselves up to the researcher's time requests, tasks, and observational gaze. The time commitments required of the researcher often limit the bounds of the work. Thus, many samples are reflective of the most suitable arrangements possible given time, expense, and willing volunteers.

Study samples may truly be formed by convenience, more often than supposed given the ideals of science. Sometimes researchers exert some criteria, or purpose, for forming their samples. For example, they might choose some schools deemed to be high performing and some not, based upon school accountability measures. Finally, sometimes researchers work to create what is called a stratified sample, attempting to replicate within a sample some characteristic of the population. As an example, two of us reside in Milwaukee, where the demographics of individual schools in the public school system reflect the highly segregated living patterns of the city. If we wanted to create a stratified sample of Milwaukee schools, we would attempt to select a number of schools with mostly African-American children roughly equivalent to their percentage in the overall school district population, as well as select a number of schools serving Latino/a children also roughly equivalent to their percentage in the population. If we selected only schools in African-American neighborhoods, we would not represent the *overall* district well, because the demographics of schools in the various neighborhoods of the city vary so tremendously.

In conclusion, researchers typically work with constraints in forming a sample for their studies. It is important for them to thoughtfully consider how best to form a sample and equally important that they describe this sample as thoroughly as possible for readers. It is then up to the reader to evaluate the sample. Who is represented in the sample? Does it seem adequate to test out the researchers' questions? What are the limits of generalizability with this sample?

Deciding Upon Instruments and Measures

In quantitative studies, data is collected via the measures utilized by the researchers. Deciding upon the instruments and measures to be used in a study is a key task that impacts the promises and pitfalls inherent in any piece of research.

Before going any further, it is important to define how researchers conceptualize variables for their studies. Recall that in Chapter 4, we described that quantitative researchers measure the concept of interest via the use of numbers. The concept of interest, or construct, being studied, is denoted by a variable that is represented numerically. The theory underlying the research describes how the variables are connected.

Let's use Denham et al.'s (2015) study of executive function as an example. In this study, there are several variables. Executive control was one construct of the study. The researchers used one instrument as a measure of hot executive control, one variable of the study. They used a second instrument as a measure of cool executive control, another variable. Denham and her colleagues were also interested in several other areas of children's functioning. These constructs included social competence and classroom adjustment. These constructs were measured by instruments completed by the teachers of the children. One variable is denoted as social competence and another variable is denoted as classroom adjustment.

In Denham et al.'s (2015) study, the measures of executive control were used to predict children's social competence and classroom adjustment. Because they are predictors, or come first in the research question, the measures of executive control are independent variables. Independent variables are considered to impact or have some influence on other variables. The measures of social competence and classroom adjustment are dependent variables because they come last in the research question, and the researchers are interested in how they are impacted, or influenced, by the independent variables. In the researchers' stated expectations, it is clear how the independent–dependent variable relationship is theorized: "we expected that CEC [cool executive control] would be more highly associated with classroom adjustment than HEC [hot executive control], with the converse true for social competence" (Denham et al., 2015, p. 215). Note that the independent variables (CEC or HEC) come before the dependent variables (classroom adjustment and social competence) and are considered to influence them.

Interestingly, while the science of research includes the concepts of independent and dependent variables, in research articles, these terms are not always used explicitly. Rather, readers have to infer which is which based upon the question of what variable(s) is being assumed to influence or impact what other variable(s).

This portrayal of independent and dependent variables is the simplest form of an equation that reflects research questions. Frequently the equation is made more complex with the use of intervening variables, such as moderating variables and control variables. A moderating variable operates as its name implies, impacting the relationship between the independent and dependent variables from 'in the middle.' A control variable is used in the statistical analyses to isolate the impact, or influence, of the variables in the study. In essence, a control variable is used to express, 'Let's remove the influence of the control variable from the equation and see what is left in the relationship between the independent and dependent variables.' We will explain more in the next chapter on understanding these analyses. For now, in looking at the Denham et al. (2015) study on executive function, we see in the research questions that control variables were used. One aim of the study is described as being to "describe associations of PSRA [measure of executive function] components with teachers' reports on children's social competence and classroom adjustment, after holding child characteristics constant" (p. 215). The control variables are child characteristics, in this case gender, age, and maternal education.

Moving to Sheridan et al.'s (2014) family engagement study, we find the following research questions: "What are the effects of the Getting Ready intervention on preschool children's learning-related behaviors (e.g., agency, persistence)?" (p. 750). Here, the independent variable is the intervention that was received by those in the treatment group, which is being compared to the control group, families that did not receive the intervention. The dependent variables are children's learning-related behaviors. The second research question was, "Does parental depression moderate the effects of Getting Ready on children's learning-related behaviors?" (p. 750). Parental depression is the moderating variable operating 'within the middle.' The researchers could control who got the intervention and who did not; they could not control who was experiencing depression. But they believed depression could impact how the families participated in the intervention, so they measured level of depression and included it in the analyses. We must note that Sheridan et al. also utilized two control variables, the child's gender and the presence of an identified disability as reported by the parent. These control variables are not included in the research questions, as was the moderating variable depression, but instead are mentioned in the Methods section under a header "Study Variables and Instrumentation" (p. 756). This exemplifies how important it is to read a research report carefully and thoroughly; sometimes information is located in various places.

The first step in understanding the instruments and measures used in a study is to comprehend how variables are defined and related to each other, as we have just described. From there, readers must examine how researchers chose to measure the variables.

In many cases, variables are measured through the use of instruments. The instruments are described in the Methods section of a research paper. Often researchers make use of instruments that have been devised by others, although sometimes they do develop new instruments for a study.

In Denham et al.'s (2015) study on executive function, the researchers used several established instruments. Hot and cool executive control were each measured with an instrument that directly assessed children. The dependent variables, social competence and classroom adjustment, were measured by surveys completed by the children's teachers. For each of the direct assessments, Denham and her colleagues described what children were asked to do and how scores were established. For example, for hot executive control, the children were asked not to peek while the child assessor spent a minute wrapping a toy. The variable was measured as the number of seconds (up to 60) before the child took a first peek, as well as the presence of peeking (or not) and the number of peeks during the 60-second process. Denham et al. do note, however, that they only used the time until the first peek in their analyses for the study. In regard to each of the teacher surveys, Denham and her colleagues identified how many items each survey contained and described the subscales contained within each by naming the subscale and offering an example item.

When researchers describe the instruments used, they should provide enough information to help readers understand the nature of the instrument. Our explanation in the previous paragraph of the executive function study shows how these researchers accomplished that task. In addition, harkening back to our discussion in Chapter 4, researchers should also offer information about the validity and reliability of the instruments. Denham et al. (2015) addressed this in regard to internal consistency and interrater reliability for the child assessment instruments and internal consistency and validity for the teacher-rated surveys.

In the experimental study of family engagement by Sheridan et al. (2014), recall that the independent variable was the Getting Ready intervention program. What we find in this Methods section is a description of the strategies that form the components of that program. In addition, the researchers measured the fidelity with which teachers implemented the intervention. The researchers cite other published papers in which they described the fidelity measure more thoroughly, but stated here, "A variable accounting for both quality and quantity of strategy use was created by computing the product of adherence and quality" (p. 755). While this explanation is brief, it does let the reader know that the researchers tracked the teachers' use of the intervention strategies.

Sheridan et al.'s (2014) dependent variables were the levels of agency, persistence, activity level, positive affect, distractibility, and verbalizations shown by children in interaction with their parents. These were rated from videotapes, and the researchers described the process of establishing interrater reliability. To measure depression, the moderating variable, the researchers had families complete an established survey about how frequently they had experienced depressive symptoms. The researchers explained that this instrument results in a range of scores (in the case of this instrument, participants rate 20 items on a scale of zero to three, resulting in a possible range of scores from 0 to 60). They decided to use the scores to categorize the participants using a cut-off score for depression. Therefore, participants whose scores were elevated compared to those of the other participants were categorized as experiencing depression. This is an example of how the researchers began with an established instrument but then created their own variable via how they chose to record scores. They might have merely recorded the score on this instrument for each participant (e.g., A scored 14, B scored 5, C scored 31, etc.) and used it in the analyses. Instead, they decided that a score of 21 or higher was used to categorize some participants as depressed (e.g., A, B, and so on are not depressed; C and so on are depressed).

In addition to the use of instruments, researchers take smaller bits of information to create measures used within their studies. For example, demographic information (age, gender) is frequently used for measure in research. Background information about participants is also utilized often in early childhood research, such as teachers' level of education, teachers' years of related experience, and family members' level of education. Researchers sometimes simply name the variables used and sometimes provide some information on how unique variables were created.

Returning to Denham et al.'s (2015) executive function study, the researchers used measures of child gender and age. The researchers reported how many children were 3, 4, and 5 years of age at the start of the study. The researchers also surveyed parents about their educational level and created an education variable that had two levels, mothers who had a high school diploma or less (low education) and mothers who had an associate degree or higher (high education). We might question, incidentally, how a mother with some college coursework but not an associate degree would be categorized on this dichotomous (two-level) variable.

Often educational level is used to denote just that—how much education a participant has completed. Denham and her colleagues stated that they were utilizing maternal education as a "proxy for socioeconomic risk status" (p. 216). Thus they moved back and forth in their paper, referring to "children of mothers with less formal education" and "children at risk for living in poverty" (p. 220) in reference to the same variable. Proxy variables are used when something more easily measurable (such as education level here) is used to signify a more complex variable, here the chances of living in poverty. The researchers explained that some of their participating children were enrolled in Head Start programs, which do serve children living in poverty. Yet some children were enrolled in private child care centers, and this tells us little about families' potential socioeconomic situations. As well, it would be reasonable to ask if in two-parent families the mother's educational level is a reliable indicator of the likelihood of the family living in poverty. The larger question is: What does mother's educational level signify and stand for? Therefore, in the case of proxy variables, it behooves readers to consider how well they believe the proxy stands for the variable of interest.

It should be clear that deciding upon instruments and measures for a study is a complex and important process. Researchers aim to use the best instrument available but also must compromise in those decisions with the resources and constraints of the study being conducted. In addition, decisions must be made about how measures will be recorded. We have described the transformations made to create a measure of depressed/not depressed as an example of how researchers go about this task. It is then up to the reader to evaluate the logic of the researchers' decisions. Does an instrument seem an appropriate measure of a variable? Are the instruments age appropriate for children? Are reliability and validity adequately assessed?

Importantly, the instruments used by quantitative researchers make use of standardized procedures. This guarantees that all participants experience the same questions, hear the same instructions, and have the same opportunities to respond. Questionnaires have preset responses (such as the Likert scale of 1 = strongly disagree to 5 = strongly agree). Order matters, and while often the same order is used for all participants, sometimes researchers vary the order systematically to ensure that order does not influence the results. For example, in the Fisher and Ellis (1988) poetry study, the researchers determined the order of poems heard by the children over 8 days. While the order was not varied among the classrooms participating in the study, the researchers could have set up a systematically varied order for each classroom in consideration of how children might create new responses based upon an ongoing consideration of what poems meant to them over the multiday process.

We have chosen the Fisher and Ellis (1988) poetry study as an exemplar because their measures are somewhat unique among quantitative researchers. In this case, the children were asked by their teachers to comment about what they liked and disliked about poems. The teachers recorded their answers. This is in contrast to the typical closed-ended options utilized in quantitative research. However, it gave young children (first through third grades) maximum response options. After data collection, the researchers used an instrument to assign the children's comments to categories. Consider how this is different from the data analysis processes used by qualitative researchers. In the end the data was subjected to a standard measure for 'reducing' them to numerical form, the number of responses in each category.

Collecting Data

Once measures and instruments have been defined, researchers make decisions about data collection, information that is typically included in the Methods section of their papers. Unsurprisingly, the decisions harken back to the logic underlying the research questions.

In the Denham et al. (2015) executive control study, the researchers tested how children's executive control predicted (varied with) their teachers' ratings of social competence and classroom adjustment. The research team assessed children's executive control first, in the middle part of the school year (enrollment and parent report of demographics occurred in late fall to early winter). They then waited until the end of the year to collect the teacher reports. By that time, if indeed the independent variables influenced the dependent variables, there would have been time for this to occur. Thus, decisions about collecting data are made in light of expected relationships of the variables (e.g., temporal order) as well as in consideration of when participants can best offer the information needed for the study. For example, if a researcher wants children's scores on a pretest and posttest measure to investigate the impact of a particular intervention, it would be important to time the assessments as close to the beginning and ending of the intervention as possible. Too late into the intervention or too soon before its ending point, and the scores might not represent the full impact of the intervention on the children's scores.

As might be expected, procedures here are also as standardized as possible. If, for example, a researcher was observing children's peer relationships in preschool classrooms, standardization of the timing of the observations matters. Collecting data in some classrooms in the spring and other classrooms in the fall may affect the data in a biased manner, as children have had more time by spring to form relationships with their peers. Another question that readers should consider is the viability of the timing. Have teachers had time to get to know children before completing surveys? Did researchers spend enough time observing to get a strong sense of how classrooms function?

Conclusion

We began this chapter by noting that there is much to be done up front in a quantitative study. These decisions begin with forming researchable questions. They continue to enrolling a sample of participants, deciding upon measures and instruments, and planning for data collection. In a well-done study, there will be consistency and connectedness at each step of the process. When researchers veer from the direction of their logic (e.g., an instrument that doesn't quite assess the construct of interest, a data collection process with inopportune timing decisions), the limits and pitfalls associated with the study increase, while the promises decrease. Each study is a balancing act of trying to maintain the logic as closely as possible and rein in the limits. It is up to the reader to evaluate the study methods. Even in the best-planned studies, the processes of collecting data are messy and sometimes unpredictable. Teachers leave positions unexpectedly, children leave programs, surveys come back only partially completed. Thus, any critique of research must also keep in mind the real-world issues that will always intervene, no matter how meticulous the planning.

Reading and Understanding a Quantitative Study

Purpose/Research Question

Task: *Identify the research question.*

Look for: The question is often introduced at the outset of the study, but it is often stated most clearly at the end of the literature review. Examine the question(s) to determine *who* this study involves, *what* is of interest, and *how* the researcher expects the phenomenon of interest to operate.

Task: *Map out how the study is framed within the literature base.*

Look for: To begin to build your understanding of the literature review, look for the headers used to identify topics. Read the topic and concluding sentences of sections or paragraphs carefully to set up your understanding of main points. Examine how the researcher set the stage for this study by describing what has been found in previous research and how this study addresses gaps and/or ongoing questions.

Methods: Sample

Task: *Record who is represented in this study.*

Look for: Note the descriptions given of the participants in the research. How much does the researcher tell you about their backgrounds? What do you wish you knew that isn't reported? How sufficient does this group of participants seem (e.g., number involved, their local contexts)? How did the researcher find the participants, and if pertinent, group them (note: if this is not detailed, most likely it was a matter of convenience)?

Methods: Variables and Measures

Task: *Identify what is being measured and how it is being measured.*

Look for: Note the concepts that are involved in the study and their role in the research questions. Researchers often do not label variables as independent and

---

dependent, so it might be helpful to consider what is *up front* in the research question and what is *resulting* in the question. How clearly and concisely did the researcher define the variables? Read the descriptions of each instrument used in the study. Are *reliability* and/or *validity* addressed? How closely tied, or representative, of the concept is each instrument? Look for promises (the instrument is closely tied to the concept), pitfalls (there is some disconnect between what the researcher wants to measure and this particular instrument), and limitations (the connections are variable or perhaps partial).

Methods: Data Collection

Task: *Identify the procedures used to collect data.*

Look for: Note *when* the data was collected, *how often* (if applicable), and *by whom*. Were the procedures standardized to ensure that data collection remained the same throughout the study and for all participants? Do the responses to questions of *when* the data was collected make sense for the research questions (e.g., if teachers are making reports about children, have they had sufficient time to get to know the children?).

8

STATISTICAL ANALYSES IN QUANTITATIVE RESEARCH

It is likely the case that some readers skimming the table of contents had a sharp intake of breath as the title of this chapter appeared. A lack of comfort with statistical analyses is a challenge to being a confident consumer of research. We acknowledge that many or most readers may have never taken a course in statistics. Our goals for this chapter are to acquaint readers with major types of analyses conducted and to scaffold an understanding of how to locate and understand pertinent information about the results of analyses.

We will continue to make use of the studies described in the previous chapter. We will follow a similar structure to that chapter, explaining first descriptive data presentations, then correlational analyses, and finally comparative analyses. It is important to note that the topic of statistical analysis includes a wide array of possibilities. We are unable to explain the full range of analyses used in early childhood research but instead will focus on predominant types.

Descriptive Data Presentations

In the previous chapter, we explained that presentations of descriptive data frequently frame the opening of the researcher's presentation of a study's findings. As a foundation to this chapter, we begin with an explanation of the nature of data. How data is described and analyzed is dependent upon these differences.

Some forms of data are categorical, meaning that discrete groups are recorded. For example, gender is invariably coded as male or female by researchers. Similarly, racial and ethnic heritage is coded categorically.

When data is categorical, researchers report the frequencies of each category or type within the variable. Sometimes a type of shorthand is used in researchers' reporting of frequencies. For example, Denham, Bassett, Sirotkin, Brown, and Morris (2015) reported, "approximately 50% of the participants were male." In this case, the reader then infers the percentage of females—although in the case of a 50–50 split, the math is quite easy.

Other data is continuous in nature. For example, age ranges along a continuum of possible data points, as do possible scores on many standardized assessments used with children. Similarly, but in a more restricted range, participants' responses on a one- to five-point Likert scale result in a set of data points located along a continuum.

One of the most important descriptors for continuous data is the mean. The mean is the arithmetic average of a variable. When a mean on a one- to five-point Likert scale is reported as 1.78, we can visualize where responses tended to cluster on the item. The symbol used for a mean is $\bar{X}$ (or sometimes the abbreviation M). For a continuous variable, the range is also often presented. This represents the smallest and largest values for the variable.

Another important descriptor of continuous data is the standard deviation. This number reflects how 'spread out' the data is. Given a sufficient sample, there is an assumption that data tends to spread around the mean in a predictable manner, producing the normal bell curve, with more responses clustered around the middle of the curve and fewer in the tails. The standard deviation, abbreviated as SD, indicates the spread of data points for a variable.

The standard deviation is calculated such that approximately 34% of the data points will fall within one standard deviation above the mean and another 34% fall within one standard deviation below the mean. Thus, about 68% of the data points fall within ± one standard deviation. Approximately 13.5% of the data points fall between one and two standard deviations above the mean, and conversely, another 13.5% fall between one and two standard deviations below the mean. In sum, about 95% of data points are within two standard deviations in either direction from the mean. Please see Figure 8.1 for a representation of the normal bell curve.

In making sense of the standard deviation, look for how it compares to the mean and range. The smaller the standard deviation figure, the more closely packed-in the bell curve is; the larger the standard deviation, the more spread out the curve becomes. For an example of the standard deviation in published research, refer to Table 8.1. This is a table from Sheridan et al.'s (2014) study of the Getting Ready intervention. In this table the researchers reported the means and standard deviations for the child behaviors they coded from videotapes of the child and parent interacting together. These are reported for several behaviors, which were rated on a scale ranging from one to five. The various standard deviations range from .5 (meaning about 68% of scores fall between a half point below the mean to a half point above the mean) to .9 (meaning about 68% of scores fall between almost 1 point below the mean to almost 1 point above the mean). While these differences may not seem large, remember the range of possible scores is relatively restricted (1 to 5). The differences reflect that the data was more or less spread out for different variables.

By examining the descriptive data, consumers of research can begin to understand the nature of the research variables. In order to answer most research questions, however, the researcher performs analyses on the data. The descriptive measures we have described, frequencies of

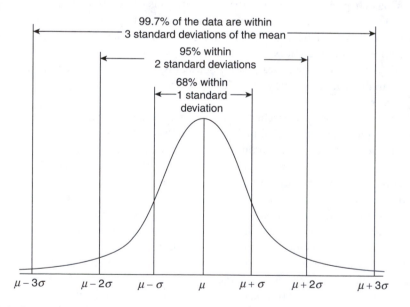

Figure 8.1 Bell Curve and Standard Deviation

Table 8.1 Descriptive Statistics for Outcome Variables at Pretest and Posttest

Child behavior code	Value	Baseline		20 months	
		Treatment	*Control*	*Treatment*	*Control*
Agency/	*M*	3.69	3.67	3.53	3.91
enthusiasm	*SD*	0.7	0.8	0.8	0.8
Persistence	*M*	3.78	3.72	4.02	3.82
	SD	0.7	0.8	0.7	0.8
Activity level	*M*	1.89	1.71	1.56	1.91
	SD	0.7	0.8	0.5	0.9
Positive affect	*M*	2.80	2.79	2.76	3.03
	SD	0.9	0.8	0.9	0.8
Distractibility	*M*	2.07	1.96	1.69	1.94
	SD	0.7	0.8	0.6	0.8
Verbalizations	*M*	2.97	2.83	2.82	3.18
	SD	0.9	0.9	0.7	0.8

Note: Behaviors were coded on a five-point Likert scale in terms of behavioral frequency: 1 = *very low*, 5 = *very high*

Source: Sheridan, S. M., Knoche, L. L., Edwards, C. P., Kupzyk, K. A., Clarke, B. L., & Kim, E. M. (2014). Efficacy of the Getting Ready intervention and the role of parental depression. *Early Education and Development*, 25, 746–769.

categorical variables and the mean and standard deviation of continuous variables, are used in these analyses, which utilize inferential statistics to test hypotheses.

Correlational Analyses

Correlational analyses indicate how strongly related variables are to one another or the degree to which some variables predict another variable. Sometimes researchers are interested in questions of relatedness as their research goal. At other times they want to identify relationships that may impact other analyses, such as when variables are unexpectedly related to each other or when the relationships affect the questions and analysis of variables. In the latter case, researchers may use what is found regarding related variables to adjust subsequent analyses.

Relationships: Bivariate Correlations

A simple correlation—how two variables relate to each other—is measured by a bivariate correlation, or the Pearson correlation. The comparisons for the two variables are determined for each pair of scores contributed by individuals and then calculated to reflect the overall sample. The bivariate correlation is abbreviated as *r* and is sometimes referred to as Pearson's *r*. Bivariate correlations range from –1.00 to +1.00. In a positive correlation, the higher the value of one variable, the higher the other variable tends to be (they vary in the same direction). In a negative correlation, the larger one variable is, the smaller the other variable tends to be (they vary in opposite directions). The closer the number is to zero, the weaker the relationship. At the value of zero, there is no evidence of a systematic relationship between the two variables. Because it bears repeating, we will again make the point that these relationships cannot be assumed to be causal in nature.

To further explore bivariate correlations, please refer to Table 8.2. This is a table of correlations from a study by Tominey and McClelland (2011) who were researching self-regulation

Table 8.2 Bivariate Correlations for Children in the Overall Sample (*N* = 65)

Variable	1	2	3	4	5	6	7	8	9	10	11	12	13
1 Child age (months)	—												
2 Child gender[a]	.31*	—											
3 Head Start status[b]	0.09	0.18	—										
4 Maternal education[c]	-0.09	-.31*	-.65***	—									
5 Fall HTKS	-0.01	-0.17	-.37**	.33*	—								
6 Spring HTKS	-0.05	-0.02	-.52***	0.22	.50***	—							
7 HTKS difference	-0.04	0.16	-0.16	-0.12	-.46***	.52***	—						
8 Applied Problems difference	-0.20	0.03	-0.02	0.04	0.19	-0.08	0.08	—					
9 Letter-Word Identification difference	-0.03	-0.12	-.28*	.45***	.29*	.32**	0.03	0.11	—				
10 Vocabulary difference	-0.06	0.02	-0.15	0.14	-0.12	-.00	0.14	-0.03	0.06	—			
11 Intervention group[d]	-0.11	0.05	-0.07	0.12	0.07	0.14	0.05	0.05	0.01	-0.04	—		
12 Number of sessions	-0.09	0.06	-0.08	0.04	0.05	0.18	0.1	0.03	.28*	.28*	.94***	—	
13 School absences	-0.07	0.01	0.17	-0.13	-0.1	-.24†	-0.12	-0.13	-0.05	0.01	0.07	-0.08	—

Note: HTKS = Head Toes Knees Shoulders task.

[a] Child gender: 0 = female, 1 = male.

[b] Head Start status: 0 = not enrolled in Head Start, 1 = enrolled in Head Start.

[c] For correlations including maternal education, *n* = 55.

[a] Intervention group: 0 = control, 1 = treatment.

†*p* < .1. **p* < .05. ***p* < .01. ****p* < .001.

Source: Tominey, S. L., & McClelland, M. M. (2011). Red light, purple light: Findings from a randomized trial using circle time games to improve behavioral self-regulation in preschool. *Early Education and Development, 22,* 489–519.

interventions with young children. The table presents the correlations among all of the study variables, which include the child's age, gender, participation or not in Head Start, and mother's education level. In addition, there are variables representing measures of self-regulation and math and language/literacy skills. Finally, there are variables to represent whether the children were in the intervention or treatment groups, the number of intervention sessions they experienced, and the frequency of their absences from school. Each of these variables is located in the left-hand column. You can note that some of these variables are categorical (e.g., in intervention or treatment) and some are continuous (e.g., number of intervention sessions). It is possible to calculate correlations between categorical and continuous variables, as we will describe in what follows.

To read the table, look at the column labeled 1. This represents the variable numbered 1 from the far left-hand column, child age. There is no number in the space that represents the intersection of row 1 and column 1 because a variable is perfectly varied with itself. But continue down this column. The next number (.31) is the correlation between 1 (the column—child age) and the row within which it lies, child gender. Child gender, a categorical variable, is marked by the superscript a, which corresponds to a footnote stating that for gender, males received a score of 1 and females a score of 0. This translates to 'boys are higher; girls are lower' on this variable (this scoring allows for a correlation to be calculated). There is a positive relationship between age and gender, meaning that the older the child, the more likely the child is a boy. Thus, girls had some tendency to be younger. The relationship is closer to zero than to one; this signifies the relationship was not particularly strong. Continuing down this column, it is evident that the remaining variables are correlated negatively with child age (except for Head Start status), but the strength of those correlations is quite weak, as most of the results are less than −.10.

Now move to the column labeled 3. The first correlation is between maternal education and Head Start status, another categorical variable. The footnote tells us that 'Head Start is higher; not in Head Start is lower.' Here the relationship between the variables is stronger than other correlations on the table (−.65), with children in Head Start more likely to have mothers with lower levels of education.

One final detail is important in understanding this table. There is a series of symbols in the last footnote, which present numerical equations around the value p. In inferential statistical analyses, the probability of the outcome occurring by chance alone is calculated. This is referred to as p, or the significance level.

A statistical analysis begins with the assumption that there is no relationship between the variables. Once the analysis is performed, there is a calculation of how likely it is that the result would have occurred *if indeed there is no relationship between the two variables*. Obviously, in the case of a bivariate correlation, the further a value gets from zero, in either direction, the more likely we are to expect there may well be a relationship that is not just occurring by chance. But we can't assume this from the value itself; whether this was a likely or unlikely value depends upon the nature of the particular set of data. Thus, the p value tells us how likely this value was for this particular set of data.

In research, there are accepted conventions about what value of p is worthy of our attention. There are three p values marked with asterisks on the table ($p < .05$, $p < .01$, and $p < .001$). The asterisks are used in the table to denote which analyses reached these levels of significance. Thus, the .31 value between child gender and age reached a significance level of .05 and the −.65 value between maternal education and Head Start status reached a significance level of .001.

What these significance levels indicate is the chance of a correlation of this strength occurring just by chance if in fact there was no relationship between the two variables. So we interpret the finding between child gender and age this way: If there was indeed no relationship between child gender and age, the chances for the bivariate correlation to be .31 are less than .05, or less than 5 in 100 (read the *p* value as five hundredths). This finding has reached the level of unlikelihood (this is certainly a tricky word!) that researchers have agreed to accept. But how should we make meaning of this? Applying what we know about gender and age in young children, we might speculate that the finding may well be due to the luck of the sample. It may be similar to the situation in which a classroom ends up with 15 boys and three girls, although we know that boys and girls are about equally distributed in the population of young children. It is not very likely, but it does happen every so often. Thus, while we know the odds are pretty low for a correlation linking age and gender at this level to happen by chance, in this sample there was a relationship at a significant level. We shouldn't assume that it generalizes to 'older children are more likely to be boys' in the overall population. Significant findings in quantitative research do not always lead to greater understanding of a phenomenon, and as this case illustrates, the luck of sampling may result in a group that is not truly representative of the larger population. In a case such as this, researchers may make adjustments in subsequent analyses to 'correct' for the fact that boys tended to be overrepresented among older children.

For the relationship between maternal education and Head Start status the interpretation is: if there was indeed no relationship between maternal education and being enrolled in Head Start, the chances for the bivariate correlation to be −.65 are less than .001, or 1 in 1,000. Mothers whose children were in Head Start were more likely to have less education. Since this program serves families of very low incomes, this finding would appear to reflect something we would expect in the larger population.

In summarizing significance levels, in order for researchers to accept that something is indeed 'at work' here, the odds for the result to occur just by chance (without some systematic something 'at work') have to be quite uncommon. In addition, the presence of a significant finding may not add meaning to our understanding of the research questions. Finally, if we accept the odds that the finding could have occurred '5 times out of 100 by chance alone (unlikely, but possible), then sometimes the finding might have occurred just by chance. This is referred to as a false positive. Although the chances of a false positive being reported are relatively low, it is still an ongoing possibility. Furthermore, the more analyses that are conducted, the more likely it is that a false positive can crop up. Recall that in Chapter 7 we explained that quantitative researchers aim for a parsimonious set of analyses; this is due to the nature of the statistical analyses, in which a false positive is a potential issue.

Before leaving this topic, we want to note that Tominey and McClelland (2011) also labeled results with a level of *p* < .1 in the table reproduced in Table 8.2. This corresponds to a finding occurring by chance 1 time in 10. As we noted, the standard convention accepted by researchers is the .05 level (5 in 100). Some researchers choose to report the .1 level to indicate that the relationship in the data is 'approaching' a significant level. The message tends to be along the lines, 'something *might* be happening.' Others choose not to report this value of *p*. Their thinking is along the lines, 'well it was close, but it just didn't make it.' It's up to the reader to decide how to interpret results that are in the margins and how much importance to attach to them.

Prediction: Regression Analyses

Correlational relationships are at the heart of regression analyses as well. In regression analyses, the researcher aims to determine how accurately a dependent variable can be predicted based upon some set of independent variables. The logic is as follows. For a dependent variable, there is some range of values found for the participants in the study. Because we will be using Denham et al.'s (2015) executive control study for our example in this section, let's consider one of the study variables, social competence. Remember that teachers rated the social competence of children participating in the study. Children's social competence scores will differ based upon any number of factors. The totality of all these differences amongst scores is referred to as variance. If we consider all of these social competence scores residing within an area enclosed by a circle (the variance), the aim of regression analyses is to 'rope off' areas of that circle by determining some percentage of the total variance of social competence that relates to each of the independent variables. In other words, can the researcher find the predictive power of an independent variable for determining the dependent variable? How much of the total variance of a dependent variable can be explained by knowing this independent variable and knowing that independent variable? For quantitative researchers, the ability to predict suggests understanding something about the phenomenon of interest. Once again, we must remind readers that regressions are correlational analyses, and correlation does not imply causation. It could be the case that the relationships found in regression analyses are really due to some other, unmeasured variable.

Multiple regression analyses are performed in a couple of different ways. In a standard multiple regression, all of the dependent variables are analyzed at once to determine their relationships to the independent variable. In a hierarchical multiple regression, independent variables are entered in sequential groups, resulting in analyses that are reported as consisting of two or more steps. If researchers are using a hierarchical regression, they must determine the logic for how to sequence the steps used to enter the independent variables. As will be evident in the examples that follow, both categorical and continuous independent variables can be used.

Finally, researchers also have the option of inserting interactions as a predictor. An interaction is the unique relationship between two independent variables. Say, for example, that two independent variables are gender and age. The researchers may want to examine if gender has a specific relationship to social competence at certain ages; perhaps previous research has shown the differences are wider between boys and girls at a younger age than at an older age. By entering an interaction as a predictor, the research question is, does the relationship of gender and social competence depend upon the age of the child? This is obviously a relationship that implies some conditions, as in how well gender predicts children's social competence is conditional upon the children being younger or older. When interactions are used in a regression analysis, they are usually represented as 'variable 1 × variable 2.'

Denham et al. (2015) used a hierarchical form of regression analysis in their study of executive control. One of their research aims was to "describe associations of PSRA components [executive control tasks] with teachers' reports on children's social competence and classroom adjustment, after holding child characteristics constant" (p. 215). What does it mean to hold a characteristic constant? In this case, Denham et al. entered child characteristics (gender, age, and maternal education) into the regression analyses first. They determined how much of the variance in social competence and classroom adjustment was predicted by these variables; effectively, they 'roped off' this portion of the variance. Then they entered the scores on executive control tasks to see *how much more* of the variance of the independent variables (social competence and classroom adjustment) could be predicted, in other words, how executive control tasks added predictive potential above and beyond what was already shown to be predicted by child characteristics. By "holding child characteristics constant," as the researchers said they did (p. 215), they are in effect saying, 'Let's assume those pieces are taken out off the top.'

In Table 8.3, we have reproduced the table from Denham et al. (2015) in which the regression analyses are displayed. Let's examine the results first for social competence. The child characteristics are listed under Block 1, meaning that they were entered into the analyses first. Note the symbol β along the headings under social competence; this refers to beta weight, and there is a corresponding value for each variable. The beta weight value indicates how much

Table 8.3 Prediction of Social Competence and Classroom Adjustment, Given Age, Maternal Education, and Gender

		Social Competence			Classroom Adjustment			
		B	SE B	β	ΔR²	B	SE B	β	ΔR²
Block 1					.162 ***				.122 ***
	Age	0.021	0.005	.217 ***		0.012	0.004	.173 **	
	Maternal education	−0.095	0.033	−.157 **		−0.033	0.025	−0.076	
	Gender	0.42	.082	.280***		0.312	0.061	.285 ***	
Block 2					.019 *				.036 **
	CEC		0.002	−0.019		0.002	0.001	.118+	
	HEC	0.005	0.002	.156*		0.004	0.002	.149 **	

+ $p < .10$. * $p < .05$. ** $p < .01$. *** $p < .001$.

Source: Denham, S. A., Bassett, H. H., Sirotkin, Y. A., Brown, C., & Morris, C. S. (2015). "No-o-o-o peeking": Preschoolers' executive control, social competence, and classroom adjustment. *Journal of Research in Childhood Education, 29*, 212–225.

that dependent variable increases or decreases (depending upon if a negative sign is indicated) if the independent variable increases by one standard deviation. Thus, the numbers are decimals in these tables, indicating the proportion of increase in the standard deviation for each dependent variable. These beta weights are marked by asterisks denoting they were significant at p levels of .01 or .001. Age positively predicted social competence; children who were older tended to be rated as more socially competent by their teachers, with the increase being .217 of a standard deviation.

Denham et al. did not discuss these individual beta weights in their paper, instead focusing only on the fourth column, marked by ΔR^2. This symbol is read as 'delta R squared.' The value of R^2 indicates how much variance in the independent variable is predicted by the group of variables entered in the block. The 'delta' refers to the change in R^2 that is achieved by that block of variables. In this example, the value of ΔR^2 is .162 for Block 1. The interpretation goes like this: approximately 16% of the variance in social competence was predicted by the child characteristics (transform the figure to a percentage by moving the decimal point two places to the right). This means that knowing all of the variables in Block 1 allows a researcher to predict 16% of the variance in social competence. Clearly, that leaves quite a lot of the variance unexplained. Moving downward to Block 2, the ΔR^2 value is .019. This means that an additional 2% (approximately) of the variance in social competence was predicted by executive function. This is obviously a small value, but the asterisk indicates it was significant (a good example of how the value of a number itself is not necessarily a good indicator of its likelihood of reaching significance). When we examine the individual variables for executive function, we see that only one, hot executive control, was a significant predictor, with a beta weight of .156. The positive value indicates that children who scored better on this measure were rated as more socially competent by their teachers. The analyses in this table are described this way by Denham et al. in the text of the paper: "after controlling for significant contributions of age, maternal education, and gender, HEC [hot executive function] contributed to a significant increment in variance explained for social competence" (p. 218).

These findings point to an obvious question about quantitative research—the findings may be *significant*, but how *important* are they? With regression analyses, the importance is intuited by the R^2 value. In the Denham et al. (2015) study, both child characteristics and executive control were significant predictors of children's social competence ratings. By entering child characteristics first, in the first block, Denham et al. showed that hot executive control related to social competence in ways above and beyond the relationship of child characteristics to social competence (the additional ΔR^2). However, executive control predicted only a small portion of the variance in social competence (approximately 2%) when child characteristics were entered first. Part of the research consumer's task is to consider how much importance to attach to this measure of executive function as a predictor of social competence based on the values reported from this analysis, remembering once again that prediction does not imply causation.

Comparative Analyses

Recall from Chapter 7 that some research questions are comparative in nature. In this case, researchers are interested in comparing two or more groups, examining one or more dependent variables.

Comparing Categorical Dependent Variables

As we explained earlier, categorical data is summarized by noting the frequencies occurring within each group or level. In the poetry study conducted by Fisher and Ellis (1988), the researchers recorded how many times children's comments about poetry reflected certain types of content, for instance, whether the comments reflected knowledge, interpretation, application, or judgment. The researchers also categorized children by grade level, either first, second, or third grade. For each of these sets of variables, frequencies make sense (i.e., how many), but a mean or average would not be meaningful.

In order to examine the question of whether children at the various grade levels were more or less likely to make comments reflective of different content, Fisher and Ellis (1988) used a chi square analysis. The symbol for chi square is χ^2. For this analysis, the frequencies for each cell are recorded (e.g., number of knowledge comments in grade 1, number of interpretation comments in grade 1, and continuing for each grade and each content area). The assumption underlying the analysis is that each cell is independent from other cells, meaning that there should be no systematic patterns for children at the different grade levels employing different areas of content. If the chi square analysis does reach significance, the interpretation is that there are systematic differences among the cells at a level unlikely to occur by chance.

Fisher and Ellis (1988) did report finding several significant chi square analyses, in all cases noting the p level. Again, the p level is the chance that the results would occur purely by chance, assuming no systematic differences. The authors reported the results of their analyses by reporting which cells had frequencies that differed from what the expected levels would be if the variables were independent (e.g., one cell is 'interpretation by first graders,' while another cell is 'application by first graders,' etc.). It is typically the case that only some cells show patterns of deviating from the expected, unsystematic patterns. For example, Fisher and Ellis found that first graders made more-than-expected numbers of responses that reflected application (relating the poems to some aspect of their own lives). Second graders showed a tendency to make comments reflecting judgment at a higher-than-expected level, while the same was true for third graders in regard to comments reflecting interpretation. Finally, second and third graders were less likely than expected to make comments that reflected knowledge. This interpretation comes from the size of the numerals in the cells. Numerals greater than 1.0 indicate a greater-than-expected level frequency for that variable. Numerals less than 1.0 indicate a lesser-than-expected frequency. Readers can make sense of this by noting that if the frequency is as expected, the numeral would be 1.0, meaning, in essence, that the odds are roughly equal. The numerals reported are essentially related to the odds of the frequency occurring. Other researchers may report the numerals associated with the data in the chi square cells.

What this analysis shows is how the comments of the groups of children compared and differed in some systematic ways. The results do not provide us with a clear understanding of how important these patterns may be. It is up to the reader to make sense of the results that differed from expected patterns.

Comparing Continuous Dependent Variables

Once researchers have generated means and standard deviations from a data set, analyses are available to compare two or more groups. These analyses operate under the beginning assumption that the groups are equal. If indeed the dependent variables being analyzed between or among the groups are found to be sufficiently different that an acceptable level of significance (p) is reached, the researchers are able to conclude that there is reason to believe that there are differences between or among the groups.

In its simplest form, two groups might be formed based upon an independent variable, for example gender. The scores for these two groups can be compared on the dependent variable, say executive function. In this case, the researcher may use a t-test. This is a simple comparison of two means to see if they are significantly different from each other. However, the same comparison can be made (and is often made) using an analysis of variance, abbreviated as ANOVA. The score for an ANOVA is represented as F. The analysis for a simple ANOVA or t-test can be represented visually this way:

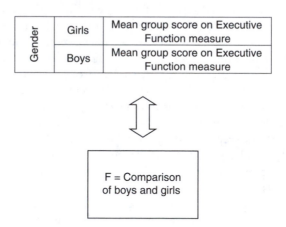

Analysis of variance can also be used for more complex configurations, such as three groups formed from a single independent variable (for example, children at 3 years of age, 4 years, and 5 years) being compared on a dependent variable such as executive function. These comparisons are called a one-way analysis of variance. The possible comparison here is, first, whether the scores for the three groups are significantly different and then where those differences are, for example between 3-year-olds and 4-year-olds, between 4-year-olds and 5-year-olds, and so on.

Age	3-year-olds	Mean group score on Executive Function measure		F = Comparison of 3-year-olds to 4-year-olds to 5-year-olds
	4-year-olds	Mean group score on Executive Function measure		
	5-year-olds	Mean group score on Executive Function measure		

In yet another variation, the participants might be categorized using two independent variables, such as age and gender, again being compared on a dependent variable such as executive function. This is referred to as a two-way analysis of variance. In this example, the comparisons can be made in several ways, between boys and girls and between children of different ages. These are referred to as main effects; this is because they represent the analysis of the independent variables. In addition, a comparison can be made of what is referred to as an interaction: whether there are differential patterns within the groups. For example, perhaps for boys age matters in different ways than it does for girls. This is represented visually in the following figure.

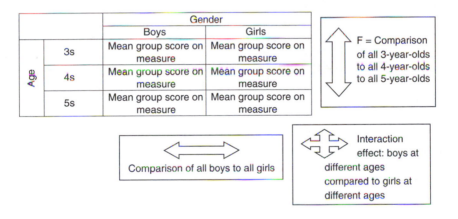

The group comparisons can become more complex with other ANOVA models. There may be two or more dependent variables in the comparison (such as two forms of executive control), referred to as a multiple analysis of variance, or MANOVA. Also, when the dependent variable has been measured at more than one point in time, for example at different points during an intervention, then the analysis used is a repeated measures analysis of variance. Finally, in an analysis where researchers want to 'take off the top' the variance associated with a variable, they use ANCOVA or MANCOVA, the analysis of covariance. Covariance refers to a variable being controlled in the analyses. For instance, say that gender has shown a significant correlation to an independent variable. Yet in this study, the researchers are not interested in gender as an independent variable. When they 'control' the variance associated with gender, they remove it 'from the top.' In effect, the analyses from that point on reflect a situation in which gender is no longer involved—as if the differences associated with gender are no longer in the picture. While this may be difficult to wrap one's mind around—in fact, gender can't 'disappear'—by controlling its impact, the researchers can assess what is happening among the independent and dependent variables without the effect of the variable that is being controlled.

In the end, the analysis-of-variance models are concerned with determining where the variance in a dependent variable(s) may be attributed.

While it is not vital that readers remember each of these various forms of the analysis of variance, what is important to remember is this: Two or more groups can be formed (sometimes reconfiguring the participants along two different independent variables) to compare on one or more dependent variables. To assist in understanding a study in the future, it may be helpful to draw a figure such as we have provided in order to visualize the comparisons being made.

The Denham et al. (2015) study on executive control utilized a MANOVA analysis. The independent variables included children's gender (boy or girl), age (3, 4, or 5 years), and maternal education (high school or less or associate's degree or more). The two independent variables were hot executive control and cool executive control. We have reproduced their table of results in Table 8.4. In what follows, we will explain how the analyses worked.

Main Effects

While they have not explicitly named it as such, Denham et al. (2015) reported the main effects for their MANOVA analysis. The main effects are the results for the analysis of each independent variable. Thus, Denham et al. reported the results of the analysis of gender and of age and of maternal education in their table. In order to fully understand the analysis, readers of the article must read the narrative as well as consult the table. When there are three or more independent variable groups and/or more than one dependent variable, follow-up analyses must be conducted to determine more specifically which of the possible comparisons were significantly different.

In looking at Table 8.4, we look first at each of the three comparisons labeled at the top of the table. Immediately under each heading is the value of F, along with asterisks indicating the level of significance. By the way, the numbers in parentheses are called degrees of freedom, and they relate to the number of means being used in the analysis and the number of participants contributing data. An explanation is beyond the scope of our text; throughout this text we have made decisions about what to explain and what to set aside to help readers develop basic understandings of research. In reality, several texts would be necessary to fully understand qualitative and quantitative research design and analysis!

Table 8.4 Age, Gender, and Maternal Education Comparisons for HEC and CEC

| | Gender | | Age | | | Maternal Education | |
| | $F(2,272) = 4.08*$ Partial $\eta^2 = .029$ | | $F(4,544) = 22.70***$ Partial $\eta^2 = .143$ | | | $F(2,272) = 10.24***$ Partial $\eta^2 = .070$ | |
	Boys	Girls	3-yr	4-yr	5-yr	High School or Less	Associate Degree or More
CEC	52.41 (2.57)	57.83 (2.64)	28.14 (3.73)	61.32 (2.49)	75.90 (3.23)	47.12 (2.69)	63.13 (2.51)
HEC	38.64 (1.83)	45.98 (1.88)	29.50 (2.66)	46.08 (1.77)	51.36 (2.30)	42.08 (1.92)	42.54 (1.79)

Notes: CEC = cool executive control; HEC = hot executive control. Fs evaluated by Pillai's Trace. Standard errors in parentheses.

$*p \leq .05.$ $** p \leq .01.$ $*** p \leq .001.$

Source: Denham, S. A., Bassett, H. H., Sirotkin, Y. A., Brown, C., & Morris, C. S. (2015). "No-o-o-o peeking": Preschoolers' executive control, social competence, and classroom adjustment. *Journal of Research in Childhood Education, 29,* 212–225.

Returning to Table 8.4, there was a significant result for the age analysis. We must return to the narrative to understand which scores were significantly different from each other. Denham et al. (2015) wrote, "Older children showed more EC [executive control]; follow-up one-way ANOVAs showed that age differences were significant for CEC and HEC" (p. 218). What this means is that first the researchers ran the largest, most complex analysis (everything in Table 8.4). Finding a significant result for age allowed them to return to examine the dependent variables, CEC (cool executive control) and HEC (hot executive control), separately. In both cases, the results were significant. This means that among the three age groups, there were differences in both dependent variables. But given that there are three age groups, we still do not know if the differences were between each pair of age groups or only some pairs. Returning to the text, "Bonferroni multiple comparisons for age differences in CEC showed a linear progression, with groups scoring higher as age increased. Similar comparisons for age differences in HEC showed only differences between 3-year-olds and both other age groups" (p. 218). To put the results another way, the follow-up analysis showed that for cool executive control (CEC), the 4-year-olds scored significantly higher than the 3-year-olds, and the 5-year-olds scored significantly higher than the 4-year-olds. Each year in age was marked by a significantly higher mean score. On the other hand, for hot executive control (HEC), there was a significant difference between the 3-year-olds and the other two groups, the 4s and 5s. The means for the 4s and 5s, however, did not differ significantly between the two groups.

In this section of the reading, Denham et al. report the results of other follow-up analyses, and we suggest readers consult the table and deliberate on these portions of the text: "SES [socioeconomic status] differences favoring children less at risk [recall that the authors have declared low maternal education a risk] were found only for CEC . . . and gender differences favoring girls were significant only for HEC" (p. 218). In summary, a MANOVA table will alert readers to which of the overall analyses reached significance. It is important to locate the follow-up analyses that pinpoint the specific differences; consequently, careful reading and comparison of the tabled and textual information is essential.

Interaction Effects

Unfortunately, Denham et al. (2015) did not report any interaction effects. To briefly illustrate the concept of an interaction, we will move to another study. Anthony, Williams, Zhang, Landry, and Dunkelberger (2014) conducted a study of the impact of several different models of literacy support for young children. They compared children's scores on print knowledge at the beginning and end of the year and, in between these assessments, implemented versions of the literacy support interventions in different classrooms. In Figure 8.2, we have reproduced a figure from the study illustrating an interaction. An interaction indicates that, within groups, there were differential relationships to an independent variable. Here Anthony et al. showed how children with differing levels of pretest scores were impacted by the interventions. The researchers found a significant main effect for the Family intervention—this is reflected in the fact that children in the Family group consistently scored higher.

The interactions are 'read' in the distance between the lines connecting groups at each of the three points indicated on the bottom axis, where children are grouped by the level of their pretest scores. Looking at the right side of the figure, the children who began with higher scores at pretest, one can see that the three groups, labeled Control, Family, and RAR, are at close to the same point for end-of-year scores (the scores are indicated on the axis at the left of the figure), although with a slight advantage for the Family group. In the case of high pretesters, children benefited only slightly more by being in the Family group. Moving to the left side of

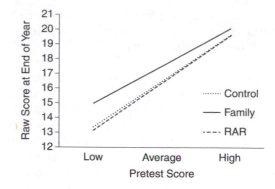

Figure 8.2 Interaction Effect for Pretest Scores

Source: Anthony, J. L., Williams, J. M., Zhang, Z., Landry, S. H., & Dunkelberger, M. J. (2014). Experimental evaluation of the value added by raising a reader and supplemental parent training in shared reading. *Early Education and Development, 25*, 493–514.

the figure, the children who began with low pretest scores, one can see that there is a larger gap between the Family group and the Control and RAR groups for end-of-year scores. In this case, children who began with lower scores benefited more by being in the Family intervention group—their scores were higher than the other two groups by a greater margin. The interpretation of this interaction is that the Family intervention was particularly effective, compared to the other interventions, *when children began with lower scores*. Researchers often use figures to illustrate interactions because the visual so effectively shows the differential effects indicated by a significant interaction.

In summary, comparative analyses are used to find significant differences between and among groups. Groups are determined by the independent variable(s). These comparisons can be made more complex by the addition of more variables, whether independent, dependent, or control variables. Comparisons can be made between groups and also within groups when there are more than two subgroupings.

As we have mentioned before, the question lurking beneath significant findings is how important those results may be in the daily realities of life. With comparative analyses, researchers are more often being expected to publish a statistic called effect size. For example, assume researchers conducted a study of two different early literacy interventions and included a third comparison group conducting 'business as usual.' Both Intervention A and Intervention B were found to have significant impact on the study's dependent variables measuring literacy skills. The question then becomes, should we institute either of these interventions on a wide-scale basis? Do either of them have practical significance? Effect size can help in those determinations.

Effect size is calculated based upon the standard deviation of the sample, most commonly using a statistic called Cohen's *d*. The effect size indicates how much the mean of the groups of interest 'moved' away from the mean of the comparison group. This movement is expressed as a decimal of the standard deviation. Standard conventions call for considering an effect size of .2 to be 'small.' In this case, the intervention group mean would have moved 20% of a standard deviation unit away from the comparison mean. Effect sizes of .5 are considered to be 'moderate' and of .8 or more to be 'large.' Thus, if Intervention A in our example had an effect size of .11, and Intervention B had an effect size of .72, we would weigh those differences in practical significance in our recommendations for which intervention to recommend (considering other factors, such as cost, ease of use, and so on).

Hierarchical Analyses

The analyses described in the previous section have been in use for decades in educational research. Recently, hierarchical analyses are being used more often because they account for a unique feature in educational settings. The types of groupings we have described in the previous section result when researchers divide a sample according to an independent variable, such as age, gender, or maternal education. When researchers conduct studies in early childhood settings, they come upon a situation in which children are already subdivided into groups based upon classrooms. We must assume that there are unique features of classrooms that can impact children; how a group of children and a teacher come to function together is a complex and unique experience. Thus, hierarchical analyses take into account the reality that children are 'nested' within classrooms. Children within classrooms share some experiences that are common to them and are not necessarily shared similarly with children in other classrooms. In what follows, we will explain a study in which hierarchical analysis was used.

Polly et al. (2014) conducted a professional development initiative focused on mathematics with elementary teachers. Their dependent variables included the teachers' beliefs about mathematics teaching and learning, their content knowledge, their self-reported instructional practices, and the children's assessment scores at the end of each of three curriculum units. The research team used hierarchical linear modeling, abbreviated as HLM. Their model had two levels, taking into consideration that the variable of children's assessment scores was nested within the teacher-level variables (their beliefs, content knowledge, and practices); each teacher had about 20 children in the classroom contributing data to the study.

The presentation of an HLM model can be confusing. From the Polly et al. (2014) article, the model is described as follows:

Level 1 (no student-level variables were considered as level-1 predictors):

$$\Upsilon_{ij} = \beta_{0j} + r_{ij}$$

where

Υ_{ij} = the dependent variable that represents the gain in mathematics skills during the first round of assessment for an individual student i in the classroom of teacher j

β_{0j} = the true mean student gain in mathematics skills during the first round of assessment in the classroom of teacher j

e_i = a random error.

Level 2:

$$\beta_{0j} = \gamma 00 + \gamma_{01}(Belief\_Teach)j + \gamma_{02}(Belief\_Learn)j + \gamma_{03}(Belief\_Math)j$$
$$+ \gamma_{04}((practice)j + \mu_{0j}$$

where

γ_{00} = the grand mean gain of all students in the first round of assessment

γ_{01} = the unique effect on student gains in mathematics skills associated with teacher beliefs in teaching mathematics

γ_{02} = the unique effect on student gains in mathematics skills associated with teacher beliefs in learning mathematics

γ_{03} = the unique effect on student gains in mathematics skills associated with teacher beliefs in mathematics

γ_{04} = the unique effect on student gains in mathematics skills associated with teacher practices in the classroom

μ_{0j} = the residual teacher-specific effects and was assumed normally distributed with mean 0 and variance τ_{00}

Source: Polly, D., Wang, C., McGee, J., Lambert, R. G., Martin, C. S., & Pugalee, D. (2014). Examining the influence of a curriculum-based elementary mathematics professional development program. *Journal of Research in Childhood Education, 28*, 327–343.

What is most important for readers to take forward is to try to understand what is included at each level of the model. In this study, the researchers explained initially that children were nested within the classrooms, with teacher variables coming in at the classroom level of the model.

Later in the article (Polly et al., 2014), we find,

> The intraclass correlation coefficients were .41 for the first round of student assessment, .37 for the second round of student assessment, and .46 for the third round of student assessment, justifying the need to use HLM because nearly 40% of the variability of student gains in mathematics skills can be explained by teacher-level variables.
>
> (p. 337)

What this means is that the children's scores had relationships with the teacher variables, so that being in the classroom of one teacher or another mattered. When the intraclass correlation coefficients (ICCs) are sufficiently high, it indicates that the data should indeed be treated as nested.

The results of Polly et al.'s study (2014) are reproduced here in Table 8.5. There are three major subsets of data, presented as the first, second, and third rounds. These represent the three units on which children were assessed. The various dependent variables are listed in the left-hand side of the table. The first is 'knowledge gains,' which is the gains teachers displayed in their content knowledge as measured with a pretest and posttest. There was one significant relationship for this variable and children's achievement scores, found in the first round. Note that the coefficient is negative, indicating a negative relationship. The authors described this in the text as follows:

> This means that students taught by teachers with relatively less content knowledge at the beginning, who gained more content knowledge through the professional development, had relatively less gains in the curriculum-based assessments at the beginning of the professional development. This difference, however, diminished as teachers were more exposed to the professional development.
>
> (p. 338)

We will not explain the other significant findings, as they require extensive explanation of the variables, but readers can note where the findings are marked by asterisks and trust that these could be understood by reading about each of the variables in the study.

Table 8.5 Parameter Estimates of Two-Level Hierarchical Liner Models About the Impact of Teacher Knowledge, Belief, and Practice on Student Performance in Mathematics Assessments

	First round		Second round		Third round	
	Coefficient	SE	Coefficient	SE	Coefficient	SE
Knowledge gains	−1.53	0.57*	−0.38	0.45	0.55	0.66
Belief in teaching						
DC toT	−10.31	7.91	3.2	7.43	24.31	4.95***
T to DC	−1.33	7.78	5.93	8.09	19.1	10.53
Learning						
DC toT	−6	6.34	2.52	9.17	−17.8	13.54
T to DC	1.89	6.71	−14.77	6.77*	−6.81	19.8
Mathematics						
DC to T	−8.44	7.03	17.48	10.97	−14.88	9.57
T to DC	5.37	6.01	−13.12	3.62**	−34.06	19.48
Teacher practice						
T to S	−10.9	4.72*	−4.55	6.14	4.07	9.78
T to T	9.15	13.99	−9.07	5.71	4.3	8.5
T to S vs. T to T	−20.08	13.37	4.36	5.77	−0.44	9.66
Effect size	0.55		0.42		0.58	

Note: DC to T = teacher beliefs changed from discovery/connectionist orientation to transmission orientation: T to DC = teacher beliefs changed from transmission orientation to discovery/connectionist orientation, the comparison group was teachers whose did not report a change of their beliefs: T to S = that teacher practice changed from teacher centered to student centered: T to T = that teacher practice stayed as teacher centered, the comparison group was teachers whose practice stayed as student centered: T to S vs. T to T = a comparison between teachers whose practice changed from teacher-centered to student-centered versus teachers whose practice stayed as teacher-centered. Effect size represents the proportion of variance the teacher-level variable accounted for student mean gains in each round of assessment in mathematics.
* $p < 0.05$. ** $p < 0.01$. *** $p < 0.001$.

Source: Polly, D., Wang, C., McGee, J., Lambert, R.G., Martin, C.S., & Pugalee, D. (2014). Examining the influence of a curriculum-based elementary mathematics professional development program. *Journal of Research in Childhood Education, 28*, 327–343.

In sum, hierarchical analyses are also concerned with understanding how the variance in a study can be attributed to the variables. The important thing to remember is that the use of hierarchical analyses indicates that the data are nested in some way, such as children in classrooms or the unique features of a classroom being nested in teachers. The jargon is extensive, and so the Results sections of these studies can be intimidating. Make it a goal to identify the levels and do the table/text comparisons to find the results.

Continuing Forward to Understand Statistical Analyses

We understand that while readers may feel they have followed our explanations thus far, it is quite a different thing to apply this knowledge to understanding a new study on one's own. In this section, we offer some general advice for working through the Results section of a quantitative study.

Prior to reading the Results section, it is important to have a firm understanding of the research questions. Labeling variables as independent, dependent, or control variables also helps. Remember that independent variables are used at the front end, and researchers are interested in their relationship to or impact upon the dependent variables.

The next task is to identify the analysis being used and what intent it serves. Even if the analysis is unfamiliar, look for its purpose. Is it being used to examine how variables are related, or are variables being compared? By puzzling out the purpose of the analysis, it is possible to think about the results, even with a limited understanding of the intricacies of the analysis.

Results are portrayed both in the text and in tables or figures. Read the text first to identify any findings described therein. Researchers do identify the significance level in the text, if they present the analysis only in the text, so watch for the p symbol. When tables or figures are used, the researchers will refer readers to them at the point in the text at which they are pertinent; this can help in the task of matching text and table. Tables have titles, which help in identifying the type of analysis.

In examining results in tabular form, looking for the asterisks allows a quick move to where findings were significant. This can be the first place to build a meaning of the results. Attempt to line up those significant findings with the research questions. It is important to not stop there, however. Take note of where significance was not reached. Looking back to Table 8.5, it is apparent that most of the comparisons did not reach significance. This is important to notice. Polly et al. (2014) did take note of this, commenting, "We were expecting more student gains for teachers who . . ." (p. 338). Oftentimes researchers do not explicitly discuss the *lack* of findings, but this is part of the story of a study. While statistical analysis can be intimidating, regarding the study as a story in which the reader's task is to identify the details and how they connect to each other may be a helpful attitude to take toward the work.

Reading and Understanding a Quantitative Study

Findings/Results

Task: *Review descriptive statistics to get a sense of the findings.*
Look for: Typically tables are used to present information such as means, ranges, and standard deviations for study variables. Examine these to make meaning of the variables. For example, were children scoring higher or lower on average on a measure? Were teachers showing higher or lower levels of a variable?

Task: *Map out the results of statistical analyses in relation to the research questions.*
Look for: The results of analyses are often detailed in tables as well as described to some level verbally. Look at each piece of the analysis. What research question was being addressed? What was the researcher looking for—a correlation, a prediction, a test of differences? For each analysis, locate the findings that were significant and relate them to the research question. Take note of what was not significant, keeping in mind the relative balance (e.g., was there a greater or lesser proportion of analyses that were significant or not?). If effect size is reported, note that and how the researcher described the importance of the effect size. Your goal will be to map out the research questions and the relevant findings, making the connections between what was asked and what answers resulted. Which research questions

resulted in significant findings and which did not? Most often the discussion by researchers centers on the findings that were significant, so it is important to note what the results failed to show as well.

Discussion

Task: *Evaluate the researcher's claims about the research.*

Look for: Examine how the researcher describes the results. Does this discussion seem to match the pattern of significant and nonsignificant findings from the Results section? How does the researcher relate the results to other studies? Does the researcher seem to take a realistic stance toward both the study's findings and its limitations?

Part II

EXAMINING RESEARCH QUESTIONS

9

RESEARCH QUESTIONS ABOUT CHILDREN

We begin with research questions about children because this seems so central to the concerns of the early childhood field. Those working with young children are interested broadly in knowing about their development, learning, and well-being.

What Interests Researchers?

The central questions framing researchers' interests set out what is important to learn more about and know. It should be unsurprising that researchers within the qualitative and quantitative paradigms take different approaches to defining their interests. The interests of qualitative researchers revolve around firsthand access to children's perceptions and lived experiences:

- What is this experience like for this child?
- What does it mean to him/her?
- How can we come to some understanding of the child's own life?
- How are our understandings about children impacted by contexts and structures that are unexamined?

On the other hand, the interests of quantitative researchers are reflected by questions that fit these types of sentence frames:

- How well can children . . . ?
- What is the impact of variable x on how well children . . . ?
- Under the conditions of variable y and variable z, how well can children . . . ?

We are not asserting that all questions in quantitative research follow these forms. However, most questions revolve around an appraisal of children's abilities, behaviors, and/or thoughts framed within a sense of what is normative or desirable.

Both qualitative and quantitative researchers aim to 'know' children. What 'knowing' means within either paradigm differs. In essence, the interests of qualitative researchers collect around developing understandings of children that are informed by the children themselves.

The interests of quantitative researchers may be described in a nutshell as 'taking stock' of the child. Sometimes this begins with data that come straight from children themselves, but quantitative researchers use this information in the form of variables they have defined. Thus, what comes from the child is shaped either by or into the researcher-defined variables. In addition, sometimes quantitative researchers use information from others who know the children.

Asking Questions

We have selected some recent qualitative and quantitative studies to illustrate the differences in the questions asked by researchers in each paradigm. Our choices were based as well on representing a range of data collection strategies among the studies.

Qualitative Studies

In the vein of creating greater understanding of children's lived experiences, Tempest and Wells (2012) conducted a qualitative study focused on one child interacting with two peers during play. The researchers chose this particular child because he had "persisting speech difficulties" (PSD), defined as unclear speech accompanied by difficulties in being understood by others, with an unknown cause. They narrowed their research question to examining instances of peer arguments, based upon literature that indicated potential concerns for negative peer interactions for children with other types of speech and language issues. They examined the children's conversation with peers to answer their research questions about how alliances were formed and maintained between and among children and how arguments developed, paying careful attention to turn-by-turn interactions among the children in a microanalysis of the conversations. This allowed them to describe the experiences of the focal child, as well as the other two children, in aligning with a peer (inclusion) and protecting the play from interruption from others (exclusion).

Interested in how children produce and appreciate what they regard as humorous, Loizou (2011) conducted a qualitative study with a small group of young children. Her research question included an investigation of the humorous aspects of photographs the children took both at the time the photos were produced and after a period of 6 months had passed. The children themselves defined how they regarded the photographs as humorous.

Researcher Perspective

Iheoma U. Iruka, Ph.D., Buffett Early Childhood Institute, University of Nebraska

Growing up in a community in which some youth seemed to be on the path of 'success' and others not raised a host of questions about why, especially when the youth came from similar economic, social, and cultural backgrounds. It was the question of what makes one resilient in the face of many obstacles, including single parenting, poverty, and violence. My interest in understanding this phenomenon began to center around the family constellation and parenting behaviors, but especially how and what families with lesser human and social capital do to create an environment of success and achievement, especially in the face of challenges, such as poverty, racism, and limited education. Thus, my research agenda primarily centers on uncovering family processes, especially families of color and those living in poverty, and behaviors and attitudes they engage in that ensure their child's success in school and life.

My approach to addressing this broad question has taken many approaches, but one of the first steps I took was to review the current literature, ranging from peer-review articles, reports, and new articles, and to continue reading the literature. My review of the literature was to understand how scholars frame and theorize about parenting and its influence on child development and how it, as a system, is being influenced. Beyond reading and reviewing other work in this area, I engaged (and continue to) in multiple conversations and discussion with diverse individuals (parents, organization, school personnel, policy makers, funders) about

Quantitative Studies

Turning to an example of quantitative research, Harrist et al. (2014) began with an examination of interactions among sibling pairs and related this data to children's peer interactions in kindergarten. The independent variables included the structure of the sibling pair in regard to age difference and the family structure (one or two parents living in the home). The researchers hypothesized that these variables would be associated with the frequencies of complementary interactions (hierarchical; differential power between the two) and reciprocal interactions (collaborative). Next, the researchers pursued the question of how the variables for sibling interactions (levels of complementary and reciprocal interactions) related to dependent variables in kindergarten: the children's engagement with peers, social status, and presence of behavior problems. They examined whether family status predicted these relationships uniquely. In this study, the research questions fit with a sentence stem similar to 'under the conditions of variable x [sibling structure] and variable y [family structure] how well can children . . . in kindergarten?"

Becker, McClelland, Loprinzi, and Trost (2014) investigated the relationships among active play, self-regulation, and academic achievement (letter knowledge and math). The research questions included these topics: the relationship between active play and children's self-regulation skills, the relationship between active play and children's academic achievement, and the relationship between self-regulation and academic achievement. In determining these relationships, the researchers looked specifically at whether self-regulation mediated the relationship between active play and academic achievement. In other words, they looked for evidence of a chain of relationships—active play predicting self-regulation predicting academic achievement. This allowed them

their perspectives regarding parenting and its value in children's long-term success. Reflections on current literature, conversations with diverse individuals, and personal experiences refined my thinking to one that is more culturally based rather than one that assumes parenting behaviors, approaches, and intentionality are universal. For example, my question morphed from 'What is the link between parenting and child outcomes?' to 'To what extent does the link between parenting and child outcomes vary by culture?'

As a means to really understand the extent to which the relationship between parenting is linked to child outcomes varies across cultural groups, I have utilized existing large databases, such as the Early Childhood Longitudinal Study and Early Head Start Research and Evaluation Study. The benefit of these datasets is that they provide a large culturally diverse sample with key constructs of interests. The downside is that they don't necessarily capture the full breadth of particular constructs. Nevertheless, these large datasets provide the avenue to examine key phenomenon of interest that will then allow a researcher to have a basis and rationale for additional data collection, especially more qualitative data. I have begun to expand my methodological and analytical approach to be more multifaceted and aligned with my inquiries of interest. The reason for this shift is because while quantitative analyses and approaches can provide evidence of relationships, linkages, and effects, they are less likely to help us understand why relationships between key constructs may exist or even uncovering phenomena such as 'tough love' (often noted with African-American parenting) or 'familism' (often noted with Hispanic/Latino parenting). Inclusion of qualitative approaches through to determine if one of the ways in which active play might be important for children's learning is that it impacts their self-regulation positively, which then is related to better academic achievement. This is referred to as an indirect effect for active play and achievement, in that the relationship is realized through the impact on self-regulation. The research questions fit the sentence stem, 'What are the impacts of active play and self-regulation on . . . ?'

The research team of Bumgarner and Lin (2014) was interested in children's development as reflected in the English language skills of Hispanic immigrant children when they entered kindergarten. The independent variables in their study included attendance in center-based early childhood education (ECE) programs prior to kindergarten entry and the families' socioeconomic status (SES). Just as Becker et al. (2014) hypothesized a chain of linked variables in the study described earlier, Bumgarner and Lin hypothesized that SES would moderate the association between program attendance and English proficiency, using the sentence stem 'What are the impacts of SES and ECE attendance on . . .' They

interviews and focus groups with diverse groups of parents, mostly mothers, has allowed me to better contextualize why certain behaviors and practices are meaningfully different due to culture and contexts. Understanding how culture, beyond ethnic membership, directly and indirectly influences one's schema, point of view, and leaning is critical in addressing societal issues from the opportunity/achievement gap to income inequality.

In my attempt to address the opportunity/achievement gap through uncovering the value and promise of parenting, especially as it manifests in one's expectations, attitudes, and practices, I continue to seek to understand how culturally based forms of parenting are key in this effort. In addition to understanding these cultural variations, I also seek to inform policies and practices that respect, acknowledge, and value these differences, especially as the United States becomes a majority-minority country and rates of poverty increase.

expected that children from families with lower SES would show greater gains in English proficiency than children from families with higher SES following attendance in an ECE program.

To summarize, we have shown in this section how the questions posed by qualitative researchers tend to focus on an in-depth understanding of the experiences and perspectives of children, questions that they believe must be addressed by children themselves. Meanwhile, quantitative researchers tend to ask questions based from a definition of normative development and learning, focused on assessing where children stand and what factors might influence those processes.

Choosing Methods

Different methods were utilized in each of the studies discussed. Next, we will highlight how the studies exemplify the options available for researchers.

Qualitative Studies

In the two qualitative studies, the researchers relied upon hearing directly from children in the children's own words and ways. One study, the examination of arguments by Tempest and Wells (2012), stayed closest to children's everyday lives by drawing data from their play. The researchers described filming for a 6-week period, but how much time this translated to spending with the children is unclear. Filming allows for fine-grained analysis of what is being observed, as analysis can occur over and over again with replaying of the resulting tapes. In addition, in this study, filming allowed the researchers to produce a transcript for their analysis. The filming occurred during what the researchers called "'free play' with no teacher present" (p. 61). This would lead us to expect that the filming constituted a relatively short portion of the school day. In addition, they noted that the focal child chose two other children as "play partners at each data collection session" (p. 61); coincidentally, it appears the child always chose the same two peers. We suspect, then, that the filmed sessions were especially conducted, since in most classroom-wide play periods there would not be control over who played with whom. In sum, the researchers used filming to capture children's naturalistic play, although we the readers cannot be sure about whether the play sessions occurred as a matter of typical classroom activity or were set up by the researchers. Here we have illustrated the types of reasoning that must be applied when the researchers' description of methodology is truncated.

To answer the specific questions posed within this article, the researchers first identified specific incidences in their tapes in which the children participated in arguments. They utilized a definition of arguments that was marked by specific criteria related to qualities of the children's interactions (an interruption in cooperative play, a conversational turn by one of the children marked by opposition) and quantity (lasting for three or more conversational turns). By defining their criteria for an argument quite clearly, Tempest and Wells (2012) allowed others to evaluate their decision making.

Finally, the research questions were examined via a turn-by-turn analysis of the conversation in 2 of the 12 recorded arguments. In this way, the researchers (Tempest & Wells, 2012) were able to offer thick, rich descriptions of the children's interactions, showing how conversational turns built upon previous turns to accomplish the children's purposes (building an alliance, negotiating an argument).

In the other qualitative study, the children played a part in generating the data through interaction with the researchers. Loizou (2011) studied children's humor by giving disposable cameras to six children. After the 38 pictures they each had taken were developed, Loizou asked the children to pick the 10 most humorous. She interviewed individuals about what they had photographed and why they thought it was funny. She repeated this process 6 months later to see if children were consistent in their perspectives on humor. Loizou's use of photographs accomplished two things. First, it allowed her to explore the content of the children's photographs, and she described where they took pictures and who/what was photographed. Second, this method provided an entry point to talking with children about what is humorous. As Loizou noted, "The cameras worked as another form of language and allowed children who might have been unable to verbally explain their understanding of humour to have a different way of exhibiting their perception of humour" (p. 161). This type of methodology illustrates inventiveness in accessing children's perceptions when they may not be as adept or willing as adults to engage in lengthy dialogue. For example, we found ourselves, as 'early childhood people,' smiling when reading one transcript portion in which Loizou asked "Why is it funny?" and the child replied "Because" (p. 157). The researcher persisted in rephrasing the question, and the child did eventually explain his/her perspective with more words, but this illustrates the occasional difficulties in generating data with young children.

Quantitative Studies

The three quantitative studies included in this section reflect a variety of strategies for knowing children. This includes information from children themselves and from others involved with children. Predictably, how that information is generated varies substantially from qualitative methods.

Researchers used observational methods in this group of published studies. In the Harrist et al. (2014) study of sibling interactions and children's social development in kindergarten, research assistants conducted two visits in each child's home, each lasting 2 hours. The family members were asked to carry on with their typical early-evening routines. To record data, the observer hand-wrote "detailed" notes about the social interactions of the target child and other family members; these were broken down into separate "social events" (pp. 207–208). Later, other research assistants coded aspects of these events based upon a set of 37 different categories drawn from the literature and further developed by the research team. Obviously, the coding is dependent upon the strength of those initial notes from the observers; any missing details could impact the coders' decisions. So it was incumbent upon Harrist and colleagues to provide extensive training to the observers. Offsetting this challenge is the concern that family members might be more uncomfortable if they were being filmed and that filming multiple individuals coming in and out of the video can result in issues with the audio quality.

In the study by Becker et al. (2014), the researchers harnessed the power of technology as another form of 'observation.' As a reminder, in this study the researchers examined how physical activity was correlated with children's self-regulation and how self-regulation was correlated with academic achievement. Children in this study were given a belt with an accelerometer, which measured their motion during a recess period outside. The resulting variable was minutes spent in active play, when children were engaged in moderate to vigorous physical activity as measured by this device. Using technology in this way resulted in a much more precise measure than is possible through simple observation.

Other forms of data collected by quantitative researchers are based upon direct

Researcher Perspective

Sophie Alcock, Ph.D., Victoria University of Wellington, New Zealand

How I used research to find out about young children experiencing playfulness in their communication: I began by reading a lot of literature and research about play, attempting to refine my research interest in that vast topic. The humor and fun in children's play became my focus area. Initial background reading revealed that most humor research emphasized individual children rather than the relational processes that occur between children. I was curious about what happens in these felt spaces between children playing together. So I'd found both a research gap and a focus.

After completing all the detailed and necessary ethics and access protocols, I carried out a small observational pilot study. As a result of that study and difficulties around defining humor, the focus broadened to include playfulness. The main research question became: How do young children experience playfulness (and humor) in their communication?

Ethnographic methods fitted with my desire to study children's evolving play processes and experiences as authentically as possible. I felt at home in ECE settings, yet as a participant observer, I wanted to get beyond this familiarity, to listen and look, to feel and think deeply, critically, differently, and reflectively about the patterns in children's playfulness. I spent hours and days gathering data, using a video camera as well as pen and paper, and reflecting on and analyzing that data. Sociocultural theory and play literature further informed this inductive analytic process.

When observing, I assumed a passive role, not interrupting children's play yet responding to requests. Researcher assessment of children. Becker et al. (2014) utilized a measure of children's self-regulation in which children are asked to do the opposite of the researcher's instructions, for instance to touch their toes when instructed to touch their heads. The researchers also assessed children's academic achievement, measuring the children's knowledge of letters and words and their knowledge of mathematics including counting, reading numbers, and simple problems. These tasks came from a standardized instrument in which scores can be interpreted based upon a normative sample of children, who are considered to represent the typical range of scores for a particular age group.

As do qualitative researchers, sometimes quantitative researchers interview children individually to collect data. In the Harrist et al. (2014) study of social interactions, research assistants interviewed each child about their classroom peers. They showed children pictures of their classmates and asked them to indicate three peers who were "good at getting others to play," three peers they liked to play with most, and three peers they liked to play with least. From these questions, the researchers defined a variable called positive peer engagement (children's nomination scores for being effective in play) and their sociometric status as popular, rejected, neglected, controversial, or average (nominations from peers for appeal as a play partner). One can see how much more 'closed' these interview questions are than the more open-ended conversations about pictures utilized by Loizou (2011).

Finally, quantitative researchers also depend upon adults who know the children as sources of information. In the Harrist et al. (2014) study, the children's teachers completed a survey for each child focused on the absence/presence of problem behaviors. Using surveys such as this provides an efficient source of information when the alternative is extensive observation or direct assessment. In

boundaries can pose interesting dilemmas. On one occasion while quietly videoing a long, involved play event, a child in the event randomly asked me to count while they hid. Still videoing, I counted to 20 and, fitting with the play, pretended not to know where the children had very obviously hidden. In such ways, I felt honoured to become part of the children's play environment, though I was not usually so integral to their play. By being there, I was part of that context, which put me in a wonderful space for observing experience.

My written observation notes consisted of three columns. One recorded what I saw and heard. Another recorded artifacts and things that mediated children's play, such as water, sand, containers, and musical instruments. The third column recorded my feelings and thoughts. Reviewing, reflecting, and analyzing these notes and video footage contributed to my increasing awareness of the rhythm, energy, and drive for togetherness in children's playful activity that was a big part of the research findings.

Rhythm and vitality expressed and felt in and between bodies was blatantly obvious when observing preverbal toddlers. Older verbal children frequently also used words rhythmically, playing with words in musical body-based ways. I recall a group of 4-year-old children becoming physically and verbally playful as their shopping-card game progressed. Zoe began singing: "open up your cards and look inside," to which Frank chimed in: "open up your heart and look inside." The group continued to develop this free-flow, improvised musical style, connecting and communicating around the activity of a shopping-card game and adding dancing to the mix.

The sound of the sung words that stuck in my mind expressed the rhythm, vitality, and togetherness of these children.

addition, surveys allow for the respondent to consider the child's typical behavior over time rather than in a single observation or assessment period.

Before leaving this section, we want to point out one other form of data utilized by quantitative researchers. The study by Bumgarner and Lin (2014) made use of an available database, this particular database being a cohort group of the Early Childhood Longitudinal Study. Databases such as this one include data from a very large number of individuals chosen to be representative of the national population of the United States. Data are collected from various sources, such as the children themselves, teachers, and parents. Ultimately, these intensive efforts to collect information are available for researchers to use. Researchers then fashion questions that can be addressed using the data available. An advantage of a database is that it gives researchers access to samples that are incredibly large and diverse compared to the samples possible when a research team is collecting its own data.

That rhythmic togetherness might have been missed, because it was so obvious had I not obsessively reviewed and reflected on the research data, looking for patterns in children's playful activity and driven by curiosity. In that sense, observation rules and is the tool of tools when combined into narrative-like events intended to illuminate children's experience of playful communication.

To summarize the methods utilized by researchers, we have noted the reliance of qualitative researchers on accessing information directly from children themselves. Methodologies vary in creating new ways to access what children are thinking, experiencing, and feeling. Quantitative researchers sometimes collect data directly from children by observation and structured interviews. They also rely on using surveys with the adults important in children's lives to report on what they know about the children.

Potential, Pitfalls, and Limitations

There is much potential within the small group of studies described in this chapter. The researchers have opened our eyes to the worlds of young children's lives.

All of the researchers utilized data generated directly with children. They asked children questions, listened to them, and observed them. We hope that readers have noted some aspects of creativity in the methodologies we have described. Giving children cameras (Loizou, 2011) or using an unobtrusive instrument to record their activity level (Becker et al., 2014) harnesses the power of technology to explore questions.

In the qualitative studies, the researchers have given us an up-close look at children's capabilities. Observing the subtleties of group conversation (Tempest & Wells, 2012) or the ability of children to stage a humorous photograph (Loizou, 2011) reminds us that young children are enormously complex and thoughtful.

The work of quantitative researchers evidenced the potential interrelationships of children's lives in multiples settings (Harrist et al., 2014) or in regard to multiple developmental domains (Becker et al., 2014). The work by Bumgarner and Lin (2014) examined trends over a very large number of children. With these sorts of data, we might more effectively answer questions about societal responses to bettering children's lives.

At the same time, all research carries the potential for pitfalls. Knowledge of where and how pitfalls occur is important to being able to evaluate research.

Some pitfalls are known ahead of time, and researchers can plan ahead to avoid them. For instance, observing children, whether using videotaping or writing notes, can be obtrusive. The technical term for this is *reactivity*, meaning that those being observed shift what they do in response to having someone in the situation 'watching.' Harrist et al. (2014) attempted to account for this in their observations conducted in children's homes. The research assistants did not begin observation for data collection until they had been present in the home for 15 minutes, providing some time for the family members to become accustomed to their presence. As another example, any large database, including the one utilized by Bumgarner and Lin (2014) has missing data. It is impossible to collect data from a large number of individuals without some incomplete attempts to reach all individuals with all measures. Bumgarner and Lin conducted procedures to impute the missing data, meaning that a complex computer program examines the relationships among the variables and creates values for the missing data. These procedures are used within quantitative studies without a great deal of controversy, but one expects to see that the missing data is not extensive.

Other pitfalls might not be foreseen. Loizou (2011) found that "the children were so excited by the disposable camera itself that they started taking photographs without thinking whether they were humorous or not" (p. 152). Loizou adjusted to this circumstance by asking the children to choose the 10 most humorous photographs. While this may have cut into the richness of her data, it may also have been an appropriate response for young children who were several months on either side of their fifth birthday. Harrist et al. (2014) encountered a pitfall when using their extensive observation coding scheme with 37 categories. Several of these behavioral categories were infrequently observed; this situation is problematic for statistical analyses. Therefore, for some of the analyses, the researchers collapsed the 20 types of complementary categories into one supercategory of complementary interactions and the 17 types of reciprocal

Researcher Perspective

Julie Nicholson, Ph.D., Mills College

The Center for Play Research conducts studies with a commitment to the value of respecting and making visible children's perspectives. As one example, we are aware that many reports have concluded over the last decade that opportunities for children to engage in child-initiated play are declining in contemporary American society. However, we are concerned that this narrative is consistently represented through the discourse and perspectives of adults. To counter this, we interviewed 98 children (3–17 years of age), the majority of whom are living in low-income urban environments, where play's decline is described as most prevalent, to gather their opinions regarding their personal play experiences. We were interested to understand whether their perspectives would complement, destabilize, and/or extend adults' stories. We also reversed the traditional roles by asking these children to comment on how they would characterize the play lives of adults. During our interviews we asked such questions as, "Can you tell me about a time you played and it was really fun?" "Do you think adults—mommies, daddies, grandmas, grandpas, and teachers—play? If so, how?" "If you could plan an entire day of play, what would you do?" and "If adults said that play wasn't important for children, what would you say to them?"

Children's ideas of fun play and the plans they imagined for filling an entire day with play emphasized relationships, outdoor play, and use of open-ended toys. Contrary to adult reports, the children we interviewed rarely mentioned digital play, although many described this as a significant form of play for adults. Further, categories into one supercategory of reciprocal interactions. Doing so enabled the analysis to proceed, but it also reduced the complexity of the data into much more general categories.

As is true of all research, each of the studies carries limitations. We will briefly note the limitations of individual studies and then consider limitations in a more general discussion.

Some of the limitations of individual studies stem from the fact that any methodology has both benefits and drawbacks. Loizou (2011) sent the cameras home with children, and we cannot know how much other family members may have participated in the process of planning and/ or taking photographs. The research assistants in the Harrist et al. (2014) study wrote notes while observing children and their family members. These notes required them to make "low-level judgments about the meaning of the observed behavior within a Social Event (e.g., whether a laugh was sarcastic or sincere) based on a variety of cues" (p. 208). With live coding rather than videotape-based coding, the decisions made by the research assistants cannot be reexamined or replayed to examine other features of the interactions. Data collection by Becker et al. (2014) was done on a one-time basis, and we must consider whether that one-time measure of physical activity on the playground is a fair representation of the children's typical play.

Other limitations speak to more general issues within a paradigm. When researchers use teacher surveys as a way to know children (Becker et al., 2014; Harrist et al., 2014), it is up to others to determine the meaning of those data. Do teacher surveys show us characteristics of the child, who they are, their capabilities and challenges? Or do they reveal to us the perceptions of adults about these children? This is a fine-grained point but one not unimportant to the task of finding meaning in research. Readers must wrestle with the issue of just what is represented in the data.

the majority of the children in our study reported that the adults they know do not play enough, a 'truth' they critiqued as problematic. We discovered that listening to children's narration of their experiences allowed for more equity by complicating, expanding, and challenging the current narratives in circulation.

The commitment to learn from children is also central to our study of children's perspectives of their play in several SOS Children's Villages around the world (Macedonia, Serbia, Bulgaria, and Kosovo). SOS villages were created to allow orphaned children to have opportunities to grow up in families and supportive communities. SOS is an international and nondenominational NGO, a federation of 116 national associations in 134 countries and territories around the world (http://www.sos-childrens villages.org/). Our research is guided by the following question, "How do children describe their experiences playing in the SOS Children's Villages?"

Inspired by the Mosaic Approach, we are gathering children's input in several ways:

(a) *Children's drawings:* Children are drawing pictures of their favorite types of play in their SOS village and then describing their pictures for us; (b) *Slide show:* As researchers, we take several photos of an SOS village and then ask children to talk about the photos and, specifically, to talk about how they play in each of the areas represented in the pictures; and (c) *Child-led tours:* We ask the children to walk around their village (always in the company of an SOS mother/father and/or staff member) and to talk with us about how they play in their village. These tours are completed in small groups and have been very popular with the children in our study.

We believe that the children's narratives will help adults create more

Quantitative researchers frequently use standardized measures, as did Becker et al. (2014) in their choice of measures for children's academic achievement. Standardized measures have been critiqued as a way of knowing children because of the very characteristics that render them to be good measurements in the technical sense. Graue (1998) argued that standardized instruments are marked by narrow conceptions of the phenomenon with an underlying reliance on assumptions of a normal distribution of characteristics within a population of children in which development proceeds universally. Is this truly how development proceeds? What are the limits of this way of knowing children? The task of finding meaning within research requires that readers wrestle with this issue and decide how to interpret these types of instruments.

equitable and welcoming classrooms. We are asking children to teach and educate *us* by inviting them to help us understand the world through their eyes. We are listening carefully to what they are saying and asking how their stories help us create a more equitable, inclusive world. Our goal at the Center for Play Research is to support children's human rights. We are striving to create opportunities for children to become active stakeholders who can influence the discourse and decisions intended to influence and affect their lives.

When using a large database as Bumgarner and Lin (2014) did, the researchers are limited by how the data was collected initially. For instance, Bumgarner and Lin had questions about children's enrollment in early childhood education programs. The database provided a variable that reflected whether children attended a center-based care arrangement before kindergarten. It was a simple yes/no variable, which leaves many unanswered questions, such as how many hours per week a child attended or the length of the enrollment. While researchers might use a database because of its size and representativeness, they cannot fashion the variables they want but must make do with what they have.

Summary

In this chapter, we have explored a number of studies that were designed to answer questions about children. We noted how qualitative researchers attempt to get close-up and rich descriptions of children's lived experiences and perceptions. We described how quantitative researchers shape their observations and interviews of children into variables, either by using an instrument that has been devised to measure a construct or by applying a coding scheme to translate observations into quantifiable variables. This can lead to questions of what exactly is being measured. Researchers operating within the different paradigms will answer this question differently, and it is a task of readers to determine what makes the most sense in their worldviews.

As is true of all research, there is potential in a well-conducted study. There are also pitfalls and limitations to the knowledge generated by research. By walking through examples of each of these in the final section, our aim has been to model different ways of thinking about these issues and present central questions for readers to puzzle through as they work to become knowledgeable consumers of research.

10

RESEARCH QUESTIONS ABOUT THE ADULTS IN CHILDREN'S LIVES

In this chapter, we move our consideration to another unit of analysis, the adults in children's lives. There are some similarities between the research methods that fit for this chapter and the previous chapter, since the focus is on people and what they do and think. Given the variety of methods available, however, we are able to discuss new research strategies. We will highlight the questions that interest qualitative and quantitative researchers and describe more about the unique methodologies used to address those questions.

What Interests Researchers?

In many ways it could be said that the interests that researchers have in the adults in children's lives is an extension of their interest in children. Children remain at the heart of the equation, as adults are responsible for supporting their development, learning, and well-being. By understanding more about the adults in children's lives, researchers hope to generate knowledge that can have a positive impact on both the adults and the children for whom they care and educate.

As was described in Chapter 9, qualitative researchers are interested in the lived experiences and perspectives of the people who participate in their research. Their questions regarding adults revolve around issues such as:

* What is this person's experience as a teacher or parent/guardian?
* What is this person's perspective on supporting children's development, learning, and/or well-being?
* How has this person come to an understanding of his/her role with children, and what is that understanding?
* How have people come to be who they are within their context, and how might we think about those structures in new ways?

The interests of quantitative researchers revolve ultimately around issues of predictability and/or control. Researchers might try to pinpoint relationships between variables or show that an intervention with adults made an impact on them and/or children. Their questions are of these sorts:

* What family/parent characteristics or actions or teacher characteristics or actions are related to children's outcomes academically and/or socially?
* Does this planned parent intervention program show benefits for parents and children?
* How does preservice preparation and inservice professional development impact the work of teachers of young children and the children themselves?

Just as was true about children, as we described in the previous chapter, both qualitative and quantitative researchers aim to 'know' the adults in children's lives. As was true about children, the interests of qualitative researchers collect around developing understandings of adults that are informed by those adults.

The interests of quantitative researchers may be described as understanding how adults and children influence each other by studying the relationships between and among variables that are used to characterize the participants. As was discussed in Chapters 7 and 8, the researchers' aims may be to determine the correlations among variables that characterize adults or the degree to which they can predict a variable based upon knowing other variables. They may also compare groups of teachers or parents or undertake causal research to determine the impact of an intervention with them. A common theme among these research goals is to learn more about how to optimize the ways parents and teachers care for and educate young children.

Asking Questions

In this section, we describe the studies we have selected to illustrate methods used to study the adults in children's lives. Our collection consists of two qualitative studies and two quantitative studies.

Doubet and Ostrosky (2015) conducted a qualitative study to understand the experiences of parents whose preschool-aged children demonstrated persistent challenging behaviors. Their research question was, "How does a young child, ages 3 to 5, with challenging behavior influence the family system?" (p. 224). They noted that there was evidence in the literature of the difficulties faced by families when children show challenging behaviors and noted the importance of fully understanding the parent perspective. Their goal was to generate rich data to help inform the field, declaring that "It is critical that stakeholders understand the parent perspective of the children they serve" (p. 231).

Bauml (2011) conducted a qualitative study to explore how first-year teachers utilized their teacher-preparation experiences in their decision making about curricula. Her research question and methods were based upon her belief that "[u]nderstanding the value of any teacher preparation program requires close examination of the practices of its students and graduates" (p. 227). Bauml's study encompassed both teachers' practices and their thoughts about their decisions, and her focus was on how first-year teachers were applying what they learned during their teacher preparation programs.

Turning to quantitative research, Hojnoski, Columba, and Polignano (2014) conducted an intervention with a small group of parents focused on introducing them to new strategies for sharing books with their young children. The researchers noted a robust literature supporting the benefits of dialogic book reading for children's language and literacy development. Hojnoski and colleagues focused their attention on children's math learning by constructing their dialogic reading intervention around parental strategies for engaging their children specifically in that area. Their research questions were "(a) Did parents increase their use of math talk during shared book reading following training? (b) Did parents generalize intervention strategies? And (c) did children increase their use of math talk during shared book reading?" (p. 471).

Swartz and Easterbrooks (2014) focused their quantitative research on both parents and early childhood professionals. Initially drawing upon Bronfenbrenner's bioecological model of development, the researchers affirmed the importance of linkages between the major settings within which children live their lives. Their focus was on the "types of inputs" (p. 574) that contribute to the resulting quality of relationships between parents and child care providers.

In their study, these inputs included parent, teacher, and child characteristics. Their research questions were:

> Are parents' experiences with child care related to parents' and providers' perceptions of their relationships with each other? Are professional characteristics of providers (education, experience, job satisfaction, knowledge of child development) related to parents' and providers' perceptions of their relationships with each other? Are child characteristics (age and temperament) related to parents' and providers' perceptions of their relationships with each other?

> (p. 578)

For each research question, Swartz and Easterbrooks included one to three hypotheses that indicated the expected direction of a relationship. For instance, they hypothesized that when children had more difficult temperaments, parents and providers would report having worse relationships but also more frequent communication. However, researchers do not always include specific hypotheses when they communicate the intent of their study via research questions.

To sum up, this set of four studies reflects the nature of researchers' interests that we described in the previous section. Both of the qualitative studies center on the lived experiences of the participants, parents or teachers. The intent of the researchers was to achieve greater understanding of their unique perspectives. In the quantitative studies, the researchers attempted to establish predictability and/or control. In testing out a parent intervention, the study by Hojnoski et al. (2014) is aimed ultimately at developing new ways to shape adults' behaviors to support children's learning. Swartz and Easterbrooks (2014) were attempting to predict important factors in the complex processes of how parents and child care providers come to perceive each other and act in relationship to each other.

Choosing Methods

Recall that in Chapter 9, we described specific methods for understanding more about children. For qualitative studies, the methods included a microanalysis of children's conversations and interviews with children about photographs they had taken. For quantitative studies, the methods included observations of children, direct assessment of children, surveys about children completed by adults in their lives, and the use of existing databases. In this chapter, we will expand upon the methods used to understand more about people, in this case, the adults in children's lives.

Qualitative Studies

As was described in Chapter 9, qualitative researchers stay as close as possible to people's experiences. In both of the qualitative studies we use in this chapter, the researchers did so.

We first examine the methods used by Doubet and Ostrosky (2015) in their study of parents whose children demonstrated challenging behaviors. An important task the researchers faced was defining this phenomenon in a clear enough fashion to locate an appropriate sample. The criterion they decided upon to define challenging behavior was that the child had to have been expelled from a child care program, or the parent must have been told that the child would be expelled if the behavior did not improve. Doubet and Ostrosky clarified that by 'expelled,' they meant either that the child had been disenrolled or the family asked to leave the program.

To recruit participants, Doubet and Ostrosky (2015) posted notices on bulletin boards in child care centers and asked the directors of centers to include a notice in newsletters. Interested families then contacted the researchers. They formed a sample of seven families. The parents reported on the types of persistent challenging behaviors shown by their children. With these brief descriptions of the children, along with descriptions of the family structure/members and family activities, the researchers helped situate the parents in their unique contexts for readers.

It should be clear by now that interviewing is a key method in qualitative research. Doubet and Ostrosky (2015) used semistructured interviews, reflecting the emergent nature of qualitative data collection methods. Following transcriptions of their initial interviews with the families, they formed questions for a second interview. These questions were particular to achieving greater depth on topics raised by a parent in the first interview.

To code the data, the two researchers (Doubet & Ostrosky, 2015) discussed emerging categories following their individual review of the transcripts. Then they individually coded the same three transcripts before meeting again to discuss and refine their categories. Individual work on coding the remaining transcripts was followed by more joint discussion. Thus, the analysis was an iterative process in which the researchers shared their interpretations of the data. Researcher reflexivity was both an individual and a joint process. Doubet and Ostrosky offered a list of actions they had undertaken, such as investigator triangulation, external auditors, and peer debriefing, as evidence for the 'credibility' of their study.

We now turn to Bauml's (2011) case study of novice teachers. Her research reflects an example of extended involvement and data collection in the qualitative tradition. Recall Chapter 4 and our use of Souto-Manning's (2014) research in a classroom; she collected data via conducting observations and

Researcher Perspective

Jennifer Keys Adair, Ph.D., The University of Texas at Austin

My work is about the cultural and political nature of early childhood practices. I am really concerned about why young children from wealthier, white families often get to have a sophisticated, dynamic, discovery-based set of learning experiences at school while young children from marginalized communities are offered more task-oriented, quiet, sitting-still learning experiences. Qualitative research is often about the 'why' of things. And I want to know why inequality in terms of learning experiences persists in early childhood education.

I use a research method called video-cued ethnography, sometimes referred to as the Preschool in Three Cultures Method after the 1989 study by Joseph Tobin and his colleagues. Professor Tobin is an anthropologist who watched his own young children go from attending a preschool in the United States to one in Japan. He was struck by how different the practices were in each country. He made a film of preschools in each country and then added China to the study. He would take one of the films, from the U.S. for example, and show it to teachers in Japan and China. Their reactions—what they liked and didn't like, what they would not do in their own classrooms—pointed out what made the practices cultural. It turned out that the countries in the study had very different ideas about early childhood education.

I do the same thing in my own work but usually with a twist. Lately I have been focused on two research questions: 'How do administrators, teachers, young children, and their parents conceptualize agency in early learning?' and interviews with the teacher and collecting classroom artifacts. Bauml used many of these same methods.

Bauml's (2011) study began with the identification of five teachers who were currently in their first year of teaching jobs. Bauml described her own positionality when she reported previous relationships with these young teachers during their college field experiences. She cautioned,

> While the rapport I had established with these 5 teachers during their preservice education enabled me to probe and question participants about their work from a position of trust, I acknowledge the possibility that participants' responses may have been impacted by my role during their professional formation.
>
> (p. 229)

Bauml (2011) interacted with her study participants over the course of the entire academic year. She conducted interviews with each participant at three points in time, the beginning, middle, and end of the study. Bauml described the content of the interviews generally, noting they focused on questions about how the participants knew how to make their curricular decisions, how coursework they had taken was helpful to them, and the role of their preservice field experiences in their first-year teaching.

In addition, Bauml (2011) observed each teacher, took field notes, and concluded each visit with informal conversations. While Bauml clarified that she spent 22 hours in observation with each teacher, she did not provide information about how many observation sessions were entailed. She collected several artifacts, including lesson plans from the teachers and curriculum examples from their district or school. Finally, she also asked each participant to conduct lesson planning once with her present and the teacher talking aloud through her planning process. She referred to this as "think-aloud, also known as process tracing" (p. 229).

'How do conceptualizations of agency affect what kinds of learning experiences are offered young children from marginalized communities?' To answer these questions, I made a film in a first-grade classroom where young Latino children of immigrants have a lot of agency in their learning. They get to design projects, choose topics, solve problems, move about the classroom, influence how they are assessed, and share their ideas with their classmates throughout the day. The film shows a typical day in that classroom.

Next, I showed the film to the children in the film as well as to their teachers and parents. They told me what they thought of the educational experiences offered to the children and whether they were appropriate or helpful or successful.

Then my research team and I took this film to many school sites in Texas and California to have groups of administrators, preK–3 teachers, parents, and first graders watch and respond to the film. Then we analyzed their answers by looking at how all the groups responded and whether there were differences in how the children spoke about agency (the ability to influence or make decisions about learning) as compared to their teachers, administrators, and parents.

As we went through the project, we noticed that teachers always considered raising hands as an act of agency. They considered this a choice that children could make, and they liked this version of a choice. Children disagreed. They thought it did not count as a choice. As one child explained, "We don't get to decide if we get called on or not."

These cultural responses to the same practice can also be more serious. Teachers often expressed doubt that their students could handle the amount of agency the children used in the film. Parents worried about safety when children

Bauml (2011) devoted a section of her paper to a description of her processes of data analysis. She began by referring to the analytic memos she had written during data collection, combing through all the data resources to assign codes. Later she read through the data within assigned codes to identify subcategories. Bauml addressed the trustworthiness of her study with this statement:

> I have attempted to substantiate trustworthiness of the conclusions with the use of multiple data sources, member checks, peer debriefing, prolonged engagement, and researcher reflexivity. In addition, I maintained an audit trail of preliminary analyses, initial interpretations, questions, and reflections . . . I tested the preliminary patterns and themes . . . with a thorough search for disconfirming evidence.
>
> (p. 230)

could make a lot of the decisions. But parents also really wanted their children to be able to help out their friends and classmates without having to get permission first. Children wanted to help their friends too but felt like that would be "being a bad student." Children often told us that "learning is quiet."

These kinds of differences have serious implications for early childhood education. If some groups are being told that learning is about sitting still and being quiet and others are being told that learning is experimenting and asking lots of questions, how can that be fair? Video-cued ethnography has been a way for me to uncover and unpack how culture and power play a role in what we offer young children at school.

In summary, both of these studies were marked by attention to trustworthiness in the descriptions of the methods. While Bauml's (2011) study is marked by more prolonged engagement, the methods used in both studies allowed the researchers to offer thick, rich descriptions of the lived experiences of their participants.

Quantitative Studies

As described, quantitative researchers' interests collect around variables that might promise the ability to predict and control. Each of these purposes is exemplified in our study set.

Recall that Hojnoski et al. (2014) developed an intervention to help parents engage in dialogic book reading practices focused on math talk. Similar to Doubet and Ostrosky (2015), Hojnoski and colleagues advertised in public settings to locate participants for the study. In this case their outlets included both child care centers and public library facilities. They achieved a sample of six parent–child pairs.

Parents were asked to read three books, chosen by the researchers, to their children during each week of the study, using a digital recorder so that transcripts could be produced. The researchers analyzed data by pulling out the utterances in the transcripts that were extratextual— meaning outside of the text in the books.

Researcher Perspective

Martha Buell, Ph.D.,
University of Delaware

How I've used research to find out about kindergarten teachers' ideas about kindergarten readiness:

I am interested in the professional development (education and training) needs of preschool teachers. Because one of

They coded each utterance spoken by adults and children in regard to whether it had content related to math and what type of utterance it was (i.e., question, response, feedback, etc.).

This study (Hojnoski et al., 2014) was conducted as a single-subject, multiple-baseline design. Here we have a new type of methodology aimed at producing descriptive data. It worked like this. Two parent–child pairs spent a week in 'baseline' reading sessions. During baseline, the parents were free to read a mix of math-related and non-math books (provided by the researchers) in any manner they wanted. These two pairs shifted into the intervention after the first week. Another four pairs began baseline reading at the same time, but two of the pairs continued baseline for a second week before beginning the intervention, and the final two pairs continued baseline for 3 weeks before moving to the intervention. In other words, two parent–child pairs were shifted from baseline to the intervention at a time.

To describe the intervention briefly, the parents were initially provided training with a research assistant. During the intervention phase, they received guides along with the children's math-oriented books; the guides included key mathematical concepts in the text and suggestions for questions to use with their children. However, each week they also received a book with only a brief summary of the content. This was considered a 'generalization' book, used to examine if parents maintained a math talk focus without guidance.

The resulting data was portrayed with line graphs that displayed the percentage of utterances that contained math talk over the entirety of the study for each participating pair. We have included a set of graphs from the study in Figure 10.1. Additionally, in the results section of the research report, Hojnoski et al. (2014) wrote verbal descriptions of the trends evident for each parent–child pair.

the goals for preschool teachers and caregivers is to make sure that the children they work with arrive at kindergarten ready for success, ensuring that we provide them with a clear understanding of necessary *kindergarten readiness* skills is a priority. Unfortunately, there is not a great deal of consensus around what constitutes *kindergarten readiness*. This is due, in part, to the fact that kindergarten has changed over time, moving from a focus on social skills and feeling comfortable being away from home to a focus on academic instruction.

Thus, in order to get a clearer picture of what has changed and what has remained the same, we examined data on kindergarten teachers' perspectives on *kindergarten readiness*. We started with administrative data that was collected in 2000, and replicated many of the readiness questions in surveys we conducted for the state in 2010 and 2013. All three surveys were administered through an Internet survey sent to all the kindergarten teachers in our state. The questions on the survey gave us both quantitative and qualitative data. The quantitative data included ratings on 1) the importance of assessment data on various developmental/academic skills and 2) specific readiness skills. Data on the importance of assessment information was generated by asking the teachers if it would be helpful to have assessment data on the following domains of development for the children upon kindergarten entry: language, academic, social, and physical. We collected information on the importance of specific skills by giving the teachers a list of 20 *readiness* skills and asking them to rank in order their top five skills. The qualitative data came from a question asking teachers to describe in their own words the term *kindergarten readiness*. We then coded this qualitative data into categories, and compiled tallies of each category for each year, essentially turning

The obvious question is how these descriptive data are interpreted. One reason for doing a multiple-baseline study is to see if there are repeated patterns across participants. In addition, because the generalization books were marked by an 'x,' one can look for patterns there. The graphs displayed in Figure 10.1 are not the graphs of a researcher's dreams (which would have low baseline values and then soaring intervention values). We can see that throughout the study, these parent–child pairs varied widely in regard to what percentage of their utterances contained math talk. Hojnoski et al. (2014) presented a measure devised to interpret these forms of data called the 'percentage of nonoverlapping data,' or PND. To determine this value, the researcher locates the highest data point reached during baseline and then calculates what percentage of data points during the intervention phase were higher than this value. In this study, the PNDs for parents ranged from 6% to 81%. Obviously, one problem with this measure is that one quite high value during the baseline, even if it is unmatched during this phase of the study, sets the bar for the PND during intervention; this is how the 6% we just reported occurred. With this study, we see that purely descriptive data are not always easily interpretable in the quantitative paradigm when the typical focus is identifying significant findings through statistical analyses.

Turning to the study conducted by Swartz and Easterbrooks (2014), we have an example of extensive survey methodology. The focus of this study was on providers' and parents' perceptions of each other. Therefore, after providers were recruited, the researchers had to ensure that at least one parent participant could be matched

the qualitative data into quantitative data for our analysis.

Our results gave us an interesting picture of continuity and change. Over time, teachers' ratings of assessment information's importance increased. In 2000, 84% of teachers identified wanting assessment data on language skills, followed by social skills at 74%. By 2013 over 90% of the teachers wanted assessment data on all four domains. While the importance of assessment data grew over time, the top five most important individual readiness skills stayed the same. The number one most important readiness skill across time was "the ability to take care of one's own bathroom needs." From the qualitative data, we found that both developmental maturity and academic skills have become more prevalent over time to the kindergarten teachers.

So what does this mean for our work? First, this data gives us insight into the importance of assessment. The ECE workforce must know how to collect, record, and interpret assessment information, to help them meet curricular needs and to support the kindergarten transition of the children in their care. We also learned that while supporting pre-academics is important, the most critical skills children need for kindergarten readiness include caring for their own needs and social maturity. So while there is much new content we must include when we offer professional development for the ECE workforce, much of what has always been important for readiness remains the same.

to each provider (the average number of parents per provider was 2). The respondents based their survey answers upon the particulars of their relationship with an individual parent or provider.

The entire data collection took place through a packet of questionnaires distributed to the participants. In some cases, there were versions of surveys that included similar content tailored

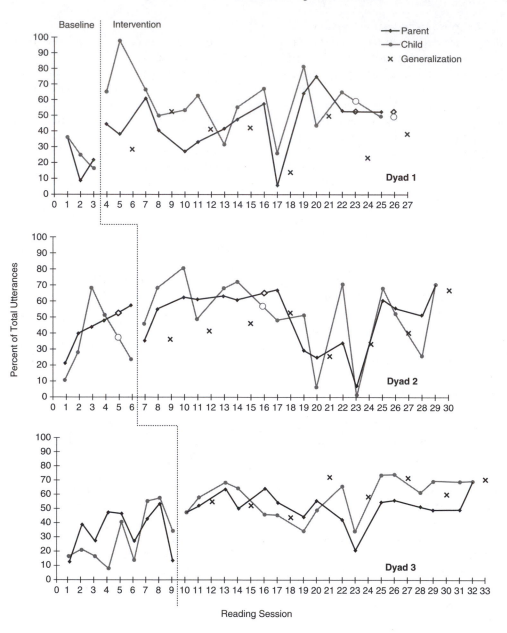

Figure 10.1 Percentage of Parent and Child Math Utterances across Baseline and Intervention Reading Sessions

Source: Hojnoski, R. L., Columba, H. L., & Polignano, J. (2014). Embedding mathematical dialogue in parent–child shared book reading: A preliminary investigation. *Early Education and Development, 25*, 469–492.

to the particular respondent group. For example, there were parent and provider versions of surveys about background/demographic information. Also, both providers and parents completed appropriate versions of surveys that assessed their perceptions of partnership and communication behaviors demonstrated by themselves and the other, as well as appropriate versions of another survey that assessed the quality of their relationships with each other (Swartz & Easterbrooks, 2014).

Each respondent group also completed unique surveys. Thus, the parents completed a survey about their use of child care with the child currently enrolled and any others. Their anxiety about separating from their child was assessed with another survey. In addition, they completed a survey that listed a number of descriptive words and phrases about children; these descriptors were sorted by content experts into 'difficult' and 'not difficult' categories. The one measure completed by providers only assessed their knowledge of child development (Swartz & Easterbrooks, 2014).

The researchers used regression analyses to test each of the questions and hypotheses posed for the study. Recall from Chapter 8 that the purpose of regression is to examine the degree to which a variable can be predicted based upon dependent variables.

In summary, one can see how much more predetermined these studies were in comparison to our qualitative examples. These studies reflected the interests of quantitative researchers described earlier.

Potential, Pitfalls, and Limitations

In all of the examples of research that we have examined, the researchers focused on ways of knowing adults that aligned with the working expectations in their paradigms. Doubet and Ostrosky (2015) and Bauml (2011) provided thick, rich description of adults that illustrated how they might be known in their own words and through a close understanding of their actions.

Both quantitative research groups framed their work around the adults in children's lives while acknowledging that these adults might positively impact children. For example, Hojnoski et al. (2014) concluded that "strategies to support early mathematical development that are acceptable to parents . . . offer an important and innovative approach to increasing parental involvement in this domain of development" (p. 489). Swartz and Easterbrooks (2014) concluded, "positive relationships among children, families, and providers are crucial to quality of care and positive outcomes for children" (p. 595). This last study was unique among the group in its effort to examine two important adult groups in the lives of children in relation to each other.

What are the pitfalls to be found in this group of studies? As we did in Chapter 9, we can look at pitfalls that could be foreseen and not foreseen.

The regression analyses selected by Swartz and Easterbrooks (2014) do not allow for us to determine the direction of effects; remember that previously we cautioned that correlation is not causation. If variables are related, we cannot ascertain that one led to the other or vice versa. For instance, the researchers found that parents who had higher levels of anxiety about placing their children in child care viewed their relationships with the provider less favorably. But did their more negative views of these relationships stem from the fact that they were less secure about using child care? Or did they express more anxious views about using child care because they had worse relationships with the providers? Swartz and Easterbrooks raised the example we have just described as one of the cautions about their analytic strategy. To us, this illustrates a potential pitfall for consumers of research; they must be aware of what can and cannot be interpreted from the data and analyses.

Another foreseen pitfall is that quantitative researchers have limited understandings of the contexts within which their participants live, dependent upon the data they have collected.

Thus, we do not know how the parents in the Swartz and Easterbrooks study (2014) located their child care agency or what they were looking for during this search and what mattered most to them. Indeed, almost 200 parents participated in the study, and what we know about them is circumscribed by the measured variables and the limits of how deeply one can investigate with a sample of that size. Nor do we know about the typical book-sharing practices of the parent–child pairs in the Hojnoski et al. (2014) study.

Other pitfalls were unforeseen. It can be extremely difficult to locate a sample via posting information publicly, the strategy followed by Doubet and Ostrosky (2015) and Hojnoskiki et al. (2014). As it turned out, Doubet and Ostrosky formed a sample of families that was small but reflected various family structures, varying educational backgrounds, and varying geographical locations, although almost all were white. The resulting sample in the Hojnoski and colleagues study were almost all college-educated and of higher socioeconomic status, representing a more homogenous group. Interestingly, half of the children in this study had individual education plans in their preschool settings, although the researchers did not have much more information about their services and/or special needs. This represents a higher percentage of children than one would expect by chance. To some degree, sampling involves luck! As another bit of bad luck, one parent–child pair dropped out of the Hojnoski and colleagues study a couple weeks into the intervention phase. The child was "not interested" in the reading sessions (p. 478), reflecting a hazard with research involving young children. To the degree that research with adults, particularly intervention-focused research, might also involve child participants, the researcher can be affected by the free will of young children who are not well equipped to consider continuing for the sake of the research endeavor, something adults might be more inclined to do.

We include one last example as an unforeseen pitfall, although in actuality we are not sure of how this issue became embedded in the research. It illustrates how reading closely can raise questions for the consumer. Doubet and Ostrosky (2015) quite clearly identified their research within the qualitative paradigm. Their presentation of methods and findings fit conventional ways of operating for qualitative researchers. Yet within their discussion of study limitations, they brought up the topic of generalizability more than once. They noted that locating participants from a wider geographical area might have increased the generalizability of the findings. They also remarked that utilizing other methodological options, such as triangulating their interview data with observations and prolonged field engagement, might affect generalizability. Recall in Chapter 4 that we explained generalizability is typically not a consideration for qualitative researchers; they acknowledge that the unique nature of context is important for meaning making. While drawing upon the concept of generalizability does not necessarily represent a 'fatal flaw' for this study, a consumer should be aware that if generalizability is the goal, there are other research methods better suited for the researcher's choice than in-depth, semistructured interviews with a smaller sample.

On the other hand, since Doubet and Ostrosky (2015) included lack of prolonged engagement as a limitation of their study, we will second that in our discussion of limitations. Qualitative studies do feature much smaller samples, but the trade-off is typically the extensive nature of the data collected, and this does require a longer time spent with participants.

We previously mentioned the challenges of finding participants in a couple of these studies. An invariable limitation of research is the consideration of who participates. Research depends upon volunteers, and consumers should always look carefully at sampling procedures and the nature of the participants to consider, 'Just who volunteers for this type of involvement?' For instance, the large number of child care centers utilized by Swartz and Easterbrooks (2014) were part of a volunteer training program study. They discussed in their Limitations section that this "poses a potential challenge to the generalizability of the findings" (p. 594).

Finally, we noted at the outset of this chapter that ultimately, researchers interested in questions about the adults in children's lives are often interested in the impact of these adults on children's development, learning, and/or well-being. Sometimes studies are extensive enough that they collect data to complete this chain from adult to children, but often this is not the case. Thus, for instance, we do not know if the children in the Hojnoski et al. (2014) study benefitted from the intervention, although the researchers stated, "the increases in math talk may have the potential to increase children's mathematical vocabulary and concept development" (p. 485). Consumers need to be aware that this point is purely conjecture and not treat it as a conclusion of the study.

Summary

In this chapter, we have used four examples of research in which the focus was on the adults in children's lives. We illustrated how qualitative researchers ask questions and generate data for thick, rich description. We also illustrated how quantitative researchers use survey data and interventions to pursue questions about positively impacting the processes of parenting and educating. While pointing out pitfalls and limitations, our goal has been to increase the readers' ability to think deeply about studies. In reality, all studies have pitfalls and limitations; in science, as in life, perfection is an extremely rare phenomenon. This does not, however, render research meaningless, except in the extreme cases in which flaws do become 'fatal.'

In the following chapters, we move to new units of analyses that take us past knowing individuals. Groups and processes will take center stage.

11

RESEARCH QUESTIONS ABOUT CLASSROOMS AND CURRICULUM

In this chapter we highlight the work of researchers attempting to understand and/or explain how classrooms work, including the interactions within classrooms and the enactment of curriculum. In the qualitative paradigm, we will focus upon the use of ethnographic methods to understand children's experiences with their peers and their experiences within the framework of the enacted curriculum. In the quantitative paradigm, we will focus upon observational methods and upon the input/output models applied to explain curricular and instructional effectiveness. As in the previous chapter, we will discuss how the interests and questions of researchers within the two paradigms result in different research emphases.

What Interests Researchers?

What happens within early childhood settings is of paramount importance to many stakeholders and so is of prime interest to researchers. Our emphasis here is on understanding both how classrooms work and what works within classrooms.

Qualitative researchers' questions will focus on the intricacies of interpersonal relationships between the teachers and children or among the children and the meaning that teachers and children give to shared learning experiences. For example, qualitative researchers may ask:

- How do teachers interpret and respond to children in the classroom?
- What happens in a classroom when or during . . . (insert a teaching strategy or curricular approach here)?
- How do a teacher and a group of children develop shared classroom cultures?
- How do children and teachers describe their learning?
- How does teachers' cultural background and/or use of power shape unique practices and beliefs in classrooms?
- What types of inclusionary and exclusionary behaviors are used by children and teachers in a classroom setting? How do the children and teachers understand these behaviors?

In qualitative research, questions are asked that require an understanding of the qualities of a classroom experience, curricular model, or interpersonal interactions. These are situated in a particular context, which is described in detail. Note that our example questions focus on 'what' and 'how.' The questions also are open ended, allowing researchers to look at a topic or issue in the classroom from different lenses. Thus, they can explore, uncover, and/or illuminate the processes, details, and multiple meanings of a lived classroom experience.

Questions about classrooms and curriculum that can be asked by quantitative researchers include:

- How effective are these teaching approaches or curricula for children's learning and development? What is the developmental impact of a certain curriculum model on children?
- What effect does the classroom composition have on children's academic achievement?
- How do groups of children experiencing different teaching approaches compare on outcome measures?

These questions often are considered so that the classroom practice being evaluated or the interactions being studied can be implemented on a wider level with some promise of effectiveness.

Asking Questions

Here we have chosen four studies to show the differences in questions and methodologies depending upon the paradigm used. Each of the four research groups attempted to understand what was happening in classrooms with teachers and children but through very different lenses. To help illustrate the differences, we have paired the studies.

Two of the studies focus on the common activities of storytelling and play in preschools. In the qualitative study of Edwards et al. (2014), in which data collection spanned 10 years, we are exposed to how a particular preschool in Pistoia, Italy, becomes a cultural center for the young through play with books, storytelling, and imaginative activities. The main question guiding the overall study was 'How does the learning environment at the Italian preschool, Filastrocca, focus on building children's language and literacy through imaginative interaction with books and storytelling?' However, as mentioned earlier, as is typical of qualitative studies in which there are often subquestions that fine-tune an overall question, there were a series of four more detailed questions that guided the study. Briefly, the research team framed their work around the following: (1) What types of activities related to books, storytelling, and the imagination were part of the learning environment? (2) How did this environment reflect the school's mission? (3) What themes emerged from gathering information from the school? (4) How can we interpret these themes in relation to North American research literature on 'best practices' in literacy?

In the quantitative study by Nicolopoulou, Cortina, Ilgaz, Cates, and de Sá (2015), the researchers explored story and play in American preschool classrooms. Their focus, however, was to examine the effects of teaching practices on young children in relation to their development in oral language, literacy, and social competence. The researchers asked if the storytelling and story-acting process, as designed by Vivian Paley, used as a curriculum module within randomly assigned classrooms, would enhance the abilities of the children in these aforementioned areas. They hypothesized that the more children participated in this activity, the greater their growth in the areas of language, literacy, and social competence across the school year. Each study asked something about story and play. While the qualitative approach explored how children learned through story and play within a context of a particular culture and context, the quantitative approach investigated the results of a particular type of storytelling curriculum.

The other two studies focused specifically on adult–child interactions and teacher behaviors within classrooms. In a qualitative study, Blank and Schneider (2011) examined the language practices teachers used during conflictual situations between kindergarten children, highlighting how conflict events in early childhood classrooms have contradictory assumptions and meaning. This study was based on examining the very common phrase 'use your words' that many teachers use when teaching children to solve problems. Blank and Schneider connected this phrase to the formal conceptualization of developmentally appropriate practice as promulgated by the National Association for the Education of Young Children. The guiding questions for the study were: "What are the ways conflicts are dealt with in early childhood classrooms? And how does that translate to language practices?" (Blank & Schneider, p. 200). Working from a critical theory perspective, the researchers' aim was to disrupt the common framing and language around conflicts used by Western teachers in classrooms and to question how these practices create contradictions.

In a quantitative study by Cabell, DeCoster, LoCasale-Crouch, Hamre, and Pianta (2013), the researchers examined teacher behavior by measuring the effectiveness of teacher instructional interactions using a specific instrument called the Classroom Assessment Scoring System—or CLASS. Like Blank and Schneider (2011), these researchers desired to understand interactions between teachers and children in the classroom. Their research aims were driven by their use of an instrument that conceptualizes teaching as being more or less effective. They used the instrument to measure instructional practices across classroom settings (such as large group and free play) and across learning activities (such as literacy, science, math, social studies, and esthetics). They did not pose hypotheses but described their study as exploratory. The authors noted, "we were . . . trying to understand the nature of the differences in instructional interactions across settings and activities" (p. 827).

Again, while both research teams investigated classroom interactions between teachers and children, their foci and purposes were very different. The qualitative study employed a critical lens to question a practice that seems common and appropriate for early childhood settings, while the quantitative study analyzed numerically coded teaching effectiveness levels in classrooms as associated with different teaching/learning contexts.

Choosing Methods

To understand the complexities of what goes on in early childhood settings between teachers and children requires extensive, complex, and thoughtful methods to finding answers to our questions. In this section, we will reveal the details of how the highlighted research studies on classroom experiences were designed and conducted.

Qualitative Studies

Using methods that create a full, rich description of the inner workings of a classroom is a main feature of qualitative studies in early childhood education. Here we have two examples of how qualitative research can examine larger contextual and societal dimensions of early learning while delving deep into the details of that lived experience. In the study of a school in Italy, Edwards et al. (2014) recognized that many educators in the field of early childhood are interested in understanding different educational approaches through engaging in international investigation and discussion around unique educational experiences. To contribute to that conversation, Edwards and colleagues chose to design a qualitative case study of a public preschool in Pistoia, Italy. The researchers identified the school setting as worthy of being researched based on a "purposeful sampling" (p. 22) in which it was deemed an exceptional case because it was so different from typical early learning settings in the United States.

A cross-national/cross-cultural team of researchers and practitioners (Italy and United States) contributed to the study. Multiple visits by the researchers were made over several days at a time, periodically for a decade. Interviews were recorded of the school practitioners and administrators, and video observations were also recorded. Documents such as parent handbooks and public presentations by school members were collected. In addition, pictures and videos of classroom artifacts—puppets and toys—were collected. Given the goal of a qualitative case study to provide rich descriptions of the context and practices within a school or classroom over a significant amount of time, Edwards et al. (2014) made a substantial effort toward that.

Collecting the data was just one part of putting together a cohesive and detailed description of the preschool. The researchers acknowledged that in qualitative research, data collection and analysis are not two distinct or separate steps but rather constitute processes that intertwine and occur simultaneously. They described their 'spiral' analysis as first beginning with material collected during a visit to the school in 2001. In their case study, the data was coded, and codes were listed and then reviewed for interpretation. The researchers noted that they employed the following strategies contributing to the trustworthiness of their interpretations: prolonged engagement (the study lasted 10 years), triangulation (using multiple data sources), thick description, peer debriefing (by presenting their ideas to other educators and researchers for feedback and questioning and clarification of ideas) and member checking among the research team and other Italian experts. What resulted is a comprehensive description of the school in relation to books, stories, and imagination. The report included details regarding the philosophy of the city and school community about young children's learning as meaning making and the history

Researcher Perspective

Amy Noelle Parks, Ph.D., Michigan State University

Before I became a researcher, I worked as a teacher in elementary schools that served many students from low-income and racial-minority families. When I entered graduate school, I was deeply shocked by the ways that these children and their families were routinely characterized in research. Much of the literature related to early mathematics focused on what these students did not know, could not do, and what their families could not provide. I found few studies that described the strengths these children brought into classrooms or the ways that schooling practices themselves made it more difficult for children and families from historically marginalized populations to engage with schools in general and with mathematics in particular. I knew I wanted my own research to take up those two challenges: documenting student strengths and articulating ways that common schooling practices disadvantaged some students. In doing this work, I have designed studies around questions such as:

- How do teacher questioning practices shape children's opportunities to engage with mathematics in a diverse third-grade classroom?
- In what ways does a scripted curriculum constrain children's opportunities to engage with important mathematics in a preschool classroom?
- How do young children experience mathematics assessment interviews?

The research methods I used to answer these questions come out of ethnographic traditions and are designed to help researchers understand their participants' experiences. In my case, this means I try to tell the story of classrooms and assessment and culture of the city. The researchers also provided outlines and description of the physical environment of the school including learning spaces and materials, the routines and rules that created the lived daily experiences of the children and families of the school, and examples of children's work and play. The themes that emerged from the case study demonstrated how early language and literacy development of children in this unique setting could be understood as a way of rediscovering and preserving traditions such as folktales, with storytelling as a cultural art form and books as objects of pleasure. Additionally, Edwards et al. (2014) described literacy learning through the sharing of the larger community and within an atmosphere of magic. Language and literacy learning in this case study came to life in a holistic view of a community.

The other qualitative study highlighted here by Blank and Schneider (2011) examined conflict resolution. The researchers collected data with one teacher and one kindergarten classroom of children over a 2-week period. While the time of data collection was not as lengthy as the Edwards et al. (2014) study, we will see how examining the details of the day-to-day interactions between and among teachers and children can also illuminate classroom experiences in early childhood.

Taking a critical lens, first, the authors framed the concept of conflict as a language practice, introducing the common phrase teachers use when conflicts arise in early childhood settings (i.e., 'use your words') as a cultural practice (Blank & Schneider, 2011). Then the authors discussed the impact of the construct of developmentally appropriate practices (DAP) which they contended influenced the teacher to use language to end conflict, but not to help mediate children's language to help resolve the conflict. Blank and Schneider then framed the classroom practice of teachers helping children with conflicts as a culturally constructed activity. This supported the reader to consider that the

interviews from the perspectives of children. Practically, this means I spend a lot of time sitting close to the children and writing down everything they say and do—which we call 'taking field notes'— and I spend a lot of time video recording, which helps me revisit moments again and again to make sense of them. Because I am interested in children's experiences, I try to keep my camera focused on the children rather than on the teacher.

My methods belong to a qualitative methodological family often called 'interpretive' and are concerned with how human beings make sense of social interactions. For example, in my assessment study, I was less concerned with showing which mathematical tasks the children got right or wrong than with helping readers understand how the interview felt to the children. I found that some children showed significant discomfort during interviews, which typically is not described in large, quantitative assessment interview studies. In the written report, I examined the ways that the children's interpretation of me—a strange, white adult asking them to do mathematics tasks—might have shaped their participation in the interviews. My hope is that a study like this can help practitioners and researchers read other assessment studies with consideration for the context under which the findings were produced and to think about the ways that context can impact assessment study results, particularly when researchers are working with children across lines of race and class difference and making claims about what they do and do not know.

Overall, my goal is to draw researchers' and practitioners' attention away from curricula, standards, assessments, and schedules and toward the experiences of children. I hope this shift in attention will work to create an educational experience that is both more humane and more intellectually engaging.

language used in conflicts in early childhood classrooms should not be taken for granted or assumed to be 'correct'. Hence, Blank and Schneider's goal of exploring contradictions in how teachers act is contextualized in the larger discourse of conflict and DAP.

Seeking to reveal contradictions and complications of practice, Blank and Schneider (2011) situated the study in one kindergarten classroom and focused on the language used surrounding the values, rituals, and everyday lived experiences. So how does a researcher begin to collect data with these intentions? Blank and Schneider began by establishing a relationship with the classroom teacher. They first interviewed the teacher to find out how she conceptualized conflict and how her classroom functioned. In the next phase of the study, the researchers observed the classroom and gave the teacher a recorder to also tape conflict events in the class. Observations of classroom conflicts were conducted by the researchers, which they combined with the teacher interviews and tape recordings of classroom interactions. From this data, the researchers were able to identify conflict events that occurred between children during class time in which the teacher intervened. A cross-case analysis of these events was conducted to determine the unique sequences of actions among the teacher and children. This data collection resulted in detailed vignettes of the teacher and children interacting. The researchers conducted a content analysis of the language used by labeling the types of language and documenting the number of times similar intents were used by the teacher. For example, some of these types of language were "determining cause" and "eliciting information" (p. 205). Using the critical lens of questioning discourse, Blank and Schneider described how conflict intervention by a teacher requesting children to 'use their words' to deal with conflict functioned more to maintain control and compliance than to empower children. Also, the language convention led to forced apologies and a regulation of negative emotions. Ultimately, the researchers deduced that while the teacher identified conflict as an opportunity for teaching, the ways in which she interacted with the children sent a message that conflict was destructive and should be smoothed over rather than having a life cycle of ongoing dialogue. Such attention to the small details of these teacher–child interactions allowed us to see what before may have been hidden under the surface of prescribed or accepted practice.

In both of these examples, we have seen how detailed examinations of teaching practice can be conducted. The case study of Edwards et al. (2014) was extensive and thus ripe with information from which the researchers made meaning. Blank and Schneider (2011) collected a more limited body of data but made meaning by examining it closely.

Quantitative Studies

Political and educational discussions often tend to focus heavily on 'what works' in schools and classrooms. Quantitative study designs allow researchers to compare programs and practices, look for relationships between what teachers do and the outcomes of children's learning, and help us evaluate or make judgments about curriculum or teaching strategies. In the two quantitative studies that are the focus in this chapter, we are able to see how standardized observational tools and child assessments address these questions.

Nicolopoulou et al. (2015) wanted to know what effect Vivian Paley's story-acting and storytelling (STSA) had for the learning and development of low-income preschoolers. To identify the effects STSA had on young children, the researchers needed to collect assessments of children who had been exposed to the STSA curriculum (the experimental group) as well as those who had NOT been exposed to the STSA curriculum (the control group). The researchers began with six ECE classrooms, half of which were randomly assigned to use the STSA curriculum. After running the study for a year, the researchers invited the teachers in the control group to become a treatment group and recruited four new classrooms. Each classroom participated in the STSA curriculum for only a year. Altogether, 216 children participated in the classrooms, but a much smaller group, only 149, had a full set of data and thus constituted the sample for analysis.

A research team collected pretests (before the study/intervention) and post-tests (after the study/intervention) from the children. The children were assessed individually on measures of expressive vocabulary, comprehension of narratives, decoding skills, and pretend abilities. The children were also observed for brief periods of time (3-minute periods at two different points in time at pretest and again at posttest). Using observational information, they were rated on measures of peer play and self-regulation. In addition, the researchers kept track of how often the children in the STSA groups participated in the STSA activities by narrating stories to see if greater participation in STSA impacted assessment scores.

Nicolopoulou et al. (2015) analyzed their data with a hierarchical linear model since children were nested in classrooms. Overall, the findings revealed that in many areas, children who did participate in STSA did better on the assessments, and greater participation in the STSA was related to higher scores on the outcome measures.

Recall that Cabell et al. (2013) used the CLASS instrument to measure effectiveness of teacher–child interactions. In this study, the researchers utilized data from 314 preschool teachers of children from low-income backgrounds. The data had been collected previously as part of a larger project. In this paper, the researchers reported a 'secondary' analysis. This means that the questions for the study were not necessarily a part of the original project aims. As is often the case, however, once a large body of data exists, researchers can look to find new questions that might be addressed. In this study, the researchers wanted to know in which activities and in which settings the teachers utilized more effective strategies for teaching young children.

Researcher Perspective

Gary Bingham, Ph.D., Georgia State University

What are best practices for early childhood educators to engage in to promote the language and literacy development of young children? This is a question that I have attempted to answer during the last decade of my career. To address this question, I have conducted various professional development projects aimed at improving the quality of language and literacy practices (such as teacher read-alouds and phonological awareness instruction) teachers provide children as well as publishing papers on how children develop these skills. This work is important because children's exposure to high-quality language and literacy environments in the years before formal schooling sets a strong foundation for later academic success.

Despite my research demonstrating positive effects of these professional development projects, I became troubled by the lack of meaningful literacy practices that I was seeing in classrooms. I noticed that even when teachers received intensive support through professional development and coaching (either face to face in their classrooms or online through a website with interactive features), some teachers still had difficulty implementing instructional approaches in ways that were high quality and that 'moved' children's language or literacy development.

My experiences led me to an awareness that what was missing in these classrooms were ways for children to use their emerging literacy skills in meaningful ways. One of the most meaningful ways that children can learn literacy skills is by being encouraged and supported in early writing activities. Despite professional recommendations about the importance

The CLASS itself was designed to assess teachers' behaviors in three areas. The areas are emotional support (how sensitively a teacher responds to the children), classroom organization (including behavior management and productivity), and instructional support (concept development, quality of feedback, and language modeling). Only the instructional support area was used for this study, along with an additional measure of teachers' use of literacy decoding teaching strategies (Cabell et al., 2013). The data was collected during a single-day visit to each classroom. In general, the CLASS is used by observing the classroom for 15 minutes and then using 10 minutes to score the instrument; this constitutes a cycle. The body of data for this study included two to six cycles per classroom, with a mode (most frequent) number of cycles being four. The settings were also coded by the data collectors using the following categories: large group, small group, free choice, meals, routines, recess, and individual time. The focus of the learning activities was coded as well during these observations. A learning activity could be coded as read to, letter/sound learning, writing, math, science, social studies, esthetics, or no learning activity.

Cabell et al. (2013) used linear models to analyze the data since CLASS cycles were nested within classrooms. Their aim was to compare group differences in instructional effectiveness and literacy instruction (the dependent variables) for the independent variables of settings and learning activities. They found, for instance, that teachers' language modeling was similar in large group, free choice, and meals, all of which were significantly higher than language modeling during routines. They also found that science activities were associated with higher instructional strategy scores.

In each quantitative study, we see the necessity for large bodies of data, an intensive data collection process, and an even more statistically complex analysis of the data

of promoting writing in early childhood classrooms, relatively little research examines how teachers design environments that impact children's early writing development. Hence, my current recent research seeks to understand (a) how to measure teachers' support of children's early writing development to ensure that we can help teachers improve such practices and (b) what practices and experiences matter the most to children's writing development.

To address the first question, 'How do we best measure writing environments and practices in early childhood classrooms?' my colleague, Hope Gerde, and I validated a measure for assessing teachers' writing practices. Comprehensive observations in 68 classrooms in three U.S. states led us to develop a writing classroom assessment, WRITE, that assesses the following: classroom writing environment, environmental print, teacher modeling of writing, teacher scaffolding of child writing, and independent child writing. Results using this tool indicate that teachers vary widely in their material and instructional supports of writing in preschool classrooms. Although preschool teachers generally provide a variety of materials to support children's writing, including a well-equipped writing center, they engage in few modeling or scaffolding strategies to support children's writing development. Analysis of the quality of writing in classrooms and children's writing development suggests that teachers who provided more environmental supports for writing and engaged in more interactions to support children's writing had children with higher writing achievement across the school year.

In a follow-up study, we sought to better understand which specific behaviors teachers engaged in that promoted children's writing development. In this study,

139

to consider the many ways to look for correlations between behaviors and outcomes. We also can see how powerful the assessment tools are in framing what it means to be 'effective' in early childhood classrooms.

Potential, Pitfalls, and Limitations

What knowledge have these examples of qualitative and quantitative studies on classroom or curriculum research provided us? Each study was generative in the sense that each helped the reader examine classroom practices in new or previously unconsidered ways. Edwards et al. (2014), through engaging with a school community for a decade, were able to illustrate a way of teaching and learning with young children inside a classroom many of us may never actually see, but we are given the opportunity to imagine something different. Blank and Schneider (2011) were able to explicate a common practice in teaching young children and help question our assumptions about what that

we looked for ways in which teachers supported or scaffolded children's writing in the following domains: composing, spelling, and handwriting. We found that teachers provide infrequent support at a relatively low level (e.g., reminding them to write their names or telling them how to spell a word). Unfortunately, teachers supported children very little in connecting their thoughts (oral language) to written language (composing) but did provide some assistance with spelling and handwriting. Interestingly, examinations of children's writing skill revealed that children from classrooms with teachers who supported composing exhibited stronger writing skills. Taken together with the previous study, these findings suggest that teachers need to spend more time providing children with meaningful writing opportunities that support how children compose and less attention to the mechanics of writing (handwriting and copying).

practice might actually mean. Nicolopoulou et al. (2015) were able to show that a holistic and playful teaching practice such as storytelling and story-acting can have a positive impact on children's assessment in language, literacy, and social development. Cabell et al. (2013) helped us see how looking at specific learning activities and settings is utilized differently by teachers. In each study, we were are given data that helps reveal a new way of thinking about classroom life. However, for each study, the research processes of finding answers and insights had pitfalls that require further consideration on the part of a reader. We consider these pitfalls here.

We imagine the delicate balance required between Italian and American perceptions and interpretations in coming to a consensus on meaning in the Edwards et al. (2014) study. This research team acknowledged this, as well as that over the 10 years of study, the programs themselves changed. Since this study was carried out over such a long period of time, perceptions of the classroom activities changed and deepened as well, impacting the eventual findings of the study. This is a good example of attending to contextualization and how this greatly impacts the perspectives taken to the study data.

One of the pitfalls of work in the critical paradigm, such as the study by Blank and Schneider (2011), is that while it helps us understand the 'underside' of practice, it also can leave readers feeling a sense of frustration in terms of 'what next?' If these practices now seem questionable, what are the alternatives? How do we move forward thinking about what to do with children in classrooms? There are also unanswered questions—does the 'use your words' convention inevitably lead to practices that shut down ongoing conflict rather than allowing for exploration of it? Is it always a means of control? Because qualitative research is conceptualized as local, readers must be thoughtful in their consideration of the meaning they make of the results and any implications or applications of the findings that may follow.

In the study by Nicolopoulou et al. (2015), we note a potential pitfall for readers who might not closely follow the study description. The researchers began their description of the sample by characterizing it as consisting of 216 children. However, later they noted that there was high attrition from the classrooms, resulting in 149 children who had both pretest and posttest data and who served as the subgroup analyzed for this report. This feels like the 'fine print' in the sense that this is information that is essential to understanding the study that the reader would not necessarily learn without a careful further reading of the study. The authors report the attrition according to accepted convention, but crucial information could be left out of a reader's understanding if each section of the study is not carefully read.

Another potential pitfall exists with the measures utilized by Nicolopoulou et al. (2015). They accurately described some of their measures as being adapted or developed by their research team. This is another place for readers to take note. These measures have not been examined for their validity (recall this discussion in Chapter 4). We do not have evidence of how well these instruments measure what the researchers intended for them to measure. Thus, readers would do well to consider what children were asked to do in the assessments and ponder what meaning to ascribe to the measures. Of course, we would caution that it is always important to consider the question, 'Just what is being assessed here?'

As researchers who are familiar with the CLASS instrument, we found ourselves noting that many if not most readers would be missing information that would assist their understanding of the Cabell et al. (2013) study. Throughout the report, the researchers conceptualized the CLASS (and so the constructs being studied) as measuring teaching effectiveness. Without knowing more about the instrument, however, readers know only that teaching strategies were considered more or less effective—but how does the instrument define this? This reflects how being more of an 'outsider' can make it difficult to make meaning of research. And to assuage readers who are left with little to go on, we will briefly describe the instrument's definitions. The CLASS characterizes less effective teaching interactions as those focused on repetition of rote knowledge, with minimal feedback (consisting solely, for example, of the occasional "good job") and few opportunities for children to converse and hear complex language. The instrument characterizes more effective teaching strategies as those that facilitate children's reasoning and analysis (e.g., prediction, comparisons), provide ongoing feedback that scaffolds understanding, and offer extensive opportunities for children to talk with teachers and among themselves.

Next we consider the limitations of these studies in terms of what each can tell us about classroom practices or how the findings might be applied. In the Edwards et al. (2014) case study, readers are given information about the city and the school and some history of both. Yet it is impossible in a brief research article to provide enough information for others to fully understand the complexities of this context and the many ways in which it might both overlap and differ from the contexts of readers.

Blank and Schneider (2011) walked a fine line in their study because of their critical perspective. Working with a single teacher for data collection in a qualitative study often indicates a fairly close relationship. But if the researchers' purpose is to problematize the teacher's work, one can imagine the potential for tension. The ethics related to this relationship certainly played a part. Blank and Schneider interviewed the teacher at the start of the study. They did not utilize further interviews to learn the teacher's perspective about the particular incidents of conflict they analyzed. We do not know how they weighed this decision as researchers, but we imagine one thought may have been to create a space in which the teacher did not feel criticized through interview questions about specific practices.

Turning to our quantitative examples, we have noted in a previous chapter that direct assessments of young children offer a limited perspective of their abilities. In addition, Nicolopoulou et al. (2015) were able to assess only the older portion of their sample of children with one instrument (measuring three different skill areas) because the instrument was designed only for children 4 years olds and up. By 'respecting' the parameters of the instrument, they made the choice to lose data. The instruments Nicolopoulou et al. (2015) adapted for use as observation tools were scored based upon two different 3-minute observational periods at each data collection point. Readers can easily imagine the leap of faith necessary to assume that this small body of information represented the children fully. Finally, anyone who knows young children can imagine that they might react to direct assessment in various ways, some unlike adults. For instance, one of us witnessed an assessment in which the preschooler was being a parrot for the day and would only squawk. Luckily the assessment required only pointing on her part, which she did as she squawked! None of these limitations 'doom' the research, but they all indicate issues to keep in mind.

As quantitative researchers move into classrooms, they might, as in the case of Nicolopoulou et al. (2015), ask teachers to implement a new curriculum or teaching strategy. This can be fraught, as teachers may do this more or less faithfully. Nicolopoulou and colleagues noted that there was variation among teachers in how often they used STSA in their classrooms. Often researchers will attempt to counter this limitation by assessing the fidelity of implementation among classrooms and then using this as another variable in the analyses.

One final limitation of quantitative studies on classrooms and curriculum is that they do require rather extensive—and expensive—data collection efforts. Researchers need a critical mass of classrooms for statistical analyses, and each classroom contains many children. Because Cabell et al. (2013) observed interactions, they could collect data in many classrooms, although only one day in each. Nicolopoulou et al. (2015) had to assess many children across several classrooms. Some researchers deal with this expense by randomly selecting a small number of children per classroom to be assessed. However, readers who have had classrooms of their own can imagine the range of results that might be obtained by different samples of three particular children within the classroom. Children vary tremendously, and any small number of children will be found somewhere along a continuum of differences.

In sum, these studies show how the complexities of the human activity within a classroom are often difficult to define and difficult to capture. We believe that classrooms are extremely 'messy' places, meaning that the complexity within is enormous. And in order to capture these processes, researchers invariably slice off a piece of the whole or reduce the scope of what is being considered.

Summary

In classroom research in early childhood settings, we must contend with competing questions and questions that frame the research itself. Once again, we see that how we see the world is how we define the terms of our research. The very act of attempting to understand what is happening in the complicated worlds of teachers and children is fraught with potential missteps and miscalculations. Entering a classroom with the intention of understanding the 'whole' or even a small aspect of the experience is a challenge for the research and the participants. We often risk limiting our perspectives to only the adults' or researcher's point of view. More often than not, it is the children's voices, interests, and desires that are left out of classroom research—the very stakeholders many researchers would claim as being at the center of the work. Again, we are reminded that the process of research continues to unfold, and certainty is illusory.

12

RESEARCH QUESTIONS ABOUT INSTITUTIONS AND POLICY

In this chapter our unit of analysis is the institutions that serve young children and their families, and also the policies that frame service provision. It is true that institutions and policies have been an implicit factor in our previous chapters. For example, classrooms, one unit of analysis in the previous chapter, obviously exist within institutions and are influenced by policy. Here we will examine the interests of researchers who ask questions at this larger scale of impact.

What Interests Researchers?

Researchers who ask questions about institutions and policy are interested in several aspects of their functioning. These include the impact that institutions or programs have on those who participate in them, including effects on participants; the impact of policies on systems and/or the people within systems; the workings of institutions; and the processes involved in policy.

As we have discussed previously, qualitative researchers are interested in the lived experiences of people. Those who work within the transformative paradigm are interested in how power and oppression operate within systems. The questions of qualitative researchers regarding institutions and policy revolve around issues such as:

- What is this person's lived experience within a larger system?
- What is this person's perspective on how policy/practice relationships frame professional possibilities and limits?
- If we deconstruct the workings of an institution, how can we theorize about how structures frame the context and impact people's experiences?
- How can we examine policy to understand issues such as power and privilege?

The interests of quantitative researchers revolve ultimately around describing the impact of a policy or of an institution. Their research interests often go back to an implied concept of worth, investigating, for example, whether a program resulted in worthwhile outcomes for children or whether a policy impacted practice in the worthwhile ways in which it was intended. In fact, some researchers conduct economically based cost–benefit analyses. Quantitative researchers' questions are of these sorts:

- What are the outcomes for children and/or families who are served in a particular institution (e.g., Head Start, family child care, public prekindergarten)?
- Can we identify particular processes or components of an institution that show promise for benefitting young children and/or their families?
- Does a particular policy show evidence of providing benefits for young children and/or their families?

Researchers from both paradigms are interested in the impacts of institutions and policies. However, qualitative researchers are apt to think on the scale of individuals and examine their lived experiences and perspectives within these larger systems. Quantitative researchers are more likely to examine impacts in regard to the desired end game, the outcomes, examined as group average scores on measures.

Asking Questions

We have selected four research studies to illustrate how researchers pursue their interests in institutions and policies. As is true in any of the chapters in Part II of this text, these studies do not exhaust the possibilities but rather reflect a portion of the range of possibilities related to the research question prototypes we posed earlier.

Heimer (2005), a qualitative researcher, examined policy formulation. She based this study on literature that described policy as both a text, the statement of policy shared in the public, and as a discourse, the processes within which policy is developed, used, and interpreted. Heimer's research was based on her intent to "illustrate how the 'success' of a policy depends upon, how the policy is read and interpreted, and who has access to the policy at different stages of its formulation" (p. 20). Her study examined the work of a "policy formulation committee" (p. 21) during the 2-year period in which this group explored establishing a universal prekindergarten program in a small city. As she framed her theoretical perspective, Heimer "use[d] postmodern concepts to theorize why the collaboration of the ECC [Early Childhood Collaborative] was not effective in creating a policy that spoke to, and for all, community members" (p. 26).

Another qualitative examination of policy, this time in Australia, was undertaken by Brown, Sumsion, and Press (2011). This research team was interested in the influences on politicians' decision making around early childhood education and care (ECEC) policy. Specifically, they questioned how beliefs positioning women's roles as inextricably related to motherhood appeared in policy-making processes in the form of gendered discourses. Rather than posing a research question near the front end of the research report, they instead initially stated their findings: "Our analysis of this data suggests that despite some evidence of women's advances in political life, maternalist discourses continue to influence politicians' perceptions and understandings of ECEC and thus continue to shape the ECEC policy landscape" (p. 264). They chose to use the metaphor of dark matter to theorize about their data, arguing that their findings illustrated power relations similar to dark matter in space, exerting influence while essentially remaining invisible day to day.

In neither of the qualitative research examples do we see the presentation of a research question that we can readily convey to readers through an opportune quotation. However, the researchers' intents are described, and this is how we understand the questions of interest they held. This is an example of how readers must approach the task of understanding research by knowing how researchers frame their work. Qualitative researchers are less likely to follow a templated format in their articles than are quantitative researchers. It would be easy to declare, 'But I can't find the research question.' Instead, in these examples, readers must look for what is being analyzed and how the researchers are approaching the analysis; this constitutes the questions of interest.

Our choices for qualitative studies are situated within the transformative and postmodern paradigms. While these paradigms offer rich possibilities for examining policy, they are not the only available choices. For example, Christopher Brown, who wrote one of the researcher perspectives in this chapter, has published several case studies examining the lived experiences and perspectives of individuals relative to contexts framed by policy. Our choices for the text reflect our desire to ensure that we have offered coverage of all qualitative paradigms across the chapters in Part II. In addition to policy research conducted by qualitative researchers, there are many examples of mixed-methods evaluations of institutions in which qualitative data has formed a portion of the investigation. Please remember that our examples, of necessity, always reflect only a portion of the possibilities.

Turning now to our quantitative examples, Domitrovich et al. (2013) performed a study examining the impact of a preschool program. The program in this case was a preschool program within a city school district. This particular program was funded via both Head Start, requiring a means-tested income-based enrollment process for eligible children, and district funds, which allowed the program to be available to all other children as well. Thus, the program was rather unique, offering features typical of public schools (e.g., bachelor's-degreed teachers) and features of Head Start (e.g., home visits). The researchers were interested in the impact of 2 years of attendance (ages 3 and 4) versus just 1 year of attendance (age 4 only) on children's academic learning. Domitrovich et al. stated that they expected to find better outcomes for children who attended for 2 years.

Boller et al. (2015) undertook a study of the impact of policy on the early childhood field. Historically, much of the child care field has struggled to provide what would be regarded as quality care. State licensing policies have functioned to define operating policies that form, essentially, a floor. This means that often they represent lower levels of program quality; programs must meet the standards to operate, but too often they do not exceed these standards to meet higher levels of quality. A recent policy innovation is the Quality Rating and Improvement System (QRIS), instituted most often at the state policy level. The goal of a QRIS is to improve the quality of child care by assessing quality and services

Researcher Perspective

Christopher P. Brown, Ph.D., The University of Texas at Austin

Qualitative research and the examination of institutions, policy makers, and/or policy do not necessarily fit easily together, and because I am a consumer and producer of such research, it has created much unwanted frustration for me. Nevertheless, over the years, I have learned some 'tricks of the trade' that I think can be helpful as you embark on your own investigation into issues surrounding institutions, policymakers, and policy within early childhood education.

To begin, you will find that there may not be many qualitative studies that examine the institutional or policy issue you want to know more about as a student or researcher. This happened to me when I began my doctoral studies in 2000. I had just left teaching in a public school kindergarten context where state policy makers' high-stakes reforms drove the curriculum as well as challenged the instructional practices my colleagues and I were expected to implement. That frustrating teaching experience led me back to graduate school, and I sought to understand the emergence of high-stakes standards-based accountability reforms in the United States (U.S.), their impact on the field of early childhood education, and how those who advocate for child-centered practices might respond to and/or offer an alternative vision of teaching young children.

This was prior to the No Child Left Behind Act (NCLB), and few studies existed that examined these issues. Thus, under the guidance of my former advisor, Dr. Elizabeth Graue, I turned to the core constructs that shaped my interest: educational policy, via a rating metric and facilitating growth in quality at the agency or family child care provider level. In this particular study, the researchers asked if the coaching and grants provided in a QRIS project resulted in improvements in (1) the observed program quality and (2) the ratings achieved by providers in the QRIS rating system's metrics.

As we indicated in the previous section, quantitative researchers are often concerned with questions of the worth of an institution or policy. The two examples we have just described fit this description well. Both research teams focused on how their findings might impact ongoing policy and practice, and in both cases the ultimate interest for the public good is the benefits realized for young children.

Choosing Methods

This particular set of four studies represents opposite ends of the methodological approaches available. The two qualitative examples were conducted within the transformative and postmodern paradigms. Central to these studies was how the researchers interacted with the data, the interpretations they made as they examined the data within their selected theoretical frameworks. Their goals are to disrupt thinking about issues and/or processes. On the other hand, the questions asked by the quantitative research teams were of the cause–effect type. Recall that in Chapter 7 we explained that cause–effect questions require the most stringent of the traditional scientific methods, typically the randomized study. Thus, these studies were most driven by the considerations of the positivist paradigm.

Qualitative Studies

At the outset of this text, in Chapter 1, we suggested that approaching a research study as if it is a story can be helpful in gaining access to understand the work. In

standards-based accountability reform, high-stakes and standardized testing, developmentally appropriate practices, and child-centered learning. I also looked to research in other countries (e.g., Great Britain) that were implementing similar policies in their public education systems. Finding and reading those studies demonstrated to me how vast the field of educational research truly is, which can be a challenge.

Because the field of educational research is so expansive, you will find that there are many studies that appear to contradict each other or state that previous research failed to capture the complexity of a particular issue or policy. Part of this is because there are a lot of poorly executed qualitative research studies out there, and better research is needed.

For me, having conducted scholarly work that touches on institutional as well as policy issues within the field of early childhood education for the last 15 years, it is clear that the field of early childhood education has not done a good job of producing qualitative work that responds effectively to institutional and/or policy makers' demands. Beyond trying to address this concern through my own research, I have pursued investigations into what I consider to be key issues for the field of early childhood using qualitative metasynthesis, which is a form of meta-research, that seeks to use findings across qualitative studies to develop a refined understanding of a particular event, experience, or phenomenon. For instance, Dr. Yi-Chin Lan and I examined qualitative studies that investigated whether teachers and/or administrators were engaging in developmentally appropriate practices with their students and, if so, how such practices might influence children's cognitive development. In another study, we examined U.S. teachers' conceptions of school readiness the case of Heimer's (2005) analysis of the 2-year process toward forming early childhood policy, she in fact described her case as a "story" (p. 19). This reflects how she strove to remain close to the processes taking place in this community, since stories represent a narrative with events and actors. In Heimer's work, she sought to examine "who was included, the capital needed for inclusion, and the power related to social networks and how that shapes collaboration" (p. 19). Ultimately, she had an aim for this work, as stated, "I wonder if this story might help others think of new ways of disrupting the traditional notions of policy making in early childhood" (p. 21).

Recall that Heimer (2005) conceptualized policy as a process. She began as a participant in the Early Childhood Collaborative (ECC) and later moved to a researcher role. Her data for this study consisted of interviews, field notes, and the text of meeting minutes. Typical of the foreshortened descriptions of qualitative methods as often presented in briefer publication formats, we know little more about her methodology and analyses.

Heimer's focus was on describing the evolution of the ECC's work and then analyzing the participation structures in light of her theoretical framework. She described who was 'at the table' and interpreted this within the concept of symbolic capital. Similarly, Heimer examined the meeting structures (agendas, stated purposes, room design); she interpreted these aspects of the process within the literature about power. Heimer's report illustrates a back-and-forth process, as she described data that reflected the processes of forming policy and then used concepts from the literature to interpret this data. Because of the transformative nature of her selected paradigm, she also discussed implications

prior to and after the implementation of NCLB. This work demonstrates that there is additional need for qualitative work that provides a more nuanced picture of the institutional, policy, and/or political landscape of early childhood education.

Last, in terms of writing a qualitative study for publication that examines institutional or policy issues, the biggest challenge is providing a document that offers rich and thick descriptions of data within the prescribed word/page limit of the publication. To address this issue, I attempt to accomplish three goals in each article I produce. First, I ensure I am answering only one to two research questions in my article. Second, I define the constructs my research question is investigating and make sure I address those constructs throughout the article, for example, in the literature review, research methods, findings, and discussion. Last, I provide enough but not too much data that demonstrates to the reader that my proposed findings and implications are trustworthy.

Following these suggestions will help you come to understand the institutional, political, and/or policy issues that shape the field of early childhood education so that you can accomplish your goals as a scholar—be it advocating for a particular issue, generating your own empirical work, or engaging in effective teaching practices. Whatever you decide, I hope that you will work with me and so many others in striving to create systems of early childhood education that offer all children the opportunity to become active and reflective members of the larger democratic society.

for practice. She noted that "early childhood policies will not be responsive to the communities they serve without some reconsideration of how collaboration is defined and enacted" (p. 33). It was Heimer's intent to highlight the marginalization she read in her data to promote social justice in the field.

Recall that Brown et al. (2011) examined politicians and their decision making in their qualitative study set in Australia. They conducted interviews with nine politicians and three senior
public servants. The researchers recruited these individuals from within one particular state
due to logistics. The nine politicians represented those who volunteered from the 49 federal-
level and state-level politicians (having legislative seats) invited to participate in the study. Just
over half of the politicians did not respond, while the others formally declined. From this,
readers might surmise that study recruitment encountered some challenges. Politicians may
indeed be wary of 'going on the record' with researchers, which impacts those interested in
policy.

Brown et al. (2011) utilized a semistructured format for their interviews. All participants
were asked the same set of generic questions. In addition, "further specific questions were
devised for each politician based on additional information gathered about them" (p. 270).
The generic questions were sent to the participants prior to the interviews. As is par for the
course, the interviews were audiorecorded and transcribed, with the exception of one individual, who requested that only handwritten notes be taken during the interview. Each transcript
was returned to the participant for member checking, and the researchers specifically noted
that all of the excerpts utilized in the research report were "double-checked with the relevant
participants" (p. 270). Although the participants were identified only with a participant number and their gender, it is clear that generating data with politicians had sensitive moments. The
researchers' work toward establishing trust with this particular group of participants is reflected
in their report.

Brown et al. (2011) included detail in the description of their analyses, describing eight steps
they undertook. They stated, for example, that they identified explicit content, coding the data
into themes and identifying the regularities and irregularities in use among particular words
and phrases. They also identified implicit content reflective of ideologies and explored where
participants left a thought unfinished or unclear, among other steps.

The researchers described their findings relative to four themes. What is particular about
the work of Brown et al. (2011) is that their intent was not linked to the lived experiences
and perceptions of their participants. Remember previously we discussed that the researchers
framed their study and the analyses around the metaphor of dark matter. Thus, their discussion of findings was framed by three essential beliefs about maternalist discourses: that they
"are normalising discourses; second, like dark matter, they are difficult to detect or recognise;
and third, maternalist discourses are difficult to disrupt and dislodge" (p. 271). With a postmodern lens, Brown and colleagues sought to interrupt discourses that "politicians often
seem unaware of, or rarely publicly acknowledge" (p. 264). The researchers concluded that
with their work to "recognise and defy maternalist discourses, early childhood educators may
. . . heighten their political awareness and strengthen their political activism in ECEC policy"
(p. 279). Like Heimer, Brown and colleagues hoped to influence the field by theorizing on
their data.

Quantitative Studies

Moving to the quantitative studies, we first explore Domitrovich et al.'s (2013) study of preschool program impact. Recall that their question concerned the differential impact of 1 year
versus 2 years of attendance in a program prior to kindergarten entrance. As this is a cause–effect
question, the ideal methodology would be a randomized study. The researchers noted that there
may be differences between the families who enroll their children in a program at age 3 and
those who wait another year for the child to turn 4. This source of potential bias cannot be
eliminated when the study takes place in a publicly available program; it would not be ethical

to use randomization to serve children differentially. To improve the study's ability to address causation, the researchers used a technique called propensity score analysis. Essentially, they created two groups of children, matched as closely as possible to each other. They began this process with children who had data at the start of kindergarten. Of these children, one group of 117 had attended preschool for 2 years and another group of 151 had attended for 1 year. They conducted a complex analysis that matched pairs of children, one from each group, using a number of variables (e.g., gender, ethnicity, family structure, parent education, etc.), such that when all matched pairs were considered, all paired scores were optimally close together (or similar) on these variables. Because more children had attended for 1 year, some of these children were not matched, and their scores were not considered in the analyses. With this process, the researchers attempted to account as much as possible for any systematic differences between the two groups.

Domitrovich et al. (2013) utilized direct assessment of children to generate data for the study. In addition, they collected extensive demographic information about families from school enrollment forms. They assessed children during the fall of the preschool and kindergarten years. The Peabody Picture-Vocabulary test, which assesses receptive vocabulary, was used with both 3-year-olds and 4-year-olds, as well as in kindergarten. The remaining measures included an assessment of letter and word knowledge, an assessment of letter recognition that incorporated all alphabet letters, a writing assessment, and an assessment of mathematics knowledge. These assessments were given only when children were 4 years old, at the start of the final preschool year before kindergarten, as well as at the start of kindergarten when they were 5 years old. This research decision was based upon the age-appropriate lowest level for these assessments.

Researcher Perspective

Amanda Wilcox-Herzog, Ph.D., California State University, San Bernardino

Several years ago, my colleagues and I worked with staff at local child care centers. Our goal was to provide assessment-based training in an effort to increase child care quality and enhance children's developmental outcomes. Specifically, the Early Childhood Training Program helped local providers increase their ability to provide appropriate curriculum and teaching strategies, create suitable, safe environments for young children, promote children's health and well-being, build relationships with children, families, and their surrounding communities, increase staff professionalism and program management abilities, and assess children authentically and meaningfully. This goal was achieved by assessing providers' current skills and the skills of the children they work with and then providing targeted training designed to increase skills in each of the areas noted. It was hypothesized, based on literature indicating the importance of education and specialized training, that participating providers would show improvement in each of the areas listed.

Participants were recruited from six center-based child care programs serving preschool-age children and included program administrators, teachers, teacher aides, and enrolled children. Program administrators ($N = 6$) were assessed with the Program Administration Scale, which measures the provision of family and community relationships and ways to increase staff professionalism and program management strategies. Classrooms ($N = 14$) were assessed with the Early Childhood Environment Rating

One component of the study that reflects causal research is that the design incorporated all children who started at 3 years of age, even if they withdrew from the program later. This is referred to as "intent to treat" (Domitrovich et al., 2013, p. 708). The design follows the most rigorous standards of experimental designs; no participants are considered 'lost' due to any of the potential reasons underlying a withdrawal from the program. Thus, any children who entered at 3 years of age were included in the sample group of 2-year attendees, even if they did not finish the program when they were 3 or did not attend when they were 4.

Domitrovich et al. (2013) compared the two groups (2 years versus 1 year of pre-kindergarten) by using a multilevel model that accounted for the fact that children were nested within classrooms. They also controlled for the influence of covariates in the model, variables such as parent education and eligibility for Head Start. It is of note that some of these covariates were found to be predictive of some outcome measures. The researchers reported that on most outcome measures, the group with 2 years of prekindergarten performed better in kindergarten; they included the effect sizes for each result.

We turn now to the research conducted by Boller et al. (2015). As a reminder, they studied the impact of QRIS on child care quality. In this study, randomization was possible because the QRIS was in the pilot stage. All licensed child care providers (centers and home-based) in a geographical area were invited to participate. Those who responded were randomly assigned to the treatment group and control group using a stratified system. For example, the center-based child care providers were separated into groups based upon how many children were served, and the centers were then randomly assigned within these stratified groups. This meant that the centers randomized into the treatment group had approximately the same profile in regard to enrollment size as the control group centers.

Scale Revised and the Early Language and Literacy Classroom Observation, which measure appropriate curriculum and teaching strategies, the provision of suitable, safe environments, the promotion of children's health and well-being, relationship building with children and families, staff professionalism, and child assessment. Teachers ($N = 24$) were assessed with the Classroom Assessment Scoring System, which measured the use of appropriate curriculum and teaching strategies, the provision of suitable learning environments, teacher–child relationships, and child assessment across classroom staff. Finally, children ($N = 135$) were assessed with an author-created measurement designed to assess typical skills across five child domains.

Data from this battery of assessments was used to create workplans that were presented to providers. Workplans were based on assessment data, and providers were shown graphs of their scores on each of the assessment tools used. Scores were used to frame discussion of the workplans, and suggestions were given designed to help increase posttraining assessment scores. These suggestions led to the next phase of the project: training and support services. Providers were offered a variety of services and training opportunities dependent on their personal needs and assessment data. For example, providers were given individualized training opportunities, technical assistance, financial assistance, and observational learning opportunities.

At the end of 7 months of intervention, we found that the largest effect sizes were seen at the program administration and classroom levels and that smaller effect sizes were found at the teacher and child levels. Generally, the biggest changes occurred at the structural level. For example, we realized that before interactions could change,

The treatment group of child care providers experienced a field test of the QRIS (Boller et al., 2015). They received quality improvement grants and funds for professional development. In addition, staff members received coaching. Two of the QRIS quality standards were used to assign scores to child care providers at the outset and end of the study period; approximately 6 months passed between the baseline and follow-up assessments. The data was generated with direct observations and surveys for staff members.

The assessments measured curriculum and learning environment and education and experience of staff (Boller et al., 2015). Curriculum and learning environment were assessed with observations, using an Environment Rating Scale (either the Infant-Toddler Environment Rating Scale-R, ITERS-R; the Early Childhood Environment Rating Scale-R, ECERS-R; or the Family Child Care Environment Rating Scale-R, FCCERS-R). Each of these instruments assesses quality in a similar fashion across a range of categories. Many items focus on what is provided in regard to materials, activities, and scheduling. Additionally, interactions among the child care providers and children were observed and assessed with the Arnett Caregiver Interaction Scale (Arnett CIS). A total score was used in this study; the measure itself includes components such as sensitivity, harshness, and detachment. The researchers conducted analyses with these two measures. Additionally, the researchers recorded caregiver experience and education collected via surveys using the metrics of the QRIS rating system, and these were analyzed. For the final analyses of the study, the metrics of the QRIS rating system were used to calculate the child care providers' scores for two component standards, curriculum and learning environment and professional development and training.

To analyze the data, Boller et al. (2015) first compared the treatment and control groups at baseline. Differences that were found at baseline were used in the analyses as controls. They conducted separate analyses of center-based and home-based providers. This is important because the two types of providers required different manipulations of the data. For example, observational scores for child care centers had to incorporate the scores of separate classrooms. Hierarchical linear models were used to estimate the impact of the QRIS treatment, above and beyond the baseline differences that existed between the treatment and control groups. They found a positive impact of participating in QRIS on the Environment Rating Scale instrument in both provider groups, a positive impact on the Arnett CIS for centers but not for home-based providers, and finally, no impact on staff education/experience or the rating received via the QRIS scoring rules.

Interestingly, in both of the quantitative studies, the description of study results comprised less than a page in the research paper. Far more space (3–4 pages in these examples) was necessary to describe procedures. This illustrates how concise the quantitative paradigm can be in summarizing both the research question (typically a paragraph) and the results of statistical analyses.

---

providers needed assistance in increasing their supply of play-based materials, arranging their classroom environments to create functional play-based learning spaces, and considering daily schedules better suited to child-directed, play-based learning. Therefore, the training period focused heavily on these structural aspects of the classroom environment, and less attention was given to process quality dimensions such as classroom tone and teacher–child interactions. In the future, more training time would be beneficial. Many of the providers who participated in the training program noted that they felt that they were just getting started and getting the hang of the changes being encouraged when the program ended.

Potential, Pitfalls, and Limitations

This set of four studies reflects various potentials. Both Heimer (2005) and Brown et al. (2011) set out to disrupt the common perceptions of phenomena and events, exposing influences that they found in their data that are not necessarily recognized. Their intent was to have an impact on how the future might be realized. Both Domitrovich et al. (2013) and Boller et al. (2015) sought to establish whether programs offered for the benefit of children and families met their potential toward those goals. Their results did show some positive impacts, based upon the differences found between groups.

As we have made the case previously, it is essential that readers keep potential pitfalls in mind when evaluating research studies. Among our four exemplar studies, there are several potential pitfalls that must be taken into account.

In both of our qualitative examples, the theorizing of the researchers is important to consider. Heimer (2005) utilized concepts from the literature to theorize about collaboration in policy making, and Brown et al. (2011) utilized the metaphor of dark matter to theorize about influences on policy making. In both cases, it is the task of the reader to decide: Does this metaphor work and is it supported by the data? Has the warrant been made—in other words, does the evidence offered by the researchers match the interpretations and claims made? Do the implications offered by the researchers fit with the way that they have attempted to disrupt unexamined processes? Regarding these questions, there are not cut-and-dried answers to be identified in qualitative research. In our examples, the researchers have conducted theorizing, proposing how data can be understood. Readers must decide for themselves if this theorizing is meaningful and coherent.

Regarding the quantitative studies, there is one important pitfall to recognize. As we mentioned, the results are based upon differences found between groups. The positive impact found for 2 years of prekindergarten or for a QRIS program is an average from among all participants in the study. One can never surmise that all participants will experience similar impacts; the average is formed from those with lower and higher scores on any outcome measure. Thus, what might happen for any one child, family, or institution cannot be assumed to be similar to the average.

In addition, readers must carefully consider the measures used in quantitative studies. Particularly with young children, the possibilities are more limited. What do we want to know about what they know, and how can we find this out? As we discussed in Chapter 9, standardized instruments measure a narrow range of children's knowledge and skills. The stakes are high when we make decisions about children based upon these instruments. However, they remain high when these are our best, and perhaps only, options upon which to make decisions about the programs we offer them. Ideally, outcome measures are consistent with program purposes and assess important things for children to learn. This is a challenging ideal, however, and we do not have good instruments for some of the important things that children might learn.

The options for measuring classroom quality are limited as well. The Environment Rating Scales utilized by Boller et al. (2015) have been widely used, both in research and in QRIS initiatives. Previous research has shown some positive impacts of higher scores on the instruments for children's outcomes (Clifford, Reszka, & Rossbach, 2010). Recently, questions about how much these instruments predict child outcomes were raised by Sabol and Pianta (2014), who found little relationship between environment rating scale scores and children's outcomes using a national database. Certainties are few and far between in research!

Finally, as is true of all research, there are limitations to these studies. We hope that readers will recognize by now that the qualitative studies represent only certain perspectives of complex and multifaceted stories. Both Heimer (2005) and Brown et al. (2011) had deeper stores of data than were utilized to produce these research reports. We ourselves know how frustrating it is as researchers to present only part of a more extensive project, as if that part exists in a sufficient manner outside of the larger and more complex project. Similarly, it can be true that readers find it limiting to consider only a part of the project, and yet policy makers and the public, even other researchers as well, often want to read something concise.

All research occurs within a unique context marked by time and place. In both of our quantitative examples, the unique context was noted as a limitation of the studies. Because limitations are cited near the end of quantitative reports, it is sometimes not until the end that readers can learn more about the unique context. For instance, Domitrovich et al. (2013) conducted their analysis of a prekindergarten program during the first years of its implementation. It is possible that results could vary after several years of implementation if it is true that new programs need time to take root. In the QRIS study, Boller et al. (2015) noted that the 6-month period from baseline to impact measurement precluded examining the potential for changes in staff educational status. They attributed the short follow-up period to "the need to provide research results to inform policy and program development" (p. 314). In other words, sometimes there is a demand for researchers to produce answers rather quickly. But consider the Domitrovich and associates study, in which children were followed for up to 2 years (through 2 years of prekindergarten to the start of kindergarten). It is often the case that questions about institutions and/or policy do require a significant period of time to allow for the institutions or policies to do what they are intended to do.

Finally, the questions pursued by quantitative researchers often involve complex chains that are incompletely represented within a single study. For instance, Boller et al. (2015) did not have data on child outcomes, which are the ultimate end point of a QRIS initiative. And while we know some of the major features of the preschool program studied by Domitrovich et al. (2013), much of it is considered a 'black box' in that we do not know how program features mattered to the effectiveness of the program. In fact, Domitrovich and associates proposed that future research be conducted with a focus on components of the program, speculating that "it may be that a more intense year of programming that included specific components would result in student outcomes comparable to longer exposure to a standard program" (p. 711).

Summary

The examples we chose for this chapter allowed us to illustrate research in the transformative/postmodern paradigms, as well as research focused on causal relations. At the same time, the researchers have used methods to generate data that are similar to those described in previous chapters. What is unique are the interests described at the beginning of the chapter—the impact of system-related phenomena on adults and their work and children and their experiences. While we began this section of the text with children and worked our way up to institutions and policy, given the pervading influence of these structures, we could just as well have started at the institution/policy end and moved through the systems nested within to reach children.

13

TEACHER RESEARCH

In Chapter 1, we stated that research is a form of inquiry that relies upon evidence, or data. In this chapter, we will discuss teacher research as practice-focused inquiry. Teacher research is *practice focused* in that it addresses real problems in real classrooms. *Inquiry* is the basis of teacher research. However, teacher research is a distinct and non–scientifically based form of inquiry conducted by teachers, individually or collaboratively, to gain insights into their teaching practice and children's learning. In this chapter, we address some underlying assumptions associated with teacher research and how it redefines what it means to be a teacher. As a form of research, we will focus on the types of data generated by teachers, considering them within the framework of qualitative and quantitative approaches. After a brief discussion of the historical roots of teacher research, we discuss the processes that teachers go through when they do research, followed by a discussion of the value of teacher research as a potential means of improving professional practice and contributing to the knowledge base in education. We end the chapter by discussing some of the formats and publication outlets in which teachers and teacher educators have shared the results of their teacher research.

What Is Teacher Research?

Teacher research is a legitimate form of educational research. In general, educational research is a systematic investigation involving the analysis of information (data) to answer a question or contribute to our knowledge of theory and practice. The late British educator Lawrence Stenhouse (1981) defined research as intentional, systematic, critical inquiry made public. Teacher research contains all of these elements. Teacher research is intentional and systematic data-based inquiry designed, conducted, and implemented by teachers to address the everyday practical problems they experience (Cochran-Smith & Lytle, 1993, 1999; Stremmel, 2002).

Let's examine this definition a bit more closely. Teacher research is *intentional* because the particular questions teachers wish to pursue emerge out of a curiosity about some aspect of their classroom life. It is *systematic* in that teachers follow specific procedures and carefully document these from the formation of a question through data collection and analysis to conclusions and outcomes. In other words, they develop a research plan that moves the inquiry away from being haphazard or random. Systematic inquiry relies on teachers using methods that are appropriate to their everyday practice (e.g., observation, document collection, journaling, conversations with children) to generate data that cannot be captured by traditional methods of research but which produces credible and verifiable results. For teachers, this means demonstrating that the knowledge generated has the appearance of truth (verisimilitude), that a particular teaching technique works, or that a particular decision or action is defensible. Research is *critical* when the teacher challenges her assumptions and findings, asking such questions as 'How do I know?'; 'Are there any other reasons to believe that what I have found is true?'; 'Is this the best way to do something?'; or 'Is this the right (most defensible) choice?' Finally, the processes and results of teacher research become *public* when we allow it to be critiqued by others. However, in making public their findings, teachers use their own forms of expression, indigenous ways of telling and sharing what they have come to know through inquiry.

Purposes of Teacher Research

Teacher research has two main purposes. The more immediate one is to improve practice. When teachers engage in research on their practice, their immediate goal is to get better at what they do. The second purpose is to gain a better understanding of the context in which teaching and learning are immersed. This better understanding is in some ways equivalent to the generation of knowledge. However, the knowledge a teacher produces is located spatially and temporally and can be shared with others as stories or other forms of narrative. Teacher research, whether done individually or collaboratively, is done primarily with an intentional aim to make changes or improvements in classrooms, schools, and professional lives, as opposed to generating findings that can be applied to other settings (Hatch, 2002; Stringer, 1999). However, teacher research *can* contribute to the knowledge of teaching and learning in early childhood settings, a notion that will be explored later in this chapter. Because profound changes in practice can be brought about through teacher research, it has the potential for rethinking, resisting, and reforming the ways we currently think about teaching and learning (Cochran-Smith & Lytle, 2009).

Assumptions About Teaching, Research, and Who Can Do It

An assumption we make is that teaching, at its best and in its most complete sense, involves bringing together teaching (typically thought of as doing, acting, carrying out, and/or performing the work of the profession) and research (questioning, hypothesizing, reflecting, observing and examining, interpreting, making visible teaching and learning processes, and taking action that will improve both teaching and learning in the classroom). Like any union, however, the whole is greater than the sum of its parts. Teaching is changed when the idea of research is introduced; similarly, the notion of research is changed when the process of doing it is undertaken by the teacher (Freeman, 1998). Subsequently, becoming a teacher is about repositioning oneself as a teacher-researcher, a knower and a learner, a doer and a wonderer, a professional decision maker who explores and examines her own practice to improve it and to enhance children's learning (Cochran-Smith & Lytle, 2009; Stremmel, 2015).

This mind shift also assumes that teachers, as professionals, are capable of deciding what they need to be effective in the classroom and that their voices must be heard if we are to have a more complete understanding of teaching and learning. Teachers are typically viewed as consumers, not producers, of knowledge. Others develop the curriculum, select materials, and decide what and how to teach and how to evaluate learning. How ironic this is, when teachers are the central sources of knowledge about teaching and their classrooms. As Vivian Paley (1997) reminds us, who better understands the demands and rewards, the conflicts and triumphs, the problems and challenges, and the moments of insight and enlightenment that are experienced every day in the complex and context specific world of teaching than teachers themselves? To be clear, it is not that no one *but* the teacher can understand the intricacies of teaching; nonetheless, it certainly is the case that no one else can understand it in the way teachers do. Thus, engaging in teacher inquiry and adopting an inquiry stance should and need not be the sole domain of academics and university-based researchers (Meier & Henderson, 2007; Stremmel, 2002).

Teacher Research Is Not Scientific Research

Teacher research may be viewed as a good story that begins with something teachers wonder about, something that perplexes or astonishes them, and in the end, something they want to make known (Hatch, 2006; Paley, 1997). Why? Because, as we mentioned, often teachers' stories are about something that no one outside of a teacher's classroom understands. In these stories, teachers make known to themselves and others matters of concern that, when investigated, enable teachers to rethink and more carefully interpret their decisions and their actions.

The telling of stories (narratives) is one of the most important features of teaching and a valid and important way to share knowledge (Bruner, 1986). Teachers routinely use stories to describe the events of their classrooms and, more importantly, to interpret and make sense of what happens there. Teachers who see themselves as researchers tell stories of how they deal with issues and problems in the classroom. This narrative way of knowing creates storied understandings that cannot be captured via scientific knowledge. Nevertheless, narrative knowledge in the form of teachers' stories of research, though not scientific, is real and valid research that enables teachers to generate and share their knowledge and understanding of professional practice (Hatch, 2006).

To expound on this a bit further, let's return to our definition of research and who typically does it. The word *research* (defined earlier as intentional, systematic, critical inquiry made public) is usually associated with the use of rigorous scientific methods to study teaching. In thinking about teacher research, the term *inquiry* often has been preferred (e.g., Cochran-Smith & Lytle, 2009). It represents both a stance and a process. However, as we will discuss later, the distinction between teacher research and scientific research is less about methodology and more about the very nature of educational practice (Anderson & Herr, 1999). According to Dewey (1933), education is best practiced as inquiry, and teacher research employs the 'scientific approach' to inquiry. A defining feature of teacher research is the teacher's dual role as practitioner and researcher within the classroom, where, like scientists and educational researchers, they encounter real problems, experience obstacles to understanding, and ponder daily why things are as they are. What distinguishes teacher research from teaching reflectively is the commitment to a disciplined method for gathering and analyzing data and the fact that it can be publicly shared (Borko, Liston, & Whitcomb, 2007).

Teacher Research Is Largely Qualitative

Conventional educational research, whether scientifically based or that which is traditionally done by academic researchers, examines teacher knowledge and practice from an outsider perspective, employing either quantitative or qualitative methods and epistemologies embedded in the academic culture. Teacher research, on the other hand, primarily relies on qualitative methodologies to examine teaching practice from the inside. Although traditional quantitative methods (e.g., surveys, checklists, questionnaires, and observational instruments) that use numerical representations of data and statistical analyses *can* be used, qualitative methods in the form of reflective journaling, field notes, interviews or informal conversations, narratives, and artifacts typically are more appropriate for addressing the complex nature of teaching and learning (Davis, 2007; Hatch, 2002; Meier & Henderson, 2007; Meyers & Rust, 2008). As we will discuss later in this chapter, growing appreciation and value of qualitative methods (e.g., ethnography, narrative inquiry, biography, and autobiography) in educational research and a concurrent shift from thinking about teacher research as something done to teachers to something done *by* teachers are the primary reasons behind interest in the teacher research movement (Borko, Liston, & Whitcomb, 2007; Zeichner, 1999; Zeichner & Noffke, 2001).

Recall that in Chapter 1, it was stated that early childhood teachers are expected to have some knowledge and understanding of the research literature and to participate in dialogue with others about where and how research links to practice. Although the research literature on children, their thinking, learning, and development is vast and ever increasing, traditional educational research, especially quantitative inquiry, does not always address the real issues and concerns of teachers (e.g., Meier & Henderson, 2007; Meyers & Rust, 2008). It is often written in a way that fails to help them understand their classroom situation (Hatch, 2006). In short, traditional research on teaching often pursues the wrong questions and offers unusable answers, in part because teachers' voices have been left out of the research literature (Cochran-Smith & Lytle, 2009; Davis 2007; Stremmel, 2002). When teachers conduct their own systematic research into the problems they encounter in their classrooms and schools, they not only address issues that existing research has not and perhaps cannot address, they attempt to create new knowledge about teaching and learning from the direct study of their work in classrooms.

A few examples may be helpful. Quantitative research may employ observational instruments and statistical analyses to pursue the question of what teaching methods are most effective. Teacher research, on the other hand, may allow teachers to use reflective journaling, participant observation, document analysis, and conversations with children and other teachers to pursue the specific question, 'How or in what ways am I effective in helping children learn?' The emphasis is on what it means to teach, as opposed to the technical aspects of teaching, enabling teachers to better understand and interpret their own teaching in context. A similar example pertains to the question 'What motivates children to learn?' Shifting the focus to 'How does *my* motivation affect children's ability to learn in the classroom?' may help a teacher systematically observe and critically reflect on her attitudes, thoughts, and feelings and be more responsive to the children and the particular demands of her classroom.

Teacher research validates a more comprehensive and accurate view of what it means to be a teacher. Viewing teachers as researchers affirms their professional status and acknowledges their important responsibility to both theory and practice. Rather than implementing a prescribed curriculum or following the methodologies of others, teachers must eventually become the source and creator of the theoretical basis of their own teaching techniques. In this way, knowledge of teaching and learning originates in teaching that is grounded in research (Stenhouse, 1975).

Historical Antecedents of Teacher Research

In a seminal article in *Educational Researcher*, Ken Zeichner (1999) proclaimed that teacher research is "probably the single most significant development ever in the field of teacher education research" (p. 8). Teacher research in the United States is not a new activity, and it has a long tradition. The origins of teacher research are found in the movement for the scientific study of education and the progressive educational philosophy of John Dewey (1938). Dewey believed that inquiry was an essential element of teacher practice and that knowledge about teaching and learning originated in the systematic study of teachers' experiences with children. Like Dewey, those who have embraced a constructivist view (e.g., Duckworth, 1997; Fosnot, 2005; Piaget, 1965) have employed careful observation to suggest that children are natural inquirers who construct meaning as they explore their environments. Teachers, also, must carefully observe their students to develop an understanding of what they know and bring to learning. Therefore, it is a natural extension to view teaching as including inquiry in the classroom.

The social psychologist Kurt Lewin (1948) argued that the ultimate aim of inquiry was understanding and improvement. Lewin is widely cited as the originator of action-based research having ethical, political, and practical aims, which he termed *action* research (Meier & Henderson, 2007). But it was Stephen Corey (1953) and others at Teachers College of Columbia University who introduced and defined the term *action research* as the process through which practitioners study their own practice to solve meaningful problems (Stremmel, 2002; Zeichner & Noffke, 2001). In the education literature, teacher research and action research are often used interchangeably, the latter being the preferred term in Britain (Cochran-Smith & Lytle, 1993). However, not all teacher research is action research, as noted by Meier and Henderson (2007). Although teacher research has the goal of some type of action to improve practice, action research typically focuses on behavior or organizational change through inquiry conducted collaboratively among researchers (not necessarily teachers) and those who will benefit from the action. Teacher research takes many forms and serves a range of purposes, but it is conducted by teachers, individually or collaboratively, with the primary aim of understanding teaching and learning in context and from the perspectives of those who live and interact daily in the classroom (Meier & Henderson, 2007; Zeichner, 1999).

Interest in teacher research since the 1970s can be traced, in part, to the work of Lawrence Stenhouse (1975). Stenhouse is widely recognized for initiating an international teacher research movement in 1967 in England, which prompted many educators to form research communities within their schools (Hubbard & Power, 1999). He argued that rather than implementing outsider researchers' ideas in their classrooms, teachers should take an active role in curriculum research and development, testing ideas in their own classrooms. Stenhouse firmly believed that a research tradition that is accessible to teachers and feeds teaching must be created if education is to be significantly improved.

A new teacher-as-researcher movement emerged in North America in the 1980s in response to several factors, primary among them growth in the use of qualitative methods in educational research as previously noted. Among the pioneers who have engaged in teacher research are teachers like Nancy Atwell (1987), who conducted case studies on the teaching of writing, and Vivian Paley (1981, 1990), who has written reflectively about her teaching using narrative inquiry. Narrative inquiry is a method of studying and understanding experience through storytelling or narrative and values multiple perspectives (Clandinin & Connelly, 2000). Another form of teacher research that has emerged is self-study, which uses inquiry of self to examine identity, personal biases, perceptions, and understandings to look at how the self affects students, with the goal of improving interactions (Meier & Henderson, 2007). Since the 1990s there has been an increased emphasis on these and other forms of teacher research in university teacher education programs (e.g., Cochran-Smith & Lytle, 1993; Hill, Stremmel, & Fu, 2005; Meier & Stremmel, 2010). At the same time, the reflective practitioner movement inspired by the work of Donald Schon (1983) has led to changes in the ways teachers view themselves as professionals. Reflective teachers purposely frame, examine, and learn from their professional experiences and the changing conditions of teaching to improve their practice (Meier & Henderson, 2007; Zeichner, 1999).

For a more cogent and comprehensive documentation of the history of teacher research, we refer interested readers to Zeichner and Noffke (2001).

Processes of Teacher Research

Let's turn now to the question of the research process. John Dewey (1933) saw the research process as a cyclical process of inquiry involving observation and reflection, leading to new ideas, which are then tested by action. In the process of testing by action, new observations are made, further reflection occurs, and new understandings result. Observation involves careful and respectful watching and listening; it requires attentiveness, openness, and an implied willingness to act on the ideas of children. Reflection involves the teacher's deliberate scrutiny of her own interpretive point of view, rooted in personal and formal theories, culturally learned ways of seeing, and personal core values. Teacher researchers learn about themselves as teachers as they try to understand children's learning. Like traditional forms of research, teacher research involves:

- framing the initial question or problem;
- determining what previous research says about the question or problem;
- framing a research question or hypothesis;
- designing a plan for collecting data to address the question, problem, or hypothesis;
- analyzing and interpreting the results; and
- generating conclusions.

We will examine each of these steps from a teacher research perspective.

Getting Started: Identifying a Problem and Questions

The first step in the teacher research process is identifying a problem of meaning (something that puzzles or perplexes). We refer to problems in teaching as problems of meaning because they are real problems or dilemmas that teachers encounter in their classrooms with their children. The problems and dilemmas of teaching are all around. They arise from curiosity and interest in wanting to find out more about one's teaching decisions or behaviors or how children learn and attempt to understand. Problems may arise in trying to develop some new teaching method or trying out a new idea or in the need to understand a way of thinking about a particular decision and acting on it.

The ability to see teaching as problematic or to give voice to meaningful questions requires an attitude or way of thinking and being in the classroom. Earlier we stated that teachers must view teaching as an inquiry stance (see Cochran-Smith & Lytle, 2009). Adopting an inquiry stance means learning to recognize and interpret key moments in the life of the classroom; it means learning to question or challenge both what teachers do and what they are asked to do with children in the classroom; it means taking children's questions seriously and helping them pursue those questions to satisfaction; and it means working within communities of learners or trusted colleagues to generate knowledge and understanding of what it means to teach and to learn.

Teacher researchers must examine the professional literature to see what others have learned about the issues and concerns they face as teachers of young children. Teachers want to value and utilize all of the best information available as they design and implement their research. By utilizing the most relevant and reliable information to inform and shape their teacher research, teachers can justify their claims that they are constantly improving their practices to provide the best experiences possible for the children they teach.

After expressing a problem and examining what the literature may say about it, teacher researchers typically draw upon a combination of theory and intuition; experience and knowledge of children; observation and reflection; and perhaps the experiences of valued colleagues to develop questions and assumptions (hypotheses) relevant to the problem. The process of developing questions is very different from one used by academic or university-based researchers, who may have little or no knowledge of the particulars of the teaching setting. Meaningful questions are those teachers and children care about, questions that they are genuinely puzzled about, questions that ask, 'How is this possible?' They are questions asked with a spirit of wonder and surprise. Where might this lead? Who knows? Teachers pursue questions like: 'How can I make a connection with those children who seem distant and unwilling to interact?';

'How do children react when I use praise?' and 'What kinds of learning activities promote interaction among peers?' These questions and the assumptions underlying them form the basis of important decision making and action that will have subsequent influence on children and teaching practice. Teacher research, then, provides a more nuanced, in-depth understanding of the encounters, relationships, teaching practices, and student learning that occur daily in the classroom.

Data Collection and Analysis

Once a question is decided upon, teachers must have a systematic way of collecting data and time to reflect upon what they are discovering. Reflections should be noted in a research journal as well as in discussions with members of an inquiry group. Because teacher research is largely qualitative, the research question and plan will be modified continually to create a closer fit with the classroom environment and/or what teachers want to uncover about their teaching. This is important, because data collection must accurately represent what is going on in the classroom setting and not be based upon a dogmatic insistence on a specific form of data collection (Hatch, 2002). Inquiry groups, consisting of fellow students or teachers, can help in casting and recasting questions as well as in developing and modifying the research plan for how to collect data. Data collection is a disciplined undertaking, and teachers need to be continually aware of what they are collecting and why they are collecting it.

There are many ways to collect and analyze data, and it is important to remember that even though teacher research is primarily qualitative, many studies use a combination of both qualitative and quantitative methods. However, the key questions to keep in mind are: 'What am I looking for and what am I hoping to learn or discover?' In other words, what is the purpose of the study; what data should be collected and how; is it enough data; and does it address the question?

Some of the common methods of data collection in teacher research include direct classroom observation, audio or video recordings, and field notes, typically in the form of anecdotal records that are time based (e.g., recorded every 5 minutes) or unstructured to fit a specific purpose. Other observational methods include the use of room maps, which are visual representations of how space is used in the classroom, or patterns of movement as the teacher or children move from one activity or another (Rust, 2007). Conversations and group discussions with children, parents, and other relevant persons are part of everyday teaching and learning; group discussions, in particular, provide opportunities for children and teachers to engage in dialogue on a focused topic. Surveys and questionnaires are sets of written questions designed to focus on a specific topic or area of inquiry. A variant of the basic interview student teachers have found helpful, especially when time is a factor, is the 2-minute interview (Hill et al., 2005). In this method, the teacher asks two brief questions, usually during a break, group activity, or informal activity. Instead of recording the response(s) immediately, the teacher recalls the children's answers and writes them down as soon as she can later. Because the questions are brief and nothing is recorded at the time of the interview, the 2-minute interview is nonintrusive from the interviewee's point of view, and it seems more like a simple question-and-answer exchange.

Data analysis is a systematic process of data reduction. In qualitative data analysis, especially from a constructivist perspective, the result is only one of several possible representations of the meanings that the collected information may reveal. How a teacher represents data in a narrative will vary depending on what analysis approach is selected and a commitment to reflection. It is recommended that data is read and reread thoroughly and carefully many times, all the while keeping track of themes, hunches, interpretations, and recurring ideas (Taylor &

Bogdan, 1985). The researcher looks for emerging themes, patterns, and common threads in the data. These may include conversation topics, special vocabulary used by children, recurring activities, meanings, and feelings and ideas. In the end, there is no 'one' way to conduct data analysis. Being systematic is critical. Documenting everything and examining the data in as many ways as possible is important.

There are a number of useful books available to teacher researchers about collecting and analyzing data (e.g., Hubbard & Power, 1999; Meier & Henderson, 2007). Most of the ideas presented in these books are things teachers already do in the normal course of teaching. As stated earlier, the methods of teacher research must be imbedded in that what teachers already do. But like any sound research, teacher research must be systematic and carefully documented. Multiple approaches to inquiry using multiple sources of data and multiple methods of data analysis are essential to the quality and authenticity of teacher research and to ensure that the teacher researcher achieves the goal of addressing the question (Cochran-Smith & Lytle, 2009; Stremmel, 2015). This triangulation of the data helps minimize bias and increase the confidence in what is being discovered.

Inquiry Narrative: What Was Learned From Doing Teacher Research

In the last phase of teacher research, one tries to make sense of what was found or discovered. As we indicated at the beginning of the chapter, teacher researchers tell their stories of how they have addressed real problems using intentional and systematic data-based inquiry. These stories form the basis of an inquiry narrative that summarizes findings, particularly interpretations, thoughts, and reactions to these findings, in some formal way. A good teacher research study ends with a reflective discussion on what was learned, what will be done with what was found, how the results will be shared, and what new questions may have emerged.

Before concluding this section, it is important to emphasize or reassert that teacher research must be well designed and rigorous. In addition to being relevant to problems of practice and generating results that provide a legitimate basis for action, teacher research must be trustworthy. That is, 'Can the findings be trusted enough to act upon them?' Moreover, they must be believable, or have verisimilitude, which addresses the question, 'Do the findings appear to be true or real in the experience of teaching?' Teacher research that illuminates the complexity of teaching is likely to be viewed as credible to other teachers who can identify with the problems under investigation. When well designed, following a process of reflective inquiry, the so-called 'scientific approach' to inquiry (Dewey, 1933), teacher research has the potential to contribute substantially to the knowledge base of teaching and teacher education, a point we will discuss in more detail in the final section of this chapter.

The Teacher Research Literature

If teacher researchers are to make a large-scale impact, they need to have appropriate and accessible outlets for their discoveries. Over the last 20 years, there has been an increasing number of professional book publications devoted to teacher research (see, for example, Hubbard & Power, 1999; Meier & Henderson, 2007; Mills, 2000; Perry, Henderson, & Meier, 2012). Additionally, there have been a growing number of published studies of teacher research appearing in both research- and practitioner-oriented journals. For example, the journals *Teacher Research: A Journal of Inquiry*, *Educational Action Research*, and *Studying Teacher Education: A Journal of Self-Study of Teacher Education Practices*, and the newly released *Journal of Practitioner Research* are devoted entirely to teacher research. Several other journals, like *Harvard Educational Review*, *Teaching and Change*, *Teaching and Teacher Education*, and *Journal of*

Early Childhood Teacher Education (a publication of the National Association of Early Childhood Teacher Educators), are very open to publishing the work of teachers, students, and teacher educators who engage in reflective inquiry (Castle, 2013; Stremmel, 2002). Moreover, NAEYC's early childhood practitioner journal, *Voices of Practitioners*, is the only peer-reviewed online journal in the country solely devoted to publishing teacher research by early childhood practitioners and welcomes all forms of teacher research.

Increased interest in inquiry-based curriculum, Reggio Emilia–inspired practices (e.g., pedagogical documentation), and renewed interest in the philosophy of John Dewey may be associated with the growing amount of teacher research being published (Hill et al., 2005; Meier & Henderson, 2007). In a recent study of the state of teacher research in early childhood education, Castle (2013) indicated that one fifth of the articles in the *Journal of Early Childhood Teacher Education* from 1990 through 2010 were early childhood teacher research studies. Moreover, the NAEYC publication, *Our Inquiry, Our Practice* (Perry et al., 2012), demonstrates the profession's commitment to teacher research, with roughly half of the chapters from this book having originated in *Voices of Practitioners*. The examples of teacher research in this book may serve to inform and encourage both current and future early childhood teacher researchers.

While the publication of teacher research has increased, much of it is shared orally at regional and national teacher research or teacher education conferences such as the NAEYC's Annual Conference and Professional Development Institute and at the American Educational Research Association's Annual Meeting. Although there is a tendency to think of the products of research as a publication or presentation directed to academic audiences, teacher research must be first and foremost accessible and relevant to those who conduct it and those in situations to which it is immediately applicable. Teacher research must have the potential to make a difference in the lives of those who confront real issues and problems in particular sites, at particular moments, and in the lives of particular individuals and groups. To that end, teachers and teacher educators have been sharing the results of their research within professional learning communities and teacher networks for some time (Castle, 2013; Meyers & Rust, 2008; Perry et al., 2012). Teacher networks can nurture and validate the work of teacher education by continuing to develop the skills and dispositions associated with being a teacher researcher and by bringing their voices to issues and decisions that affect teachers directly (Stremmel, 2012).

The Value of Teacher Research

At the beginning of this chapter, we stated the primary purposes of teacher research were to improve practice and to better understand the context of teaching and learning. Teachers who engage in research become learners in their own classrooms by reflecting on what they believe and why they do what they do. Increasingly, teachers are expected to be accountable and must be more deliberate in documenting and evaluating their efforts. Moreover, teachers have a strong desire and need to know what is happening in their classrooms, and they want to know that they are effective. Teacher research is one means to that end.

Teacher research has the potential to be transformational. It can help teachers develop professional dispositions of lifelong learning, reflective and mindful teaching, and a better understanding of themselves, their classrooms, and their practice (Mills, 2000; Stringer, 1999). There is evidence that teacher research has a positive impact on teachers' perceptions of themselves as professionals and the relevance of research to their teaching, as well as their professional knowledge and actions (Cochran-Smith & Lytle, 2009; Fu, Stremmel, & Hill, 2002; Harrison, Dunn, & Coombe, 2006).

Teacher research has the potential not only to add to the knowledge we have about teaching and classrooms but also to change the kinds of questions we ask and the kinds of understanding that is produced. Thus, teacher research represents a distinctive way of knowing about teaching and learning that can alter, not just add to, what we know in the field (Stremmel, 2012). Finally, the notion of teacher as researcher validates a more comprehensive and accurate view of what it means to be a teacher. Viewing teachers as researchers affirms their professional status and acknowledges their important responsibility to both theory *and* practice. It also suggests that the aim of teacher education is not the development of teaching expertise or effective teaching techniques but the development of an ability to study and learn from teaching practices (Loughran, 2006; Stremmel, 2015).

Part III

CONCLUSION

14

RESEARCH AND PRACTICE
Promises, Pitfalls, and Limitations

So here we are! We hope the journey has been interesting and informative. We have aimed to ply readers with enough information to be competent consumers of research in early childhood education. As we have seen, there is a lot of territory to cover, and we hope that we have not only provided a comprehensive overview but also have piqued interest in finding out more. There may be readers out there who decide to become researchers themselves; we hope we have provided the starting place to think about what kinds of questions might be of interest, what types of methods would help get to those questions, and what types of research are needed in the field. It is a generative venture, and we are glad to have new participants in the quest!

We also know that many readers of this text are practitioners in the field or are studying to be so. We additionally hope that we have guided these readers to better understand what research can tell us and how and when research can be applied to educational settings. We hope that we have made the body of research seem a bit more friendly and a go-to resource when those inevitable questions about the daily work of teaching arise. We further hope that we have helped develop a curiosity that pushes practitioners in the field to listen, observe, and ask questions that can help improve their work with young children. The process of informal research on one's own classroom or educational setting can certainly be engaging, productive, and enhancing. Approaching our spaces as places teeming with questions, inquiries, and problems to solve can become a habit of mind and a way to enrich our professional lives and the ways we work.

For this chapter, we attempt to gather the 'big ideas' from the book as a whole—what did we want to make sure the readers broadly understood and would come away with? In what follows, we discuss these 'take-away' ideas.

We propose the following as big ideas that shaped the text. We also acknowledge that readers might have their own perspectives on our big ideas.

- Research is a process, and this process is governed by the culture and principles developed by generations of researchers. These processes are dynamic, not static.
- There are many ways to do research and many more ways to discuss the merits of those processes.
- In the process of research, the researcher must make many decisions, each of which shapes the process and the results.
- Many research projects are done well. Some published studies are not done very well or might not be communicated very well. Thus, being a knowledgeable consumer of research demands an evaluative stance.
- Evaluating research requires that the individual have general knowledge of research processes. While evaluating a study, it is important to pose questions about the research processes, consider the potential and limitations of the study (all studies have both!), and examine the connections among the components of the research process.

- Readers will inevitably read a study in which the processes are confusing. Some of the most intricate quantitative methodologies tend to be confusing to us! In those cases, it helps to sketch out what is known and not get too tied up in what is confusing. Just as early readers are advised to read on when a new word is confusing, we urge the same to consumers of research. In the end, it is often the case that some level of understanding can be achieved.
- Engaging in discussions with other early childhood professionals and those outside our field about early childhood research is a valuable endeavor and a necessary contribution to the development of our field.

Our first desired take-away is that research itself is complex. As we stated at the beginning, it is not enough just to say, "Research says. . ." because, as we have demonstrated, that can mean a whole host of things, perhaps some unintended by the use of the phrase. In order to make a claim about research, one needs to have read beyond the abstract of a journal article and have at least a basic understanding of the processes and claims of any study. One must be able to distinguish between quality research that can inform and broaden our thinking and less-rigorous attempts that could actually be dangerous if applied to situations for which it is not appropriate to do so.

Research can be invaluable in the attempt to afford probable explanations for phenomena and can be a powerful tool in helping us manage the ambiguity of the educational enterprise. Teachers and others working with young children engage daily in a complex set of behaviors and decision making. Information that helps us organize that complexity and helps guide us in good decision making regarding the lives of young children is certainly important. Similarly, information that helps us rethink our actions and take new, innovative, and productive approaches to our work in ways that benefit our young charges is also important. Finally, research can also provide information that helps to reveal what might have been hidden, subconscious, invisible, or not considered. The extent to which research can help us broaden our perspectives or ways of thinking about teaching, learning, children, and families is very important to our work.

Research has to be complex in order to represent or capture the complexity of real-world phenomena. And given this, it is important to keep in mind that research simply cannot tell us everything. Healthy skepticism of what any research actually can tell us is a perfectly acceptable stance. Even in research that aims to make a causal link between a particular variable and an outcome, it does not mean that the same results will follow in other similar research attempts or nonresearch contexts. Research does not determine destiny but rather is a way to help us organize and gain a picture or representation of what *may* be occurring. Very rarely should any research finding be unreflectively applied to a child's life without considering the real-world variables and contexts that a research study simply cannot fully capture. The value of research lies not in its being definitive but in the tentative stance of research as something to be explored, confirmed, or rejected in light of new evidence.

In being reflective about our own processes for this book, it was interesting to us, as we were writing the chapters, how much we struggled with our explanations because of the complexity of research. We all are researchers ourselves, so, in part, the struggle was in trying to explain processes and ideas that are very familiar to and habits of mind for us. Anyone who has tried to explain how to do a complex task to a young child, a parent, or a new teacher understands the dilemmas we faced. We struggled to figure out how much detail to go into. We had long conversations about what to include and what not to include. We each wrote long passages that then had to be cut or reduced. Finding the balance between providing enough information to be comprehensive and informative without going too far down the rabbit hole of a particular paradigm or method was tricky at times.

One thing this suggested to us was, despite our beliefs in our own open-mindedness about research, we all do hold allegiances to our various paradigms and approaches that go unexamined. As anyone reads research, it is important to keep in mind that researchers tend to be passionate about the things they study and the preferred ways of studying them. This is not a negative thing, but should always be taken into consideration when applying findings to the real world. We'll share an anecdote here. File and Mueller constructed the glossary of terms. File, a quantitatively trained researcher, took the first pass and (by her own admission) believed she had produced a comprehensive listing of terms. Mueller, a qualitative researcher, had to point out that the list overrepresented terms used in quantitative projects and had to add several terms from the qualitative paradigm. In some ways it is too overwhelming to think about it all at once, which is why, in the end, we created this guide. This is also why we believe the best way to understand the complexity of research is to take advantage of multiple sources of expertise. None of us could have, on our own, written a guide to understanding all types of research. Similarly, it can be helpful to discuss research with others—the insights offered by them help enrich the understanding any individual brings to the task.

Another take-away that is important to us is the understanding and willingness to acknowledge that research on and about children is both particularly interesting and particularly fraught. We believe it requires an approach of care and an extra layer of ethical consideration. It needs to always be remembered that children, as a whole, are a vulnerable population, and within the whole there are groups that are even more vulnerable. We have to take good care to protect their interests and to see things from their young perspectives. The 'do no harm' part of ethics in early childhood research must take on even more import. That said, over time, we have been encouraged to see a move toward the importance of children's perspectives in our field. We think it is accurate to credit the interpretive turn in research with helping us to see children not simply as research 'subjects' (to use the more outdated term) who provide the adults with information. There has been a push to consider children as having viewpoints that are worth trying to access, as having ideas worthy of study, and as having agency in their own lives that adults need to better understand. It is incumbent upon us as a field to try and figure out the best ways to connect with children to be able to truly tell their stories and capture their points of view. At the same time, given how much language dominates our own constructed understanding as adults, we must remember that young children construct their worlds in their own ways and that we cannot always access those meanings through our language-dependent methods, particularly when we 'listen' as adults.

Another important thought to us is reiterating the idea that as a good consumer of research, one's own expertise and experiences as a practitioner are important to consider alongside research. And research should be considered in light of actual practice. Our practical wisdom and craft knowledge are important and should not be discounted. We definitely believe that one of the responsibilities of being a professional in the field is to keep up to date on research findings to improve and enhance our work with children and their families. Research findings can influence our decision making in practice, and this should occur with contextualization into what we know about children, teaching, and learning. What might a particular finding mean in relationship to our specific group of children? Does a research finding make sense given what we know about our own classroom? What does it mean that curricular materials are 'research based'? We tend to believe that this means that findings or curricular decisions can and should be applied whole cloth and then we will have success. We must practice due diligence as professionals, learn about and know our children and educational settings, and have a dynamic relationship with research that informs our practice as well as honors our expertise and experience.

In the end, we all operate our daily lives with working theories about what it is we do. And we operate in the world with those theories, even if we are not aware of them. This includes theories of how children learn, behave, function, and develop and what it is we need to do as we intervene in these processes. As we know, as early childhood educators, this can have huge consequences for children. Research can be used as a means to formulate and understand those theories, to test ourselves to ensure that we have as much information as possible, and to tweak, broaden, enhance, or change those theories as we both read research and practice our craft. We all want to be the best early childhood professionals that we can in our various roles. We need to continue to fine tune our theories, and research can and should play an important role in this process. Both teachers and researchers theorize, question, and seek to discover new meaning and understanding. We ask readers to consider how this statement impacts the meaning of what it is to be a teacher and how teachers might use research information.

Finally, we hope that we have given the reader pause to reconsider research and to continue to both question and embrace what it is research can tell us and do for us—and what it cannot. We hope that this pushes readers to understand the responsibility to include research as part of their professional lives. We hope that we have helped generate more intellectual curiosity about teaching, learning, and caring and the role that research can play (and not play) in bringing forth the important questions that will make us better at what we do—for the children!

GLOSSARY

Abstract: A brief description of a research study or other larger work that appears at the beginning of a paper. An abstract may summarize the scope, purpose, and results of the work.

Analysis of variance (ANOVA): A statistical procedure that analyzes the mean differences between two or more groups by comparing the variance of between-groups and within-groups.

Axiology: The philosophical study of value or goodness, often related to ethics.

Bias: A systematic error in research sampling or testing that causes a result to deviate from the 'true' result through the selection or encouragement of one outcome over another.

Case study: An in-depth, descriptive analysis of a single participant, group, or event. Data may be gathered from a number of sources using several different methods (e.g., interviews, observations) and may continue over an extended period of time.

Cause-effect: A relationship between variables in which a change in one variable results in a change in the other variable.

Chi square: A statistical measure of how observed results compare to the expected results according to a specific hypothesis.

Coding: An analytical process by which qualitative or quantitative data is categorized or is assigned scores for later analysis.

Comparison group: A group of participants in an experiment or study with demographics that closely resemble the experimental group and are exposed to the same conditions as the experimental group except for the variable being tested.

Constructivist approach: A theory of knowledge that maintains that humans construct knowledge about the world through the interaction of their own thoughts and ideas and their experiences in the outside world.

Construct validity: How well a test or tool measures the constructs or theory it was designed to measure.

Content validity: The extent to which a measure is relevant to and representative of the elements of the construct being measured.

Context: The background, environment, setting, or framework that surrounds a phenomenon.

Contextualization: The dynamic process by which a phenomenon draws meaning via the context in which it occurs and the context is understood given the phenomenon therein.

Control group: A group of participants in an experiment or study that does not receive the experimental treatment and is simply observed. The control group is used as a comparison to determine the effects of the experimental treatment(s).

Correlational study: A quantitative research method that suggests (but cannot prove) whether a relationship exists between two or more variables (i.e., whether a change in one variable corresponds to a change in another).

Critical approach: A social theory that focuses on reflection and critique of social and cultural phenomena with a goal of making change to society.

Data: Information that can be gathered and analyzed in an effort to gain knowledge or make decisions.

Dependent variable: A variable or outcome of interest in a study that is observed and measured by the researcher. A dependent variable's value is hypothesized to be determined by the value of the independent variable.

Descriptive statistics: Statistical analyses used to quantifiably summarize and describe data in a meaningful way.

Developmentalism: Often attributed to Piaget, adherence to developmental theory in which human development over the lifespan is divided into distinct stages, each with specific and qualitative differences in behavior.

Effect size: A measure of the difference between group means (i.e., a quantified measure of the "strength" of a phenomenon).

Empirical: Gaining knowledge through measurable and observable phenomena and experiences, rather than through theory or belief.

Epistemology: The study of the nature of knowledge—its structure, conditions, sources, and limits.

Ethics: A branch of philosophy that focuses on organizing and recommending ideas of right and wrong conduct.

Ethnography: A qualitative research approach designed to obtain a systematic, in-depth description of people and cultures and an interpretation of their everyday life and practices.

Experiment (sometimes called true experiment): An investigation in which external variables are held constant as much as possible, except for one factor (the independent variable). An experiment tests a hypothesis by isolating the changes brought about by alterations to the independent variable.

Focus group: A qualitative data collection method in which a group of individuals is selected and interviewed at the same time. The group is asked to discuss their attitudes, feelings, reactions, and experiences regarding a specific research topic.

Generalizability: The extent to which findings can be applied or extended to other settings or populations; also called *ecological validity*.

Grounded theory: A general, inductive research method that generates or constructs theory through systematic research and data analysis.

Hierarchical linear modeling (HLM): A statistical procedure that analyzes data in a clustered or 'nested' linear structure in which data is hierarchical (i.e., represented by higher-level categories, subcategories, and lower-level individual units).

Independent variable: A variable that is controlled, manipulated, or changed by the researcher in a study and is hypothesized to have an effect on the dependent variable; used to define groups of participants on the basis of either random assignment or an existing characteristic.

Inferential statistics: Statistical analyses that are used to make generalizations about the population from which the research samples were drawn.

Interpretivist: A philosophical belief that reality is multiple and subjectively based on social constructions. There is an interactive, cooperative, and participative relationship between the researcher and the research subject. Researchers aim to understand and interpret motives, meanings, and subjective experiences as opposed to generalizing and predicting the causes and effects of human behavior.

Interrater reliability: The degree to which independent observers agree or are consistent in making subjective assessments (i.e., how similarly separate raters categorize or score items).

Mean ($\bar{X}$):   The average mathematical value of a set of numbers or data points.

Median: The value or quantity that lies at the midpoint of a distribution of scores.

Member-checking: Also known as *informant feedback,* a technique used in qualitative research to help improve the validity, accuracy, and credibility of research findings or interviews. Participants are asked to evaluate a summary or restatement of the research findings and whether the summary accurately and completely reflects their views, feelings, and experiences.

Methodology: The systematic, theoretical analysis of the procedures by which researchers describe, explain, and predict phenomena and gain knowledge.

Mixed (multiple) methods: A research approach that uses a combination of qualitative and quantitative approaches to answer research questions.

Multiple regression: A statistical procedure used to predict the value of a continuous dependent (or criterion) variable based on the known value of two or more other independent (or predictor) variables.

Normal distribution: An arrangement of data characterized by a bell-shaped curve in which most values cluster in the middle of the range and taper off symmetrically toward either extreme. Psychological variables tend to show distributions that are close to normal.

Objectivity: The principle or ideal that research findings are the result of natural occurrences rather than the beliefs and values or characteristics of the researcher. Objective research strives to be precise and unbiased, with researchers remaining distant and impartial to the investigation and outcomes.

Ontology: A branch of philosophy that examines the nature of existence, being, and reality.

Paradigm: A framework or model used to illustrate the accepted procedures, processes, standards, and theories of a field.

Pearson product moment correlation (r):   A measure of the strength and direction of the linear correlation between two variables.

Phenomenological study: A qualitative research approach that emphasizes the participants' subjective experiences and interpretations of the world in an attempt to understand people's perceptions, perspectives, and understandings of an event, or phenomenon.

Positivist: A philosophical belief that factual knowledge can only be gained through observation and measurement. Research is systematic, controlled, critical, and empirical, and reality is objective. Research and researcher are viewed as independent; the researcher's role is to collect data and objectively interpret the observable and quantifiable research findings.

Postmodernism: A paradigm of thought in which knowledge is considered to be local and contextualized. Reality is neither fixed, universal, nor knowable. Research is an attempt to gain understanding of the local experiences of individuals and groups.

Postpositivist: A philosophical approach in which reality is viewed as objective and existing, but it can never be fully understood. Research is an attempt to come to close approximations of reality and move closer to truth through rigorous data collection.

Poststructural: A philosophy or approach critiquing structuralism in which social order and individual behavior are determined via established social structures including language and culture. Poststructuralists argue for deeper understanding of the agency of individuals and call for an understanding of multiple realities and truths.

Pragmatic approach: A philosophical approach that theory derives from experiences in practice rather than theory guiding practice. The purpose of research is to examine phenomena in order to address or solve a problem and to develop theory from said examination.

Qualitative approaches: Methods of collecting nonnumerical data in which unstructured or semistructured techniques are used (i.e., interviews, observations). Qualitative approaches are used to gain an understanding of participant perspectives, motivations, and experiences.

Quantitative approaches: Structured methods of collecting scientific or mathematical data using objective measurements and statistical, mathematical, or numerical analysis to quantify variables.

Quasi-experiment: An empirical study that approximates an experimental design with non-random assignment of participants to groups.

Randomized control trial: A quantitative research design that randomly assigns participants into an experimental group or a control group.

Range: The difference between the lowest and highest scores in a distribution.

Reflexivity: In qualitative research, reflexivity is the process of examining oneself as a researcher. This involves examining one's assumptions and perspectives and how these influence the research process and outcomes.

Reliability: The degree to which an assessment tool or measure produces stable, consistent responses or results; a way of assessing the quality of a measurement procedure.

Sample: A group of people selected from a larger population to be in a research study.

Standard deviation: A statistical quantity calculated to indicate the amount of variance (or deviation) in a set of data values. A standard deviation of 0 indicates that data values tend to be close to the mean.

Statistical significance: The degree to which a result is not attributed to chance alone but rather can be explained by other underlying factors (i.e., whether the difference between two groups is a "real" difference). Significance is represented by the p value.

Subjectivity: The ways that research and its interpretations are influenced or biased by the perspectives, beliefs, or characteristics of the researcher.

Theoretical framework: A conceptual model that introduces and supports the theory behind research questions. A theoretical framework guides the research process by identifying specific theoretical assumptions and providing a basis for a hypothesis and the choice of research methods used.

Theory: A set of statements or ideas offered to explain how and why variables are related.

Thick description: An intensive, detailed description of observed behavior or phenomena that provides enough cultural context and meaning from which broader cultural interpretation can be made.

Transformative approach: An approach to research that suggests that the purpose of research should be to positively change the lives of the participants, group structures, or social structures, particularly to benefit oppressed or vulnerable groups.

Triangulation: Using more than one research method to collect data in an attempt to increase the believability of the research and to understand different dimensions of the same phenomenon.

Validity: The extent to which a study is able to determine a cause-and-effect relationship between the dependent and independent variables (i.e., the extent to which a study can rule out alternative explanations for the results).

Variable: A characteristic, number, or quantity that can take on different values.

Verisimilitude: The likelihood or believability of a research finding. Most often associated with qualitative research.

REFERENCES

Adair, J. K. (2014). Examining whiteness as an obstacle to positively approaching immigrant families in US early childhood educational settings. *Race Ethnicity and Education, 17*(5), 643–666.

Agee, J. (2009). Developing qualitative research questions: A reflective process. *International Journal of Qualitative Studies in Education, 22*(4), 431–447.

American Psychological Association. (2001). *Publication manual of the American Psychological Association* (5th ed.). Washington, DC: American Psychological Association.

American Psychological Association. (2010). *Publication manual of the American Psychological Association* (6th ed.). Washington, DC: American Psychological Association.

Anderson, G., & Herr, K. (1999). The new paradigm wars: Is there room for rigorous practitioner knowledge in schools and universities? *Educational Researcher, 28*(5), 12–21.

Anthony, J. L., Williams, J. M., Zhang, Z., Landry, S. H., & Dunkelberger, M. J. (2014). Experimental evaluation of the value added by raising a reader and supplemental parent training in shared reading. *Early Education and Development, 25*, 493–514.

Atwell, N. (1987). *In the middle: Writing, reading, and learning with adolescents.* Portsmouth, NH: Boynton and Cook-Heinemann.

Barnett, W. S. (2008). *Preschool education and its lasting effects: Research and policy implications.* Boulder and Tempe: Education and the Public Interest Center & Education Policy Research Unit. Retrieved from http://nieer.org/resources/research/PreschoolLastingEffects.pdf

Bauml, M. (2011). "We learned all about that in college": The role of teacher preparation in novice kindergarten/primary teachers' practice. *Journal of Early Childhood Teacher Education, 32*, 225–239.

Beatty, B. (2005). The rise of the American nursery school: Laboratory for a science of child development. In D. Pillemer & S. White (Eds.), *Developmental psychology and social change* (pp. 264–287). New York, NY: Cambridge University Press.

Becker, D. R., McClelland, M. M., Loprinzi, P., & Trost, S. G. (2014). Physical activity, self-regulation, and early academic achievement in preschool children. *Early Education and Development, 25*, 56–70.

Belsky, J. (1986). Infant day care: A cause for concern? *Zero to Three, 6*, 1–7.

Belsky, J. (1988). The "effects" of infant day care reconsidered. *Early Childhood Research Quarterly, 3*, 235–272.

Blaise, M. (2005). A feminist poststructuralist study of children "doing" gender in an urban kindergarten classroom. *Early Childhood Research Quarterly, 20*(1), 85–108.

Blank, J., & Schneider, J. J. (2011). "Use your words": Reconsidering the language of conflict in the early years. *Contemporary Issues in Early Childhood, 12*(3), 198–211.

Bloch, M. (1987). Becoming scientific and professional: A historical perspective on the aims and effects of early education. In T. Popkewitz (Ed.), *The formation of school subjects* (pp. 25–62). Basingstoke, England: Falmer.

Bloch, M. (1991). Critical science and the history of child development's influence on early education research. *Early Education and Development, 2*(2), 95–108.

Bloch, M. (1992). Critical perspectives on the historical relationship between child development and early childhood research. In S. Kessler & B. B. Swadener (Eds.), *Reconceptualizing the early childhood curriculum: Beginning the dialogue* (pp. 3–20). New York, NY: Teachers College Press.

Bloch, M. (2000). Governing teachers, parents, and children through child development knowledge. *Human Development, 43*(4), 257–265.

Boller, K., Paulsell, D., Del Grosso, P., Blair, R., Lundquist, E., Kassow, D. Z., . . . & Raikes, A. (2015). Impacts of a child care quality rating and improvement system on child care quality. *Early Childhood Research Quarterly, 30*, 306–315.

Borko, H., Liston, D., & Whitcomb, J. (2007). Genres of empirical research in teacher education. *Journal of Teacher Education, 58*(1), 3–11.

Brooks-Gunn, J., & Johnson, A. D. (2006). G. Stanley Hall's contribution to science, practice and policy: The child study, parent education, and child welfare movements. *History of Psychology, 9*(3), 247–258.

Brown, K., Sumsion, J., & Press, F. (2011). Dark matter: The "gravitational pull" of maternalist discourses on politicians' decision making for early childhood policy in Australia. *Gender and Education, 23*, 263–280.

Bruner, J. (1986). *Actual minds, possible worlds.* Cambridge, MA: Harvard University Press.

Bumgarner, E., & Lin, M. (2014). Hispanic immigrant children's English language acquisition: The role of socioeconomic status and early care arrangement. *Early Education and Development, 25*, 515–529.

Cabell, S. Q., DeCoster, J., LoCasale-Crouch, J., Hamre, B. K., & Pianta, R. C. (2013). Variation in the effectiveness of instructional interactions across preschool classroom settings and learning activities. *Early Childhood Research Quarterly, 28*(4), 820–830.

Cannella, G., & Bloch, M. (2006). Social policy, education, and childhood in dangerous times: Revolutionary actions or global complicity. *International Journal of Educational Policy, Research, and Practice, 7*, 5–19.

Cannella, G., & Lincoln, Y. (2011). Ethics, research, regulations, and critical social science. In N. Denzin & Y. Lincoln (Eds.), *The Sage handbook of qualitative research* (pp. 81–90). Thousand Oaks, CA: Sage Publications.

Castle, C. (2013). The state of teacher research in early childhood teacher education. *Journal of Early Childhood Teacher Education, 34*, 268–285.

Christians, C. (2011). Ethics and politics in qualitative research. In N. Denzin & Y. Lincoln (Eds.), *The Sage handbook of qualitative research* (pp. 61–80). Thousand Oaks, CA: Sage Publications.

Clandinin, D. J., & Connelly, F. M. (2000). *Narrative inquiry: Experience and story in qualitative research.* San Francisco: Jossey-Bass.

Clarke-Stewart, K. A. (1988). "The 'effects' of infant day care reconsidered" reconsidered: Risks for parents, children, and researchers. *Early Childhood Research Quarterly, 3*, 293–318.

Clifford, R. M., Reszka, S. S., & Rossbach, H. G. (2010). *Reliability and validity of the early childhood environment rating scale.* Retrieved from http://www.ersi.info/PDF/ReliabilityEcers.pdf

Coady, M. (2010). Ethics in early childhood research. In G. MacNaughton, S. Rolfe, & I. Siraj-Blatchford (Eds.), *Doing early childhood research* (pp. 73–84). New York, NY: Open University Press.

Cochran-Smith, M., & Lytle, S. (1993). *Inside/outside: Teacher research and knowledge.* New York, NY: Teachers College Press.

Cochran-Smith, M., & Lytle, S. (2009). *Inquiry as stance: Practitioner research for the next generation.* New York, NY: Teachers College Press.

Cochran-Smith, M., & Lytle, S. L. (1999). The teacher research movement: A decade later. *Educational Researcher, 28*(7), 15–25.

Conner, J., Kelly-Vance, L., Ryalls, B., & Friehe, M. (2014). A play and language intervention for two-year-old children: Implications for improving play skills and language. *Journal of Research in Childhood Education, 28*(2), 221–237.

Consortium for Longitudinal Studies. (1983). *As the twig is bent: Lasting effects of preschool programs.* Hillsdale, NJ: Erlbaum.

Corey, S. M. (1953). *Action research to improve school practices*. New York, NY: Teachers College Press.

Corsaro, W. (1985). *Friendship and peer culture in the early years*. Norwood, NJ: Ablex.

Creswell, J. W. (2014). *Research design: Qualitative, quantitative, and mixed methods approaches*. Thousand Oaks, CA: Sage Publications.

Crotty, M. (1998). *The foundations of social research: Meaning and perspective in the research process*. Thousand Oaks, CA: Sage.

Davis, S. H. (2007). Bridging the gap between research and practice: What's good, what's bad, and how can one be sure? *Phi Delta Kappan, 88*(8), 568–578.

Denham, S. A., Bassett, H. H., Sirotkin, Y. A., Brown, C., & Morris, C. S. (2015). "No-o-o-o peek-ing": Preschoolers' executive control, social competence, and classroom adjustment. *Journal of Research in Childhood Education, 29*, 212–225.

Denzin, N. (1978). *The research act: A theoretical introduction to sociological methods* (2nd ed.). New York: McGraw-Hill.

Denzin, N. K., & Lincoln, Y. S. (Eds.). (2008). *The landscape of qualitative research*. Thousand Oaks, CA: Sage Publications.

Dewey, J. (1933). *How we think, a restatement of the relation of reflective thinking to the educative process*. Boston, MA: Heath.

Dewey, J. (1938). *Experience and education*. New York, NY: Collier Books.

Dillon, D. R., O'Brien, D. G., & Heilman, E. E. (2000). Literacy research in the next millennium: From paradigms to pragmatism and practicality. *Reading Research Quarterly, 35*, 10–26.

Domitrovich, C. E., Morgan, N. R., Moore, J. E., Cooper, B. R., Shah, H. K., Jacobson, L., & Greenberg, M. T. (2013). One versus two years: Does length of exposure to an enhanced preschool program impact the academic functioning of disadvantaged children in kindergarten? *Early Childhood Research Quarterly, 28*, 704–713.

Doubet, S. L., & Ostrosky, M. M. (2015). The impact of challenging behavior on families: I don't know what to do. *Topics in Early Childhood Special Education, 34*, 223–233.

Duckworth, E. (1997). *Teacher to teacher*. New York, NY: Teachers College Press.

Eckholm, E. (1992, October 6). Learning if infants are hurt when mothers go to work. *The New York Times*. Retrieved from http://www.nytimes.com/1992/10/06/us/learning-if-infants-are-hurt-when-mothers-go-to-work.html

Edwards, C. P., Cline, K., Gandini, L., Giacomelli, A., Giovannini, D., & Galardini, A. (2014). Books, stories, and the imagination at "The Nursery Rhyme": A qualitative case study of a preschool learning environment in Pistoia, Italy. *Journal of Research in Childhood Education, 28*(1), 18–42.

Eisenhart, M., & Towne, L. (2003). Contestation and change in national policy on "scientifically based" education research. *Educational Researcher, 32*(7), 31–38.

Fisher, C. J., & Ellis, W. G. (1988). The literary content of children's responses to poetry. *Journal of Research in Childhood Education, 3*, 35–45.

Forry, N., Iruka, I. U., Tout, K., Torquati, J., Susman-Stillman, A., Bryant, D., & Daneri, M. P. (2013). Predictors of quality and child outcomes in family child care settings. *Early Childhood Research Quarterly, 28*(4), 893–904.

Fosnot, C. T. (2005). *Constructivism: Theory, perspectives, and practices* (2nd ed.). New York, NY: Teachers College Press.

Freeman, D. (1998). *Doing teacher research: From inquiry to understanding*. New York, NY: Heinle Publishers.

Fu, V. R., Stremmel, A. J., & Hill, L. T. (Eds.). (2002). *Teaching and learning: Collaborative exploration of the Reggio Emilia Approach*. Upper Saddle River, NJ: Merrill Prentice Hall.

Gage, N. L. (1989). The paradigm wars and their aftermath: A "historical" sketch of research on teaching since 1989. *Educational Researcher, 18*(7), 4–10.

Geertz, C. (1973). *The interpretation of cultures*. New York, NY: Basic Books.

Gersten, R. (2013). The two cultures of educational research? *The Elementary School Journal, 114*, 139–141.

Glaser, B., & Strauss, A. (1967). *The discovery of grounded theory: Strategies for qualitative research.* Hawthorne, NY: Aldine De Gruyter.

Goffin, S. (1996). Child development knowledge and early childhood teacher preparation: Assessing the relationship—A special collection. *Early Childhood Research Quarterly, 11*(2), 117–133.

Gracey, H. (1972). *Curriculum or craftsmanship: Elementary school teachers in a bureaucratic system.* Chicago, IL: University of Chicago Press.

Graue, M. E. (1992). *Ready for what? Constructing meanings of readiness for kindergarten.* Albany, NY: SUNY Press.

Graue, M. E. (1998). Through a small window: Knowing children and research through standardized tests. In B. Spodek, O. N. Saracho, & A. D. Pellegrini (Eds.), *Issues in Early Childhood Educational Research* (pp. 30–48). New York, NY: Teachers College Press.

Graue, M. E., Whyte, K. L., & Karabon, A. E. (2015). The power of improvisational teaching. *Teaching and Teacher Education, 48,* 13–21.

Guba, E. (1978). *Toward a methodology of naturalistic inquiry in educational evaluation.* CSE Monograph Series in Evaluation. Los Angeles, CA: Center for the Study of Evaluation.

Guba, E. G., & Lincoln, Y. S. (2005). Paradigmatic controversies, contradictions, and emerging confluences. In N. K. Denzin & Y.S. Lincoln (Eds.), *The Sage handbook of qualitative research* (3rd ed., pp. 191–215). Thousand Oaks, CA: Sage.

Harrison, L. J., Dunn, M., & Coombe, K. (2006). Making research relevant in preservice early childhood teacher education. *Journal of Early Childhood Teacher Education, 27,* 217–229.

Harrist, A. W., Achacoso, J. A., John, A., Pettit, G. S., Bates, J. E., & Dodge, K. A. (2014). Reciprocal and complementary sibling interactions: Relations with socialization outcomes in the kindergarten classroom. *Early Education and Development, 25,* 202–222.

Hatch, A. (2002). *Doing qualitative research in education settings.* Albany, NY: State University of New York Press.

Hatch, J. A. (1985). The quantoids versus the smooshes: Struggling with methodological rapprochement. *Issues in Education, 3*(2), 158–167.

Hatch, J. A. (2006). Teacher research in early childhood education: Questions for teacher educators. *Beyond the Journal: Young Children on the Web.* Retrieved from http://journal.naeyc.org/btj/vp/AmosHatchQuestions.asp

Hatch, J. A. (2007). Back to modernity? Early childhood qualitative research in the 21st century. In J. A. Hatch (Ed.), *Early childhood qualitative research* (pp. 7–22). New York, NY: Routledge.

Heath, S. B. (1983). *Ways with words: Language, life, and work in communities and classrooms.* Cambridge, MA: Press Syndicate.

Heimer, L. G. (2005). Voices at the table: An analysis of collaboration in the policy process for a local preschool initiative. In S. Ryan & S. Grieshaber (Eds.), *Practical transformations and transformational practices: Globalization, postmodernism, and early childhood education, Advances in Early Education and Day Care Volume 14* (pp. 19–35). Greenwich, CT: JAI Press.

Hill, L. T., Stremmel, A. J., & Fu, V. R. (2005). *Teaching as inquiry: Re-thinking curriculum in early childhood education.* Boston, MA: Pearson Allyn & Bacon.

Hojnoski, R. L., Columba, H. L., & Polignano, J. (2014). Embedding mathematical dialogue in parent–child shared book reading: A preliminary investigation. *Early Education and Development, 25,* 469–492.

Holmes, K., Holmes, S. V., & Watts, K. (2012). A descriptive study on the use of materials in vocabulary lessons. *Journal of Research in Childhood Education, 26,* 237–248.

Howe, K., & Eisenhart, M. (1990). Standards for qualitative (and quantitative research): A prolegomenon. *Educational Researcher, 19*(4), 2–9.

Howe, K., & Moses, M. (1999). Ethics in educational research. *Review of Research in Education, 24,* 21–59.

Howe, K. R. (1988). Against the quantitative-qualitative incompatibility thesis or dogmas die hard. *Educational Researcher, 17*(8), 10–16.

Hubbard, R. S., & Power, B. M. (1999). *Living the questions: A guide for teacher researchers.* York, ME: Stenhouse Publishers.

Hughes, P. (2010). Paradigms, methods, and knowledge. In G. MacNaughton, S. A. Rolfe, & I. Siraj-Blatchford (Eds.), *Doing early childhood research* (pp. 35–62). New York, NY: Open University Press.

James, A., Jenks, C., & Prout, A. (1998). *Theorizing childhood*. New York: Teachers College Press.

Janesick, V. (1998). The dance of qualitative research design: Metaphor, methodolatry, and meaning. In N. Denzien & Y. Lincoln (Eds.), *Strategies of qualitative inquiry* (pp. 35–55). Thousand Oaks, CA: Sage Publications.

Johnson, R. B., & Onweugbuzie, A. J. (2004). Mixed methods research: A research paradigm whose time has come. *Educational Researcher, 33*(7), 14–26.

Kalota, G. (2014, February 11). Vast study casts doubts on value of mammograms. *The New York Times*. Retrieved from http://www.nytimes.com/2014/02/12/health/study-adds-new-doubts-about-value-of-mammograms.html

Kinard, T. A. (2015). Anonymous green painting: An artifact of resistance as danger and hope in an early childhood educational setting. *International Journal of Qualitative Studies in Education, 28*(2), 195–215.

Kliebard, H. (2004). *The struggle for the American curriculum, 1893–1958*. New York, NY: Routledge Falmer.

Kuhn, T. S. (1962/2012). *The structure of scientific revolutions*. Chicago, IL: University of Chicago Press.

Lagemann, E. C. (1997). Contested terrain: A history of education research in the United States, 1890–1990. *Educational Researcher, 26*(9), 5–17.

Lather, P. (1991). *Getting smart*. New York, NY: Routledge.

Lather, P. (2006). Paradigm proliferation as a good thing to think with: Teaching research in education as a wild profusion. *International Journal of Qualitative Studies in Education, 19*(1), 35–57.

Lewin, K. (1948). *Resolving social conflict: Selected papers on group dynamics*. New York, NY: Harper & Row.

Lincoln, Y. S., Lynham, S. A., & Guba, E. G. (2011). Paradigmatic controversies, contradictions, and emerging confluences, revisited. *The Sage Handbook of Qualitative Research, 4*, 97–128.

Loh, J. (2013). Inquiry into issues of trustworthiness and quality in narrative studies: A perspective. *The Qualitative Report, 18*(65), 1–15.

Loizou, E. (2011). Disposable cameras, humour and children's abilities. *Contemporary Issues in Early Childhood, 12*, 148–162.

Loughran, J. (2006). *Developing a pedagogy of teacher education: Understanding teaching and learning about teaching*. New York, NY: Routledge.

Lubeck, S. (1985). *Sandbox society: Early education in black and white America*. Philadelphia, PA: Falmer.

Madrid, S., Baldwin, N., & Frye, E. (2013). "Professional feeling": One early childhood educator's emotional discomfort as a teacher and learner. *Journal of Early Childhood Research, 11*(3), 274–291.

Meier, D., & Stremmel, A. (2010). Narrative inquiry and stories: The value for early childhood teacher research. *Voices of Practitioners, 12*, 1–4. Retrieved from http://www.naeyc.org/publications/vop/teacherresearch

Meier, D. R., & Henderson, B. (2007). *Learning from young children in the classroom: The art and science of teacher research*. New York, NY: Teachers College Press.

Meisels, S. J., Xue, Y., & Shamblott, M. (2008). Assessing language, literacy, and mathematics skills with work sampling for Head Start. *Early Education and Development, 19*(6), 963–981.

Mertens, D. M. (2014). *Research and evaluation in education and psychology: Integrating diversity with quantitative, qualitative, and mixed methods*. Thousand Oaks, CA: Sage Publications.

Meyers, E., & Rust, F. (Eds.). (2008). *The missing link—Connecting teacher research, practice & policy to improve student learning*. New York, NY: Teachers Network.

Mills, G. (2000). *Action research: A guide for the teacher researcher*. Upper Saddle River, NJ: Merrill and Prentice-Hall.

National Association for the Education of Young Children. (n.d.). *Ethical standards for research*. Retrieved from https://www.naeyc.org/resources/research/ethical

National Institute for Literacy, National Early Literacy Panel. (2008). Developing early literacy: Report of the National Early Literacy Panel. Retrieved from http://lincs.ed.gov/publications/pdf/NELPReport09.pdf

National Research Council. (2002). Scientific research in education. Committee on Scientific Principles for Education Research. R. J. Shavelson & L. Towne (Eds.). Center for Education. Division of Behavioral and Social Sciences and Education. Washington, DC: National Academies Press.

National School Boards Association (n.d.). *Background on early childhood education: Key points.* Retrieved from https://www.nsba.org/advocacy/federal-legislative-priorities/early-childhood-education/background-early-childhood

Nicholson, J., Kurnik, J., Jevgjovikj, M., & Ufoegbune, V. (2015). Deconstructing adults' and children's discourse on children's play: Listening to children's voices to destabilise deficit narratives. *Early Child Development and Care, 185*(10), 1569–1586.

Nicolopoulou, A., Cortina, K. S., Ilgaz, H., Cates, C. B., & de Sá, A. B. (2015). Using a narrative- and play-based activity to promote low-income preschoolers' oral language, emergent literacy, and social competence. *Early Childhood Research Quarterly, 31,* 147–162.

Paley, V. (1997). Foreword. In I. Hall, C. Campbell, & E. Miech (Eds.), *Class acts: Teachers reflect on their own classroom practice* (pp. vii–ix). Cambridge, MA: Harvard Education Review.

Paley, V. G. (1981). *Wally's stories.* Cambridge, MA: Harvard University Press.

Paley, V. G. (1990). *The boy who would be a helicopter: The uses of storytelling in the classroom.* Cambridge, MA: Harvard University Press.

Patton, M. Q. (2015). *Qualitative research and evaluation methods* (4th ed.). Los Angeles, CA: Sage.

Perry, G., Henderson, B., & Meier, D. (Eds.). (2012). *Our inquiry, our practice: Undertaking, supporting, and learning from early childhood teacher research.* Washington, DC: NAEYC.

Pew Research Center. (2015). *"Public and scientists" views on science and society.* Retrieved from http://www.pewinternet.org/files/2015/01/PI_ScienceandSociety_Report_012915.pdf

Phillips, D., & McCartney, K. (2005). The disconnect between research and policy on child care. In D. B. Pillemer & S. H. White (Eds.), *Developmental psychology and social change: Research, history and policy* (pp. 104–139). New York, NY: Cambridge University Press.

Phillips, D. C. (2009). A quixotic quest? Philosophical issues in assessing the quality of education research. In P. B. Walters, A. Lareau, & S. H. Ranis (Eds.), *Education research on trial: Policy reform and the call for scientific rigor* (pp. 163–195). New York, NY: Routledge.

Phillips, D. C., & Burbules, N. C. (2000). *Postpositivism and educational research.* Lanham, MD: Rowman & Littlefield.

Piaget, J. (1965). *The moral judgment of the child.* New York, NY: The Free Press.

Piasta, S. B., Justice, L. M., Cabell, S. Q., Wiggins, A. K., Turnbull, K. P., & Currenton, S. M. (2012). Impact of professional development on preschool teachers' conversational responsivity and children's linguistic productivity and complexity. *Early Childhood Research Quarterly, 27,* 387–400.

Pinar, W. (2004). *What is curriculum theory?* Mahwah, NJ: Lawrence Erlbaum Associates.

Polly, D., Wang, C., McGee, J., Lambert, R. G., Martin, C. S., & Pugalee, D. (2014). Examining the influence of a curriculum-based elementary mathematics professional development program. *Journal of Research in Childhood Education, 28,* 327–343.

Popkewitz, T. (1984). *Paradigm and ideology in educational research: The social functions of the intellectual.* New York, NY: Falmer Press.

Quintero, E. (2010). Something to say: Children learning through story. *Early Education and Development, 21*(3), 372–391.

Rabinow, P., & Sullivan, W. (1987). *Interpretive social science: A second look.* Berkeley, CA: University of California Press.

Rhedding-Jones, J. (2007). Who chooses what research methodology. In J. A. Hatch (Ed.), *Early childhood qualitative research* (pp. 207–221). New York, NY: Routledge.

Richters, J. E., & Zahn-Waxler, C. (1988). The infant day care controversy: Current status and future directions. *Early Childhood Research Quarterly, 3,* 319–336.

Rist, R. (1970). Student social class and teacher expectations: The self-fulfilling prophesy in teacher education. *Harvard Educational Review, 40*(3), 411–451.

Rudolph, J. L. (2014). Why understanding science matters: The IES research guidelines as a case in point. *Educational Researcher, 43*(1), 15–18.

Rust, F. O. (2007). Action research in early childhood contexts. In J. A. Hatch (Ed.), *Early childhood qualitative research* (pp. 95–108). New York, NY: Routledge/Taylor & Francis.

Sabol, T. J., & Pianta, R. C. (2014). Do standard measures of preschool quality used in statewide policy predict school readiness? *Education Finance and Policy, 9*, 116–154.

Saldaña, J. (2013). *The coding manual for qualitative researchers* (2nd ed.). Los Angeles, CA: Sage Publications.

Saracho, O. N., & Spodek, B. (2013). Introduction: A contemporary researcher's vade mecum (redux). In O. N. Saracho & B. Spodek (Eds.), *Handbook of research on the education of young children* (3rd ed., pp. 1–15). New York, NY: Routledge.

Schon, D. (1983). *The reflective practitioner*. New York, NY: Basic Books.

Scott, D. (2008). *Critical essays on major curriculum theorists*. London, UK: Routledge.

Sheridan, S. M., Knoche, L. L., Edwards, C. P., Kupzyk, K. A., Clarke, B. L., & Kim, E. M. (2014). Efficacy of the getting ready intervention and the role of parental depression. *Early Education and Development, 25*, 746–769.

Sherwood, S. A., & Reifel, S. (2013). Valuable and unessential: The paradox of preservice teachers' beliefs about the role of play in learning. *Journal of Research in Childhood Education, 27*(3), 267–282.

Sherwood, S.A.S., & Reifel, S. (2010). The multiple meanings of play: Exploring preservice teachers' beliefs about a central element of early childhood education. *Journal of Early Childhood Teacher Education, 31*, 322–343.

Smith, L. (1990). Ethics, field studies, and the paradigm crisis. In E. Guba (Ed.), *The paradigm dialogue* (pp. 139–157). Newbury Park, CA: Sage Publications.

Society for Research in Child Development. (2007). *Ethical standards in research*. Retrieved from http://www.srcd.org/about-us/ethical-standards-research

Soukakou, E. P. (2012). Measuring quality in inclusive preschool classrooms: Development and validation of the Inclusive Classroom Profile (ICP). *Early Childhood Research Quarterly, 27*, 478–488.

Souto-Manning, M. (2014). Making a stink about the "ideal" classroom: Theorizing and storying conflict in early childhood education. *Urban Education, 49*(6), 607–634.

Stenhouse, L. (1975). *An introduction to curriculum research and development*. London, UK: Heinemann.

Stenhouse, L. (1981). What counts as research? *British Journal of Education Studies, 29*(2), 103–114.

Strauss, A. (1987). *Qualitative analysis for social scientists*. New York, NY: Cambridge University Press.

Stremmel, A. (2002). Nurturing professional and personal growth through inquiry. *Young Children, 57*(5), 62–70.

Stremmel, A. (2015). Repositioning teacher education: Teacher research as professional development. *Voices of Practitioners, 10*(2), 98–103. Retrieved from http://www.naeyc.org/files/naeyc/file/vop/VOP_Summer_2015_repostion.pdf

Stremmel, A. J. (2012). Reshaping the landscape of early childhood teaching through teacher research. In G. Perry, B. Henderson, & D. R. Meier (Eds.), *Our inquiry, our practice: Undertaking, supporting, and learning from early childhood teacher research(ers)* (pp. 107–116). Washington, DC: NAEYC.

Stringer, E. T. (1999). *Action research* (2nd ed.). Thousand Oaks, CA: Sage Publications.

Swartz, M. I., & Easterbrooks, M. A. (2014). The role of parent, provider, and child characteristics in parent–provider relationships in infant and toddler classrooms. *Early Education and Development, 25*, 573–598.

Taylor, S. J., & Bogdan, R. (1985). *Introduction to qualitative research methods* (2nd ed.). New York, NY: Wiley.

Teaching Strategies. (2010). *Research foundation: Language and literacy.* Retrieved from http://teachingstrategies.com/content/pageDocs/TS-CC-Research-Foundation-Language-Literacy_11-2013.pdf

Tempest, A., & Wells, B. (2012). Alliances and arguments: A case study of a child with persisting speech difficulties in peer play. *Child Language Teaching and Therapy, 28*(1), 57–72.

Thompson, R. A. (1988). The effects of infant day care through the prism of attachment theory: A critical appraisal. *Early Childhood Research Quarterly, 3,* 273–282.

Tominey, S. L., & McClelland, M. M. (2011). Red light, purple light: Findings from a randomized trial using circle time games to improve behavioral self-regulation in preschool. *Early Education and Development, 22,* 489–519.

Trawick-Smith, J., & Dziurgot, T. (2010) Untangling teacher–child play interactions: Do teacher education and experience influence "good-fit" responses to children's play? *Journal of Early Childhood Teacher Education, 31*(2), 106–128. doi:10.1080/10901021003781148

Truong, S., & Mahon, M. (2012). Through the lens of participatory photography: Engaging Thai children in research about their community play centre. *International Journal of Play, 1*(1), 75–90.

U.S. Department of Health and Human Services, National Institutes of Health. (2006). *The NICHD study of early child care and youth development: Findings for children up to age 4 ½ years* (NIH Pub No. 05–4318). Retrieved from https://www.nichd.nih.gov/publications/pubs/documents/seccyd_06.pdf

Walsh, D. J., Tobin, J. J., & Graue, M. E. (1993). The interpretive voice: Qualitative research in early childhood education. In B. Spodek (Ed.), *Handbook of research on the education of young children* (pp. 464–476). New York, NY: Macmillan.

Winter, S. M., & Sass, D. A. (2011). Healthy & ready to learn: Examining the efficacy of an early approach to obesity prevention and school readiness. *Journal of Research in Childhood Education, 25,* 304–325.

Wong, V. C., Cook, T. D., Barnett, W. S., & Jung, K. (2008). Evaluation of five state pre kindergarten programs. *Journal of Policy Analysis and Management, 27,* 122–154.

Zeichner, K. (1999). The new scholarship in teacher education. *Educational Researcher, 28*(9), 4–15.

Zeichner, K. M., & Noffke, S. E. (2001). Practitioner research. In V. Richardson (Ed.), *Handbook of research on teaching* (4th ed., pp. 298–330). Washington, DC: American Educational Research Association.

INDEX

References to tables and figures are indicated by an italicized page number.

children, adult presence: data coding 123; data collection 127–9; data, portrayal 126–7; extensive survey methodology, example 127–9; generalization book 126; inputs, types 122–3; intervention, description 126; interviewing, usage 123; parent/child math utterances, percentage *128*; participants, location (challenges) 130; potential/pitfalls/limitations 129–31; qualitative studies 122–5; quantitative researchers, interests 121; quantitative studies 125–9; researcher interest 120–1; researcher perspectives 123–7; researcher questions 121–2; research methods, selection 122–9; research questions 120; respondent group surveys 128–9; sample, location (difficulty) 130; study participants, recruitment 123; study, single-subject, multiple-baseline design 127; teachers, observation 124

Children Crossing Borders (CCB) Study 53, 55, 56

children, research: data collection 114–15; individual studies, limitations 118; methods 112–16; observational methods, usage 114; observation, technology (usage) 114; observed behavior, meaning (low-level judgments) 118; photographs, usage 113; potential/pitfalls/limitations 116–18; qualitative studies 112–13; quantitative studies 113–16; questions 109; safety 28; technology, usage 114; watching 117; *see also* research; study

Children's Play Narratives Project (CPN) 18

chi square analyses 95–6

claims, making (process) 71

classroom: adjustment, prediction *94*; adult–child interactions, study of 133–4; children, nesting 101; improvisational practice, usage 54–5; literacy support interventions 99; quality, measurement options (limitations) 152; teacher behaviors, study of 133–4; teacher relationship 38; young children, discussion 42

Classroom Assessment Scoring System (CLASS) 134, 138; cycles, nesting 139; design 139; instrument, familiarity 141

classroom, research questions 132, 133–4; conflict resolution, study example 136–7; cross-case analysis 137; data collection 135; interpretive method 136; linear models 139; methods, selection 134–40; potential/pitfalls/limitations 140–2; practice, contradictions/complications 137; pretest collection 138; qualitative researcher questions 132; qualitative studies 134–7; quantitative study 133, 137–40; questions, design studies 135; researcher interest 132–3; researcher perspectives 135–7,

138–40; spiral analysis 135–6; storytelling activities, study of 133

closed-ended options, usage 84

codes, list (researcher development) 68

coding, approach 68–9

comparative analyses 95–100

comparative questions/research 78

complementary interactions, frequencies 111

complex subjects, examination 4

concept/phenomenon 34

conceptualizations, completion (absence) 34

concurrent validity, assessment 40

conflict resolution, study example 136–7

conflict theory 34; application 44

Conner, J. 14

constant comparison 68

constructionism 11; paradigm 48–9

constructivist paradigms 14, 15–16

construct validity, appraisal 40

contexts 22–7; family context 25

contextualization, idea/process 56

continuous dependent variables: comparison 96–8; effects 98–9; interaction effects 99–100

control variable, usage 81

convenience decision, advantages/disadvantages 63

convergent validity 40

cool executive control (CEC): age/gender/maternal education comparisons *98*, 99; measure 76

Corey, Stephen 158

correlational analysis 89–95; usage 77–8

correlational relationships, importance 92–3

Creative Curriculum for Preschool 9

critical race theory (CRT): multivocal ethnography, combination 66–7; theoretical framework 70

cross-case analysis 137

cultural misunderstandings 66

culture 22

curriculum: inquiry-based curriculum 162; study of 23; teacher decision making, qualitative study of 121

curriculum, research questions 132, 133–4; conflict resolution, study example 136–7; cross-case analysis 137; data collection 135; interpretive method 136; linear models 139; methods 134–40; potential/pitfalls/limitations 140–2; practice, contradictions/complications 137; pretest collection 138; qualitative researcher questions 132; qualitative studies 134–7; quantitative study of 133, 137–40; questions, design studies 135; researcher interest 132–3; researcher perspectives 135–7, 138–40; spiral analysis 135–6; storytelling, study of 133

cases, illustrative examples 64; emotional life, example 71–2; emotion, feminist/ poststructural approach 58; first-year teachers, identification 124; novice teachers, case study 123–4; observation 124; practice, cultural responses 124–5; professional development (PD) 32–3; teacher–child interactions (effectiveness measurement), CLASS (usage) 138; teacher–child play interactions, untangling (research example) 19; teacher-preparation experiences, usage (qualitative study) 121

teaching: assumptions 155–62; contexts, range 64; emotion, complexity 57–8; guilt/stress/ frustration/worry 58; improvisation, usage 49; problem, understanding 159; vocabulary teaching, approach 77

test–retest reliability 41

Thai children, engagement (research example) 16–17

themes: findings narrative, organization 71; identification 67–8

theoretical constructs 51

theoretical framing 55–7; explanation 56

theory triangulation 61

time: context 153; importance 61–2

transformation, catalyst 71

transformative paradigms 14, 16–17; representation 49

transformative research, goal 16

Trawick-Smith, J. 19

triangulation, types 61

Truong, S. 16

trust, importance 27

trustworthiness: defining 40–2; issue 60; quantitative research 40–1

truthiness 41; aim 42

t-test, usage 96–7

two-level hierarchical linear models, parameter estimates 103

Ufoegbune, V. 17

unbiased information, provision 36

unlikelihood level, attainment 92

validated surveys, usage 61

validity, types 40

variables: accounting 82; categorical dependent variables, comparison 95–6; categorical variable, example 91; continuous dependent variables, comparison 96–8; control variable, usage 81; impact 93; independent/dependent variables, concepts (inclusion) 81; moderating variable 81–2; outcome variables, descriptive statistics (example) 89; relationship, correlational analyses (usage) 77–8; representation 91

verisimilitude: attainment 60–1; concept 60; notion 41

vocabulary teaching, approach 77

Voices of Practitioners (NAEYC) 162

Ways With Words (Heath) 38, 62

whiteness 51; examination 55; operation 49

Wilcox-Herzog, Amanda (essay) 149–51

within-case comparisons 69–70

worldviews, explanation 56

Zeichner, Ken 157